Armand Mattelart, editor

Communicating In Popular Nicaragua

D1299564

Armand Mattelart, editor

Communicating In Popular Nicaragua

international general

New York and Bagnolet (France)

COMMUNICATING IN POPULAR NICARAGUA
Introduction, Selection, Translations and Bibliography
© Armand Mattelart and International General 1986.
All Rights Reserved.
No part of this book may be reproduced or utilized in
any form or by any means, electronic or mechanical,
including photocopying or recording or by any infor-
mation storage and retrieval system without permis-
sion in writing from the publisher, International
General. For information please write International
General at POB 350, New York, N.Y. 10013, or 173
avenue de la Dhuys, F-93170 Bagnolet, France.

ISBN: 0-88477-024-9, Large-format Paperback

Acknowledgements:
The editor, Armand Mattelart, would like to thank his
Nicaraguan friends working in the following organizations and media: the Agencia Nueva Nicaragua, the
Asociación de los Trabajadores del Campo, *Barricada*,
the Centro de Estudios y Capacitación en Comunicación — Escuela de Periodismo (Universidad centroamericana), the Centro de Investigaciones Económicas de la Reforma Agraria, the Corporación de Radio-
diffusión del Pueblo, the Departamento de Agitación y
Propaganda del FSLN, the Editorial Nueva Nicaragua,
INCINE, the Instituto de Investigaciones Económicas
y Sociales, the Ministry of Foreign Affairs, the Ministry
of the Interior, *Los Muchachos*, the Sistema Nacional
de Publicidad, the Sistema Sandinista de Televisión, *El
Tayacán*, and the Union de Periodistas de Nicaragua.
On a more personal level, the editor is indebted to
Carlos Fernando Chamorro, Xavier Chamorro, José
Luis Coraggio, Guillermo Rothschuh Villanueva and
Rosa María Torres. A special note of thanks is due
Tomás Borge Martinez for the valuable time spent in
long and friendly discussions and for a memorable trip
to the city of Granada (Nicaragua).
For their part, the publisher would like to thank
David Kunzle and Mercedes de Uriarte for their help in
proposing the two Spanish translators, Janette Jamieson
and Don Clark.
Cover photograph by Archivo INCINE, Managua.
The book was typeset by SMC Typesetting, Bristol
and was printed in Great Britain in July 1986.

10 9 8 7 6 5 4 3 2 1

Table of Contents

ARMAND MATTELART
Communication In Nicaragua
Between War and Democracy

The East/West axis of interpretation has acquired such a legitimacy in collective representations that it is difficult to avoid when one tries to understand what is happening in Nicaragua, the subject of international news only to the extent that it feeds and illustrates the bipolarity of the world order. If truth be told, news of Nicaragua makes the front page not so much because of what is actually happening there but because of what its enemies say and think. The principal origin of the "facts" which have sparked off "news" about Nicaragua lies — need we be reminded — in the declarations of the U.S. government. It is this which explains why, in a very short period of time, this tiny country whose existence was all but forgotten during nearly 50 years of Somozist dictatorship has more than made up for its late entry onto the news market.

The East/West dimension has become the basis of a new "received wisdom" which fixes the threshold of tolerance for an increasingly intolerant discourse on Nicaragua. It determines what can be said and heard about this country. Paradoxically, in spite of the extreme politization that this East/West bipolarity expresses, its end result is, in fact, an idea of the end of politics.

Even before being an affront to intellectual honesty, this imprisonment within the East/West paradigm is an affront to the intelligence. For, by dint of stuffing everything into this category alone, one cannot offer the slightest means to understand the nature of the resistances which are multiplying throughout the world. This vision also expresses a profound resignation, a willingness to leave the world such as it is, in the West as in the East. It is surely here that we find the reasons for the incredible confusion reigning in the minds of those who can only think in terms of slogans.

Thus in France in March 1985, a group of well-known intellectuals created a "Resistance International" and published a full-page advertisement in *Le Monde*, demanding that the U.S. Congress "renew its aid to the Nicaraguan resistance in a spirit of democratic solidarity"[1]. This is a militant provocation if there ever was one. For after all, one is free to think what one likes of the policies of the Sandinistas in Nicaragua. But from there to underwrite a veritable call to crime in the name of freedom and democracy is to take a giant step backwards.

There is no confusion, however, on the part of the U.S. President when he calls the former officers of the Somozist guards "freedom fighters" and assimilates them to the U.S. founding fathers, Simon Bolivar, and the French resistance during World War II. If giving them the benefit of the doubt, one can explain the position of some of the aforementioned French intellectuals as due to naïveté or misplaced good faith, it would be ingenuous to think that Ronald Reagan does not know what he is doing when he muddles the cards to this extent. For his geo-politics moves into the political vacuum of others.

Unable to appeal to the intelligence, these crusades thrive on the current emotional wave of refusing the Other. One perverse effect of the present crisis has been the development of specific forms of racism in the industrialized countries. But there are other forms of racism (and therefore other ways of maintaining social intolerance) than the obvious ones relating to immigrant workers. Demands for internal tolerance can very well accommodate discourses on external intolerance. It is only the incredible shrinking of our mental territory, expressed by the withdrawal into the defense of "Western values", that prevents the contradictions of this new ethnocentric cosmopolitanism from becoming evident.

Camping on the East/West boundary line in order

1. *Le Monde* (Paris), 21 March 1985, p. 6. Among those who signed this text were Eugène Ionesco, Robert Jaulin, Bernard Henri-Levy, Jean-François Revel, Olivier Todd, and Emmanuel Leroy-Ladurie. The text was also published in *The New York Times*.

This text was translated from the French by David Buxton. English translation Copyright © International General 1986. This is its first publication.

to understand the world and to grasp its conflicts amounts to refusing to admit the emergence of new historical subjects on the international scene. It is to refuse to accept that, if the contradiction between East and West is a reality, the tension between the North and the South is also a reality which must henceforth be taken into account. To interpret the rebellions of others as void of all autonomy or self-will, like the games of sorcerers' apprentices on the chessboard of great empires, is tantamount to refusing the identity of others and their dignity.

To the East/West polarization which tends to stifle debate on alternatives, there are really only two responses: either repeat the ritual of liturgies celebrating the existing socialist countries, or distance oneself from rigid certainties by venturing onto the path of hypotheses. At the risk of disappointing both friends and foes of the socialist countries, it is the latter approach that we have chosen.

This study was written following a visit to Nicaragua in February–March 1985. It is the outcome of conversations, discussions and debates with journalists, filmmakers, researchers and directors of the various mass communication media, as well as with readers, listeners and viewers of these media.

THE END OF MODELS

There was a time — not so long ago — when for each revolutionary process that exploded in the world, a good number of Western intellectuals hastened to find in it a "new model". To be patented this model had to remedy the erring ways of previous revolutions and console their disappointments; but also — one forgot to add — it served to mask the real incapacity of these intellectuals to further revolution in their own countries. From the 1917 revolution to Mao, from China to Cuba, from Cuba to Chile, from Chile to Portugal, etc. until the day when many ceased to fish for models and swapped the inevitability of revolutions for the seduction of a technological "revolution".

Does the revolution in Nicaragua offer a model at this stage? No, no more than in the other cases inasmuch as models are only constructions of the mind. Seen in terms of communication, Nicaragua neither represents nor proposes a model. It does not constitute a model in the sense that it has resolved — finally! — all the questions that those before it seeking to change or reorient the legitimized models of culture and communication have or have not posed. If it is experiencing so many difficulties in resolving its own problem in this domain, it is perhaps also in part because those who have preceded it have not been able or have not wanted to pose certain questions. It does not represent a model because it does not lend itself to any unilateral approaches. In effect, it is riddled with contradictory lines of reasoning and therefore with contradictory models. One finds the

persistence of classical models related to the concept of "ideological work", itself indebted to a doctrine of agitation and propaganda, as well as the emergence of radically new practices. Depending on which of these different lines one follows, one arrives at diametrically opposed conclusions: the inevitable reproduction of vertical schemas of bureaucratic organization; or the beginnings of new social relations and therefore of a horizontal mode of social organization and communication. But even if one can allow oneself to dissect and isolate each of these approaches for analytical purposes, the reality is something else again. This system of communication and information in Nicaragua is at once one and the other; that is to say, a space where contradictory approaches with their sites of confrontation, negotiation, mediation and complicity are linked. Only the unrepentant desire to find at all costs and in spite of everything a "model" would permit one to separate the one from the other, removing a part of reality and giving it preference so as to better ignore the other approach. This is the best way to be sure of a rude awakening.

Before we begin, we should make it clear that nothing would be more false than to imagine that behind each line of reasoning there are necessarily locatable and definable groups and individuals. The same individual or group is often the bearer of two contradictory positions. It is time to break with a simplistic vision which understands the operation of social organizations in revolution — or elsewhere! — as being obligatorily influenced by party headquarters or political fractions plotting and scheming to put their project into action.

The struggle to establish the hegemony of a project, in this case a model of communication, takes on extremely varied forms. They are modelled as much from shortcomings, habits and inertia, as from networks of affinity, from voluntary or imposed circuits of solidarity. They are modelled above all from their capacity or incapacity to fathom the forces of reality and the resistance it puts up to preconceived ideas. When this incessant reference to reality and its concrete actors is no longer being made, an ideological project has begun to make the real conform to its ideological mould.

After six years of revolution, these two approaches remain. But the questions posed by some sectors of the Nicaraguan revolution on their media indicate that the search for new forms of communication is far from being of minority interest. Many journalists and filmmakers, not to mention the public, are in fact extremely critical themselves and open to criticism from others. This openness goes hand-in-hand with an ability to draw lessons quickly from these criticisms. One example among others. Knowing that Werner Herzog's film on the Miskito Indians which was later broadcast on French television, was not going to please them very much, I asked the director of a research centre on agrarian reform, one of whose responsibilities was to develop a project of autonomy along with the indigenous populations, what he thought of the film. He replied: "Yes, we helped Werner Herzog a lot to make his film. We had many discussions with him. The film isn't very favorable towards us; that's the least one could say. But he taught us a lot. And that's important."

We are no longer in the era when young revolutions ostracized anyone who dared criticize them as being a CIA agent. This capacity for criticism and self-criticism is admittedly not to everyone's taste. A professor from the University of Leipzig, a specialist in communication theory working as a technical assistant in the Nicaraguan Department of Agitation and Propaganda (DAP) said to us after having spent two months in Managua: "Here, Pavlov's theories don't work. The Nicaraguans are very critical, much too much. With criticism, one can't go very far."

For those from the Eastern socialist countries, this criticism is not the only surprise. The biggest is undoubtedly finding that the Sandinista Front does not function according to the orthodox, Leninist definition of the party: no General Secretary, but nine Commandants. For a foreigner arriving for the first time in Managua no less surprising is the discovery that in this city levelled by an earthquake in 1972 there is no physical centre but that which exists in the minds of the Managuans.

A MIXED SYSTEM

The state, the Sandinista National Liberation Front (FSLN), the private sector, and associations share the communication system which reflects the political and economic system in Nicaragua; a mixed economy and political pluralism. Only the communication media in the hands of the Somoza family and its faithful and, more rarely, in the last few years, of those who have gone over to the *Contras*, have been confiscated. The state controls about 15 radio stations, and according to unofficial statistics, the private sector controls between 15 and 25 stations. Among the six biggest stations one finds *La Voz de Nicaragua* (state), *Radio Sandino* (linked to the FSLN), *Radio Mundial* and *Radio Corporación* (private commercial sector), *Radio Católica* (the Catholic church), *Onda de Luz* (the Protestant church). The four biggest have practically the same coverage: between 70% and 100% of the national territory. The religious radios cover only half of Nicaragua.

The television is state owned. Channel 6 (TV de Nicaragua) belonged to President Somoza and became public property in July 1979. Channel 2 (Televicentro), belonging to private shareholders, some of whom were linked to the Somoza family, was

expropriated under the pressure of its personnel in August 1980. At the same time the two channels fused to form the Sandinista Television System (SSTV).

Before the revolution there was no film industry in Nicaragua. The Nicaraguan Institute of Cinema (INCINE), under the Ministry of Culture, was founded in September 1979. It produces mainly newsreels (*noticieros*) and documentaries but has two large co-productions with the Chilean film-maker Miguel Littín to its credit. The first, *Alsino y el condor*, was co-produced with Costa Rica, Mexico and Cuba. The second, *El Señor Presidente* was co-produced with France and Cuba. The private sector largely controls the film distribution circuits. Of the 130 cinemas, less than 20% are managed by the state[2].

The daily press consists essentially of three newspapers: *La Prensa* (private sector, founded in 1926), *Barricada* (FSLN, 29 July 1979) and *El Nuevo Diario* (co-operative, 1980). The circulation of *La Prensa* fluctuates between 65,000 and 70,000, *Barricada* around 100,000 and *Nuevo Diario* between 50,000 and 60,000. To understand this limited press system, one has only to glance at the genealogy of a single family, the Chamorros, who count several Conservative presidents among their ancestors. In January 1978, *La Prensa* had become a symbol of resistance to the Somoza dictatorship and its director, Pedro Joaquim Chamorro, was assassinated by the National Guard. Up until the triumph of the revolution (19 July 1979), the journalists of *La Prensa* (from whom two of the nine Commandants were issued) continued to ferociously oppose the dictatorship. The buildings of the newspaper were bombed in response. At the time, *La Prensa* was owned by Violeta, Jaime and Xavier Chamorro, Pedro Joaquim's siblings and his eldest son and namesake. Each member of the family owned a quarter of the shares.

Divisions arose very quickly. Violeta was a member of the first government junta but her resignation signified a rupture with the Sandinistas. 90% of *La Prensa*'s journalists left along with Xavier Chamorro who, with the money from the sale of his shares, created a co-operative to produce *El Nuevo Diario* in May 1980. This newspaper aligned itself with the Sandinista revolution but did not want to follow a party line. It is addressed more particularly to the professional classes. The other members of the family remained with *La Prensa* and have taken up an increasingly radical opposition to the government. However, it is another member of the family, Carlos Fernando Chamorro who founded and still directs the newspaper of the Sandinista Front, *Barricada*. Despite these family divergences, "we still see each other", Xavier Chamorro confided to me, "Obviously, we don't talk politics. We lend each other paper, ink.... The offices of *La Prensa* are practically neighbours to those of *Nuevo Diario*."

There is hardly any need to add that the story of the Chamorro family is similar to that of numerous Nicaraguan families, particularly those belonging to the

2. Carlos Ibarra, "La problemática de la exhibición cinematografica", *Ventana*, a supplement to *Barricada* (Managua), 11 September 1983, p. 3. Concerning the history of INCINE see the text of Julianne Burton in this volume.

richer classes and some sectors of the professional class, many of whom count among their families both young revolutionaries and ferocious opponents of the government, sometimes even *Contras*, or simply a relative who has preferred to emigrate to the United States.

The periodical press offers a much wider range of weeklies, monthlies and journals. The six parties

---

SABIDURIA DEL PUEBLO

La mona aunque se vista de seda, mona se queda

el tayacán

Semanario para el Pueblo de Nicaragua

C$5.00

Año 4 No. 142

Managua, Nicaragua Libre

LA BIBLIA

LEERLA Y ENTENDERLA

(Con una buena traducción)

■ Fotonovela
¿UN REMEDIO MILAGROSO?

■ Metiendo la cuchara
LO MAS TRISTE DEL PLAN DE REAGAN

■ Aprendamos a comer
El AZUCAR, ¿UN VENENO?

■ Los Chilopios

... MOVILIZARON LAS HORMIGAS ...

Y VOLVIO LA ALEGRIA
(Capítulo V)

Front page of the 13–19 April 1985 issue of *El Tayacán* (Managua), the weekly newspaper of the grassroots church community.

which participated in the general elections of November 1984 all possess their own publication and do not hesitate to use it to criticize government measures. The most virulent is undoubtedly that of the Moscow-line Nicaraguan Communist Party which has often accused the Sandinistas of restoring just another capitalist path by refusing to apply socialist policies. Also circulating are almost 20 weeklies, monthlies and revues published by research centres, Christian groups and associations. One of the most interesting weeklies is *El Tayacán*, published by members of the grass-roots church communities. It is practically impossible now to buy international news magazines or women's magazines which circulate throughout Latin America. There is consequently a widespread buying, selling and trading, particularly of photo-novels and romance novels, which recirculates the stock of magazines existing before the drying up of these imports.

As can be seen, all aspects of communication technology in Nicaragua are extremely underdeveloped even when compared to the rest of Latin America. Printing resources were so limited that for a while *Barricada* and *Nuevo Diario* were printed on the same rotary press in León as *La Prensa*. All three now have their own composition and printing facilities; *Barricada* thanks to the help of the German Democratic Republic, *Nuevo Diario* through the assistance of a Dutch foundation and *La Prensa* thanks to the Friedrich Naumann Foundation in the German Federal Republic. This shows the diversity of the technical assistance and financial aid to different sectors of Nicaraguan society.

Television was also characterized by the same lack of technical resources. The two channels, closely linked to the U.S. networks ABC and NBC which, as in most other Latin American countries, helped set them up, covered in July 1979 only the large cities, on the southern coast of the Pacific where purchasing power was concentrated. There was little production capacity and 80% of programmes were imported, with local production limited to news, game shows and some advertisements. There were few technicians as breakdowns were handled by RCA specialists sent out from Mexico or the United States. In spite of these limitations, the Somozist television offered programmes and political debates live from the United States through the Intelsat system.

Needs in this domain are enormous. The lack of foreign exchange has slowed down the expansion of Nicaragua's media potential. Many radios are equipped with worn out material over 30 years old. The majority of the population has little access to batteries for transistor radios as nearly 80% live in the country. Television is not any better off. To remedy this lack of technicians and resources, Nicaraguans have discovered the virtues of simple technologies from other South American countries. They have called on Japanese technology, revised and corrected by the Mexicans. To extend the range of coverage of their television service, they have imported small re-transmitters, manufactured by FACSA, an appendage of the Mexican multimedia conglomerate Televisa. Thanks to this inexpensive material, television is now available in two-thirds of Nicaragua. Because the countries of the southern hemisphere do not yet manufacture mobile units, the French firm Thomson-CSF was called in. To train 76 people from the technical sector (camera, videotape and lighting technicians, mobile unit crew) they were sent to Mexico (at FACSA) and Cuba. 120 people in the production sector have been trained in Nicaragua and in foreign countries with the help (in order of importance) of Spanish television, Cuba, the National Audiovisual Institute (France), the German Democratic Republic and Mexico (notably Televisa). Since no television sets are manufactured in Nicaragua, commercial or joint private-state firms import Japanese sets through the Panama free trade zone. State administrations have signed agreements with the Cuban electronics industry to import television sets for co-operatives in the north of the country. In 1984, there were 200,000 television sets in Nicaragua for a population of 3 million, half of which were in Managua.

The underdevelopment of the media and their extreme degree of dependance reflects the nature of the local bourgeoisie, a class whose formation into a national bourgeoisie was long prevented by the nepotism of the Somoza dynasty which used the state apparatus to compete with its opponents in financial speculations and commercial profits. In fact, this bourgeoisie began to become conscious of itself and to formulate another project only during the last few years preceding the popular insurrection in July 1979. It was only after the assassination of the director of *La Prensa* that this traditional class hastened to offer an alternative to the victorious advance of the Sandinist troops.

The non-existence of a national bourgeoisie revealed in turn how intimately Nicaragua was linked historically to the U.S. system of alliances, not so much because of its economic wealth — 70% of its foreign exchange came from agriculture and cattle-raising — as the place it occupied in U.S. geo-political strategy in Central America. In this capacity, Somozism intervened in the repression of popular movements in Costa Rica (1948), Guatemala (1954), and it was on its territory that the invaders of the Cuban Bay of Pigs (1961) were trained.

The underdevelopment of the media under Somoza did not, however, prevent them from forming one of the most determined centres of resistance to the dictatorship. Many struggles (strikes, marches against censorship, occupations of radio stations) in the cities were marked by actions of the journalists' unions, first by the Union of Radio Journalists of Managua, founded in 1963 to counter the association of journalists infiltrated by Somozism; then afterwards by the Nicaraguan Journalists Union (UPN), a national union founded in March 1978. In reaction to the increasingly numerous bans preventing them from exercising their profession, journalists invented a "journalism of the catacombs" whereby they occupied churches and read censored radio news from the pulpit before engaging in discussion with the congregation. The Episcopal Conference condemned this original type of protest but most parish priests ignored their superiors. It was journalists from the UPN who founded Radio Sandino in June 1978, a clandestine station which was to play an essential role in the organization and preparation of the combats which led to the overthrow of the dictatorship.[3] In 1985, the UPN has approximately 500 members representing all political tendencies, and the FSLN has an uncontestable majority. 80% of the union's Executive Council elected in March 1985 are women. The other journalist association, the Association of Journalists of Nicaragua, the APN, has no more than 50 members.

THE WAR AND ITS PRIORITIES

Nicaragua is at war. Some hasten to qualify this by affirming that "Nicaragua has declared itself to be at war", while others speak of "low intensity conflict", implying that it is not really a war in the strict sense of the word. All of this leads to an essential question: at what point does a conflict have the right to a war status on the international news market? And especially, at what point does it begin to be perceived as a war by foreign public opinion?

Whatever the reply, the reality of aggression exists. The daily incursions of the *Contras* on the Northern and Southern fronts, on the Honduran and Costa Rican borders respectively, have already caused 8,000 casualties among women, children, militia, soldiers and civilians. They have already put 10–15% of the arable land out of economic action. They have caused a total economic loss of more than a billion dollars since the beginning of hostilities. Military spending accounts for 40% of the state budget; 30% for the armed forces and 10% for logistics. In a country which

3. On the history of the media before the revolution, see Guillermo Rothschuh Villanueva's text in this volume; *La insurrección de la paredes*, Managua, Editorial Nueva Nicaragua, 1984, with introduction by Sergio Ramírez and texts by Omar Cabezas and Dora Maria Tellez; Carlos Tünnermann, *La contribución del periodismo a la liberación nacional*, Managua, Ministry of Education, 1980, and Doris Läpple-Wagenhals, *A New Development Model — A New Communication Policy? On Communications in Nicaragua before and after July 19, 1979*, Frankfurt/Main, Verlag Peter Lang, 1984, the only book written on the Nicaraguan media in transition by a European researcher. Also see the U.S. readers on Nicaragua listed in the bibliography in this volume, which often contain articles on the media, culture and education.

4. "Telcor assume grandes retos", *El Nuevo Diario*, 2 March 1985, p. 6.

has never known the draft, young people now carry out two years of compulsory military service and most spend part of this time in the war zones. War also means a commercial embargo, an economic blockade with the mining of ports by the U.S. fleet, the dislocation of the transport of oil which is entirely imported and the suspension of loans from the Inter-American Development Bank, the U.S. having the right of veto.

Whether one likes it or not, this war is an essential element for understanding how the Nicaraguan communication system and its contradictions function. The state of war fixes, in effect, certain priorities. Thus, the decentralization of the radio network is being carried out firstly in the sensitive areas of the country. The broadcasting power of local radio stations is increased in function of their proximity to the war fronts; this is especially important as the telecommunications infrastructure is extremely dispersed and the radio is also a telephone and telegraph system. This development is not limited to war needs as the policy of decentralizing radio and television is also situated in an overall policy of autonomy for the Indian populations on the Atlantic coast. But the war is the most striking aspect. When the government signs an agreement for the importation of television sets, it is for the peasant co-operatives in the north, not far from the Honduran border. The few government news reports on the communication infrastructure and policy published by the national press — generally difficult to obtain for research because they come under the heading of strategic information — bear witness to these priorities. The 2 March 1985 issue of *El Nuevo Diario* reports that TELCOR (the Nicaraguan Postal Service)

has been given the responsibility of beginning the technical work for installing radio stations which will operate in the war zones where radio broadcasts from Honduras are preventing the reception of national broadcasts. . . . Moreover, a financial and technical aid agreement is being negotiated with the Bulgarian government for the installation of microwave networks which will benefit those living on the Pacific and Atlantic coasts[4].

To understand the role that the communication media, notably radio and television, play in this war, it must be mentioned that Nicaragua is particularly exposed to foreign broadcasting. Theoretically, the television viewer can pick up about 15 neighboring television channels while the radio listener can receive about 80 foreign stations. In practice this depends on the region where a person lives and what type of equipment they own; many people in Managua can pick up U.S. television channels. The inhabitants of the town of Bluefields in the southern region on the Atlantic coast — a particularly strategic zone — receive above all the television channels in Costa Rica, which is their closest border. Even though it is only recently that it has been able to receive the national channels from Managua, this area is particularly well equipped with television sets. The contraband of electronic goods has always been a second activity for the fishing boats, stimulated by the nearby free trade zones in the Caribbean and Panama. In the north, by the Honduran border, Honduran TV channels bombard the regions of Nueva Segovia, Esteli and Jinotega. Television sets from Honduras have long-profited from that country's exclusion from the Central American common market to legalize this traffic. As for radio, the listening range is much larger and more pluralist because one can pick up Radio France-Internationale, the BBC and Radio Havana as well as the Voice of America. In terms of the war, one station in particular occupies a key position: Radio 15 de Septiembre, located on the outskirts of Tegucigalpa (Honduras). This station is directly controlled by the *Fuerza Democrática Nicaragüense* (FDN), the most important branch of the *Contras*, composed principally of ex-Somozist guards. The ARDE (*Alianza Revolucionaria Democrática*), under the orders of the former Sandinist Commandant Eden Pastora operates, for its part, from Costa Rica where it is much less well equipped. As the ARDE refuses, for reasons of principle, to join with the FDN in a common front, the latter has gone so far as to jam the radio broadcasts of the ARDE, thus hoping to force it into a holy alliance[5]. Finally, in the last few years, the Voice of America has increased its broadcasting coverage throughout the region, notably from Costa Rica[6].

The broadcasts of Radio 15 de Septiembre are dominated by anti-Sandinist propaganda. One of their main lines of attack is of "patriotic military service". Among other things, this propaganda incites women to create the conditions for a "national insurrection of mothers", while calling on young people to desert from the army by claiming such things as the so-called forced nature of recruitment, the sacrifices of youth on the altar of party interests rather than the country, the lack of military training of young recruits who are used as cannon fodder, the forced indoctrination, and the separation from the family. Another axis of propaganda presents Sandinist Nicaragua as "an obstacle to peace in the region because of its arms race and its desire to export the revolution to all Central America", "a totalitarian state aligned with the East and subject

Leaflet from the *Contra* group Fuerza Democrática Nicaragüense, "Make Up Your Mind: The Church or the Communist Sandinistas" (Reprinted from *Barricada* (Managua), ca 1984).

to the Cuba–Moscow axis". The economic crisis which the country is undergoing is interpreted as "the product of the arms race reinforced by the corruption of the administration, the appetite for gain, and the inability of the FSLN to govern". Finally, a constant theme: "the threat of the Sandino–Communists' Marxist atheism against the Catholic people, menaced in its faith and beliefs".

Psychological warfare tends to become a daily norm. All the *Contras* now carry in their haversack a manual titled *Operaciones sicológicas en guerra de guerrillas* ("Psychological Operations in Guerrilla Warfare"). These types of concerns are similar to those shown by the joint manoeuvres of the U.S. and Honduran armies ("Big Pine" in April 1985) which devoted a third of their time to carrying out practical exercises in handling a radio set, a portable printing press, and preparing a newspaper. The American experts came from the Psychological and Civil Affairs Operations Group stationed in Fort Bragg (North Carolina) along with the Green Berets.

Nothing could be more normal in this type of conflict than psychological warfare. What is less normal is the "normality" which it establishes in the field of international news. In effect, much of this "news" emerging from a context of a propaganda war is taken up as "objective" fact and projected into the international scene, becoming the raw material for the transnational news agencies[7].

Without being as directly affected as radio by this

5. Ana María Ezcurra, *Agresión ideológica contra la revolución sandinista*, Mexico City, Ediciones Nuevomar, 1983. This book analyzes in detail the attitude of national and international church organizations to the Sandinista revolution. See also the text of David Kunzle in this volume.

6. See the text of Howard H. Frederick in this volume. The radio station "15 de Septiembre" takes its name from the date of Nicaragua's day of independence (1821).

7. The invasion of Grenada in October 1983 by U.S. troops is extremely revealing on this point. For five days, the U.S. Army refused to allow journalists onto the island, giving the reasons for this blockade–censorship as "the security of journalists cannot be guaranteed". During these five days, the Pentagon, the only authorized news source furnished numerous bits of "information" such as the discovery of mass graves, which it quickly denied several days later. See P. M. Thivolet, "Les vertus de la désinformation", *Le Monde Diplomatique* (Paris), December 1983.

war of propaganda and counter-propaganda, television has also suffered from its repercussions. To attract the Nicaraguan market, television channels from neighboring countries have increased their broadcasting power and organized their programming to broadcast *telenovelas* when the Managuan channels are off the air. The Sandinista Television System has replied by beginning its programmes at noon instead of 3 p.m. and extending its transmissions until midnight.

The war has also affected film activity. To make up for the lack of cinemas, INCINE has set up mobile cinemas throughout the country. In 1984, 52 mobile units reached over 3 million spectators, many seeing a film for the first time. However, as the director of INCINE remarked:

The big stumbling block continues to be aggression. We have carried out 15,000 projections, most of them in the war zones.... Film projections and the informational and educational work they accomplish are directly aimed at the counter-revolutionary radio stations which inundate the north of the country from Honduras. For the peasants participate in debates. It's not without reason that these radio stations threaten our projectionists.... On 19 July 1984, one of our technicians was wounded in an ambush at Waslala; in another contested zone, a jeep overturned into a ravine and another unit came under mortar fire.... All of this in addition to the classic problems of the blockade of spare parts, the lack of foreign exchange and the delays caused by armed attacks[8].

For newspaper journalists, the war has meant a change in their way of approaching the theatre of operations. Now, for months on end they take part in patrols on the same terms as soldiers before returning with long articles published in bookform by *Barricada*. If they return at all: some do not return, like the journalist from *Barricada*, Juan Matus, a war correspondent, killed in 1984 at the age of 42 on the northern front.

Finally, the war makes its presence felt in the type of international news carried in the national media. One senses the real difficulty in changing from an understanding of international affairs seen principally in terms of imperialism to a vision of international multipolar alliances which is more in keeping with a project of revolution. In spite of this difficulty the dispatches of the Agencia Nueva Nicaragua (ANN), founded in October 1979, cover an increasingly complex international situation.

THE LOGIC OF WAR

The logic of war affects the media as it affects the whole of Nicaraguan society. It is beginning to seriously affect economic strategy: "We are passing from a policy of expansion to a policy whose axis is defense", as the Minister of Industry announced on the 8 p.m. television news on 8 March 1985.

The necessity of mobilizing the population to counteract the continual slogans of the *Contra* radio stations and fighting the resulting rumours, in a complex way conditions how the press, radio and television function, especially in the area of news reporting.

The logic of war reintroduces and relegitimizes the law of propaganda and counter-propaganda. Admittedly, even from this point of view, there is a noticeable evolution in the treatment of the raids of the *Contras* and armed confrontations. The initial description of the *Contras* and their allies as *bestias* (beasts) has been dropped. But the problem perhaps lies elsewhere: one can, indeed, understand the anger of a people who lost 40,000 lives during the war of liberation and suffered during 50 years the legendary ferocity of the National Guard today which President Reagan calls the defender of freedom on the subcontinent. But even if one could imagine a civilized response to an enemy propaganda which stoops to all manners of insults, ignominies and lies, the problem would remain.

The danger with the rationality of war is that it resists the idea of contradiction. Information likely to demoralize combatants or the civilian population cannot be divulged. This is the very principle of propaganda and counter-propaganda. In this perspective, there is little information which is not likely to be judged capable of undermining the morale of the troops. For example, the news that in some regions, some peasants had taken up arms and joined the *Contras* was withheld. An effective war strategy must be built not on doubts and hypotheses but rather faith and certainties.

With all the shadows of a doubt swept away, there remains only a place for the heroic style, like the billboard on the road to the Managua airport showing a close-up face of a woman with young soldiers in action in the background and the phrase: "The country; no, my son won't be a traitor. Patriotic military service". And yet, many mothers do not let their sons go to the front with the joy and pride of having brought into the world a heroic defender of the country. The counter-revolution has understood this well and has made this the central theme of its propaganda, countering the heroic style with slogans rooted in the everyday life of women and the family.

Yet what government in a state of war can allow itself to show its difficulties, its errors and its losses? What government has ever succeeded in mobilizing its people not with its heroes but with its conscientious objectors, especially when the latter flee to Miami or join the *Contras*? This is a problem that few people even ask, but it is demanded of Nicaragua that they solve it.

The rationality of the war and propaganda lead to the construction of a reality where the intelligence of things and beings gives way to emotions, and not just any emotions, for one has to respond to elementary feelings like fear, hope, desire and hate. This is the classic definition of propaganda and counter-propaganda found in the "psychological warfare" section of army manuals.

8. "Cine por todo el territorio", *Barricada*, 18 September 1984, p. 12.

CENSORSHIP

The war is at the heart of the problem of censorship because it is the state of war that is invoked to justify it. Prior censorship has existed in Nicaragua since March 1982. The organism responsible for this is the Office of Communication Media, attached to the Ministry of the Interior. Before censorship was established this organism was part of the Ministry of Culture. The question of the need for censorship is far from being a taboo subject and is amply discussed. Even if censorship above all hits *La Prensa* which offers more occasions to incur its wrath, other media are not spared either as the repeated protests of the opposition parties' press, situated to the Left or Right of the Sandinistas, remind us. During our stay in Nicaragua, we examined the news that had been censored during a full month, put at our disposal by the Office of Communication Media. The news censored from *La Prensa* was also freely available at the *La Prensa* offices. What is censored? First and foremost, news directly related to the war, such as reports or parts of reports dealing with the reactions of the mothers of soldiers, or parents of young combatants killed at the front; news on the refusal of some young people to do their military service; articles giving concrete information on the aid offered by Pastora's ARDE to young people seeking refuge in Costa Rica; the translation of an article from a U.S. magazine offering $100,000 to the first Nicaraguan pilot to desert with his new Soviet helicopter; articles outlining the simulated invasion of Honduras by Nicaraguan troops, a practical exercise imagined by Pentagon experts during the joint manoeuvres of the U.S. and Honduran armies; and, finally, articles taken from the international press accusing Nicaragua of being a centre of international terrorism (because of supposedly giving asylum and training to members of the Basque ETA, the Italian Red Brigades etc.).

Also censored is a great deal of news dealing with supply problems, the poor performance of some firms, and the irregularities discovered in some government administrations and departments. As a strict definition of war does not apply in these cases, why then is this type of information censored? A young woman lieutenant in charge of the Office of Communication Media replied honestly:

We are forced to censor some news which is not directly related to the war because our own media are not always capable of dealing with certain problems, particularly those concerning the operation of our economy where, on top of sabotage, one finds evidence of negligence and sometimes even corruption. . . . Obviously, censorship plays the role of a retaining wall and is justifiable only if there is really the construction of an alternative. If not, there is a danger of the bureaucratization and impoverishment of language. Censorship cannot indefinitely make up for the deficiencies in our communication. We would thus, for example, wind up covering up cases of corruption whereas in fact we disapprove of them and do everything we can to eliminate them.

She went on to give a series of examples illustrating how the media favorable to the revolution had failed in their task of reporting the news. In most cases, journalists dodge the issue when they have to explain why a product (such as sugar, toothpaste, petrol etc.) is lacking. A caricatural example: instead of explaining that there was a scarcity of white sugar because it earned more foreign exchange than brown sugar and the government had decided to export it, some journalists found nothing better to say than to encourage the population to consume less white sugar because it was fattening!

When I posed the same question to Tomás Borge, Minister of the Interior, he directly replied: "Many journalists should remember when you tell the truth, our people understand; when you tell them lies, they feel it".

The question of censorship was the central issue at the March 1985 UPN Journalists' Congress where the very principle of its suppression was discussed. The proposed final declaration even included a clause to this effect. However, as it did not receive unanimous support, it was withdrawn, evidence of a certain malaise among journalists. According to one UPN member, it was "a sign of tension". The eliminated passages read as follows:

The Union of Journalists of Nicaragua considers that prior censorship is not a suitable way of regulating the relations between the state and the communication media. . . . [It is necessary] to eliminate the measures of contention which do a disservice to the communication media and make us pay a high price internationally because measures like prior censorship are not acceptable to journalists either internally or externally. . . . We recognize that censorship is an instrument for the defense of the revolution but we insist on pointing out its lack of thematic definition.

At the same congress it was decided that a change in censorship rules would be directly negotiated by the UPN, which would make propositions, and the competent authorities.

The principle of the abolition of censorship seemed to be accepted. What continued to be a problem was the control of strictly military information. For Nicaragua remains at war. Lessons from history are not exactly encouraging when one remembers how the definition of "sensitive" information in wartime has become so elastic that it includes anything likely "to disturb public opinion". In other latitudes, we have often seen the tactical invocation of a *raison de guerre* transform itself into a constitutive element of normality and take the place of strategy. This type of argument, inspired by the history of really existing socialism, is at least listened to by Nicaraguans. This surely is a step forward.

The liberalization of censorship foreseen by the debates within the UPN in March 1985 has not taken place. The following 15th of October, the Sandinista government re-established a "State of Emergency" which reinforced, among other things, the control of the freedom of expression. This "State of Emergency", in fact, is simply a return to the old "State of Emergency" decreed in March 1982 and subsequently watered-down in November 1984 during the elections. To justify this new measure, the government blamed the "increased military actions by the *Contras* supported by Washington", and the "actions by their allies within Nicaragua who with the help of certain parties, media and religious institutions have intensified their sabotage of the military defense effort". The confrontation between the government and the Catholic hierarchy has amplified, especially with Mgr. Obando, the veritable leader of the internal opposition.

Have the conditions underlying censorship radically changed since the new "State of Emergency"? Here is the reply of Violeta Chamorro:

Censorship is a little more severe than before. They are a little more finicky. We send the page proofs to the censorship office around 11.00 a.m. and they only return them around 3–4.00 p.m. with the hope that they will delay publication of the newspaper (*Le Monde* (Paris), 24–25 November 1985).

According to the same source, however, the censored articles are photocopied and continue to be distributed by *La Prensa* directly to the foreign embassies and selected clients with the full knowledge of the government.

The problem of censorship certainly affects journalists. But at the same time, it completely surpasses them. As the Director of the Office of Communication Media argued: "Censorship is an indication how the whole state-government-Sandinista Front-unions-mass organizations-civil society system functions". I had begun the conversation with the criticism "Why do you sometimes censor news on conflicts in the workplace and strikes, even in firms belonging to the private sector?" She replied without beating around the bush:

Because our unions don't always do their job. In this case, communication is above all the unions' problem. They must explain what's happening. This means questioning their relations with their own members and with non-members. Otherwise, every opponent, particularly *La Prensa*, has every opportunity to use each isolated conflict against us. Our journalists can't make up for this deficiency.

To situate the debate in these terms, is to restore the discussion on censorship to its real dimension. It is also one of the only ways of preventing from the start the war from serving as an alibi for the institution of authoritarian practices by covering up all the conflicts and contradictions within the popular classes. Here again, the lessons from history are clear. After the idea of the flawless war hero comes that of a united, heroic working class, bearer of the proletarian revolution, an idea that has caused so much damage to socialism. One crack, it is argued, and the whole edifice crumbles!

9. Luis Serra, "Censura o concientización: los medios de difusión masiva en nuestra révolución", *Cuadernos de Periodismo* (Managua) I, 2 August 1984, p. 24.
10. Luis Serra, *art cit*, p. 21.

MULTIPLE LOGICS

The logic of war, and of propaganda and censorship, gives rise to a model of communication whose natural tendency is to underestimate the critical capacity of the receiver. In effect, one refuses to recognize the latter's ability to sort the mass of enemy information received and act not only as his or her own censor but especially to produce another form of information. The underestimation of the receiver has its counterpart in the overestimation of the powers of censorship and propaganda. Some are perfectly conscious of this. In a debate published in the February 1985 issue of the journal of the School of Journalism at the Universidad Centroamericana in Managua, one reads:

In the course of the last few years, we have seen that certain censored news circulates, in exaggerated form, by word of mouth. Given our people's tradition of oral communication, and the possibility they have of hearing or reading reactionary news from within the country or from other media in Central America, the effectiveness of censorship is questionable[9].

The underestimation of the receiver leads back to a privileged conception of the sender which itself is in symbiosis with a certain conception of the party:

On the one hand, one presupposes the existence of an alienated and ignorant popular audience. On the other, one presupposes the existence of a group endowed with a fully revolutionary and scientific consciousness. The group expresses in itself revolutionary ideology and, as such, then assumes the task of selecting and orienting information so that people can attain its level of consciousness[10].

It would be relatively simple to understand what is happening in the mass communication media in Nicaragua were it only for this logic of war. However, there is another logic as powerful as that derived from the war situation which coexists with it. It finds its expression in the daily construction of democratic spaces. This logic, which sees the receiver as being capable of thinking and arguing for him or herself, short circuits the logic of war behind its back.

In November 1984, general elections were held. The Sandinista Front won 67.2% of the votes cast (excluding invalid votes). Six opposition parties, The Social Christian Popular Party (PPSC), Independent Liberal Party (PLI), Democratic Conservative Party (PCD), Nicaraguan Socialist Party (PSN), the Communist Party of Nicaragua (PCN), and the Marxist–Leninist Popular Action Movement (MAP–ML) won the rest. The rate of abstention was 24.6%, and thus the FSLN won the votes of 47.4% of the enrolled voters.

Only the bad faith of Ronald Reagan, himself elected in 1980 with a record abstention rate of 47.3%, could deny the validity of this election which was observed by over 600 foreign journalists.

Whether one likes it or not, the relations of force between the various political sectors expressed by these elections is closer to reality than that imagined by those for whom the only criterion of legality would have been the defeat of the Sandinistas.

On the outcome of these elections, a National Assembly was established with the difficult task of constructing a parliamentary pluralism. In this representative assembly, censorship is obviously not acceptable. The stormy debates which are reported by the communication media testify to the openness of this forum where unlimited criticisms are made by opponents to the Sandinistas.

The creation of a National Assembly is only one of numerous signs of a project which is attempting to articulate different political and social sectors around the construction of a civil society in a country where it has always been stifled, as coercion and exclusion prevailed over a consensus.

In the realization of this project, the communication media play an important role to help constitute a political subject which substitutes a collective subject ("people") for subject "public opinion". This nonmythical people is composed of artisans, peasants, a small working class, liberal professions, ethnic minorities, and also businessmen who have their own representative association, the High Council for Private Enterprise.

The question of "political pluralism" and its relationship to popular power is at the heart of the debate. As Sergio Ramírez Mercado expressed it in May 1983:

The imperialists hope that pluralism will collapse under the pressures that they themselves lay against it, so that they can find easy excuses to isolate the revolution. So for us, pluralism is a concept essential to the revolution, maintained by not merely the recognition of certain right-wing parties so that they can function within the country, but also to make possible the political and democratic participation of different sectors of the population that never before in our history had access to that participation[11].

For the first time in the history of young revolutions, Gramsci's concept of hegemony had made its appearance, not only in discourse and programmes but also in practices. The necessity of constructing social alliances prevails over the "dictatorship of the proletariat". As Tomás Borge argued in a speech to the Propaganda Department of the FSLN on 1 March 1985:

Hegemony supposes the moral and intellectual direction of society. It implies creating a consensus around a political project. It goes much further than simple political legitimation, in the sense that Max Weber gave to this concept[12].

11. On the problem of hegemony, see the text of José Luis Coraggio in this volume, and Giulio Girardi, *Revolución en la cultura*, Managua, Editorial Nueva Nicaragua, 1983. On the question of political pluralism see "Pluralism and Popular Power: An Interview with Sergio Ramírez Mercado" in Marlene Dixon and Susan Jonas, editors, *Nicaragua Under Siege*, San Francisco, Synthesis, 1984, pp. 169ff.
12. *Intervención del Cmdte Tomás Borge en el departamento del FSLN*, 1 March 1985, published in this volume.
13. Tomás Borge, *Discurso de clausura del primer seminario sobre comunicación participativa*, Managua, CECCOM, 25 November 1984, published in this volume.
14. *Intervención del Cmdte Tomás Borge, art cit.*

It is against this background of references that emerges an alternative project to that which is now dominated by the needs of the war. Inaugurating the Center for Communication Studies and Training (attached to the School of Journalism at the Universidad Centroamericana, directed by the Jesuits), Tomás Borge further stated in November 1984:

It is necessary to set up in radio, film, television and the press a model of horizontal communication. All media must open themselves up more to the popular project — creatively and without falling into a populism or empiricism; at the same time, we should deepen marginal experiences and convince those who are not conscious of the capital importance of communication in the construction of a new society[13].

Criticizing certain propaganda practices, Borge sums up well the tension between two communication projects which characterize the current situation, even if on this specific occasion he was referring above all to the role and work of the Sandinista Front:

I think that slogans are repetitive, mechanical and boring. The masses do not have the chance to develop their capacity for creation. Slogans are imposed on them. We must let the creative torrent of the masses overflow and launch its own slogans according to the circumstances of the moment. Admittedly, the war imposes a centralization, but democratization within the party is also a strategic necessity[14].

Democracy and war, one and the other are indissolubly linked in the present period of the revolution in Nicaragua.

Though the revolution is only six years old, the role of the media has already been revised several times and the situation is far from being frozen, whereas in many past revolutions six years was quite enough for most alternatives to have been eliminated. Since the revolution, the Nicaraguans have taught themselves much about their own media and much to those who, believing they know everything, have come to help them.

These lessons are of very different types and levels; their repercussions are both theoretical and practical.

PROPAGANDA IN QUESTION

If "solidarity is the tenderness of peoples", as the Nicaraguan poet Gioconda Belli has written, it can also cover up many things which are less admirable.

If the Nicaraguans justly appreciate the generosity and self-sacrifice of the thousands of young Cubans who enabled them — often at the price of their lives — to reduce the illiteracy rate in several months from over 50% to less than 11%, if they appreciate the decisive help given by Cuban radio and video technicians, they have also been able to judge the limitations of other contributions. Not that they have been convinced by Voice of America propaganda that the Cubans are trying to indoctrinate them, but simply because they know perfectly well that ideas imported from one historical reality do not necessarily fit their own.

The Cuban revolution is certainly not a model as far as the operation of its media is concerned. Its press is boring and its television has not succeeded in developing an alternative form of fiction, and the stereotyped language of agitation and propaganda is present everywhere. On many occasions the Cuban government has not hesitated to criticize its media, but this is another story[15].

Through the Cuban channel came a heavy arsenal of traditional conceptions of agitation and propaganda. Concepts issued by Communist Party schools in the Eastern bloc for decades and illustrated by the Spanish translation of works, especially from the Soviet Union and Bulgaria, published by Editora Politica in Havana[16]. These texts have become basic manuals for agitprop militants. The level of their propaganda is equalled only by the journalism training texts that the cultural services of the U.S. Embassies distributed free to communication schools in many Third World countries during the 1960s. But if they have many defects, these manuals from the East via Cuba have at least the merit that they are free, like the series of texts published by Progress Publishers in Moscow such as *Lenin and the Cultural Revolution, Lenin and the Scientific and Technical Revolution*, and *Lenin and the Press*.

As in the first years of the Cuban revolution, the role of militants moving from the Nicaraguan Communist Party to a triumphant Sandinista Front has been determinant in the formation of the propaganda media and the peddling of these references. Like the young Castro movement, the Sandinista Front, a movement which has broken with the old Bolchevik tradition, has very few specialists in the domain of communication, here defined as "ideological work". The only ones to have accumulated elements of knowledge and some experience were hardened militants of the traditional Communist Party, pushed aside in the struggle for power by the young *guerrilleros*. These Communist militants converted to the FSLN, therefore naturally gravitated towards these strategic positions, stamping the seal of orthodoxy on this important sector where the relation masses-party is defined.

It would, however, be underestimating the critical capacity of Nicaraguans to think that these manuals are necessarily read and used in terms of the ends for which they were conceived. As one would expect, their effect has been just the opposite. The Nicaraguans are fed up with these manuals and many young Sandinistas who have studied sociology or political science in Texas or California have quickly realized that the same criticisms they once addressed to their U.S. functionalist teachers could easily be applied to these manuals.

Admittedly, the manuals remain. And they are still used. Undoubtedly it will be some time before they can be replaced by other texts from less categoric and more open horizons. But the Cubans who assisted the setting up of the schools for agitation and propaganda training are leaving. The event precipitating this departure was the approach of the elections of November 1984, a turning point for understanding the evolution of thinking and practice in the field of communication. The irrelevance of the vision of the Cuban advisors became clear. The electoral campaign required pluralist rules — informing and discussing. But Cuban information practice was based on the idea that unauthorized information by nature is secret and should not be allowed to filter outside. If they had followed this advice, the Sandinistas would have been on collision course with catastrophe. For the first time in the history of revolutions, a movement which had taken power after a long war of liberation and a popular insurrection accepted to go to the polls. This iconoclastic rupture demanded a rethinking of the communication process, barely institutionalized but already on the way to sclerosis.

And the unexpected happened. After 26 years of revolution, the Cubans are beginning seriously to pose questions about their own media. They are observing what is happening in Managua from another viewpoint. But in Havana, when the historic Director of the Agitation and Propaganda Department of the 26 of July Movement was dismissed, the only explanation the international news agencies could advance was that the chief of the Cuban revolution wanted to accentuate his personal authoritarian control over the entire party apparatus!

Here at least is one case where it is difficult to accuse Nicaragua of being a Cuban–Soviet vassal.

In reality, events have doubtless occurred in a more chaotic, less transparent way than how I have related them here. But the truth is there: a certain idea of propaganda and agitation is in crisis in Nicaragua and, in one way or another, it has affected those who have observed it.

One cannot fight one ideology with another. One fights it with reality. This is what many Nicaraguans seem to be saying. The Nicaraguans have two virtues. First, they are pragmatic and are less taken in by references to the classics of Marxist orthodoxy and thus appreciate more the contributions of other currents of thought. Second they are irreverent; from this point of view, there is no comparison with the formality of the Cuban revolution.

15. See *Documentos, intervenciones y discursos de clausura, IV Congreso de la Union de Periodistas de Cuba* (UPEC), Havana, 27–9 March 1980.

16. See for example Vasil Tasev, *Proceso ideológico y educación*, Havana, Editora Politica, 1983. An indispensable reference for those who want a general idea of this literature is the Cuban journal *Materiales sobre propaganda* published by the Department of Revolutionary Orientation of the Central Committee of the Cuban Communist Party.

MEMORIES OF CHILE

If the November 1984 elections precipitated a questioning of the role of the media, they were, nevertheless, only a detonator. For a long time already, certain sectors had often realized the specificities of their situation and measured the inadequacy of the responses of other revolutions to the question of communication. Without always having the concepts to enable them to express their doubts, these sectors realized that there were few historical references from which ideas could be drawn. The classics of revolutionary propaganda fail at the point where consumer's taste begins. The only historical situation with some similarity to that of Nicaragua was Chile under the Popular Unity government from 1970–73[17].

Admittedly the conditions were very different. The Nicaraguans hold political power. The Chilean Popular Unity controlled only the government — and barely even that — because they had to sign a "pact of constitutional guarantees" in order to gain the parliamentary support of the Christian Democrats to ratify the presidential election, won by Salvador Allende with a plurality of 36.4%. One of the clauses of this pact was the preservation of the status quo in the media.

The Nicaraguan bourgeoisie had proved itself incapable of proposing a national project. The Popular Unity government, however, was confronted by a bourgeoisie which was certainly dependant but also endowed with political intelligence arising from its long experience in managing public affairs within the framework of a representative democracy. Many other differences distinguish Chile from Nicaragua: the nature of the popular movement, the middle classes and the media system itself. But beyond these differences there still were similarities. In both cases, the Left had to confront an entrenched bourgeoisie and to accept pluralist rules. In both cases, ideological and cultural questions came to the forefront in opposition to mechanical approaches which had relegated them to by-products of the economy. In both cases, it was necessary to take account of mass culture which had become a daily life culture. Like the Chileans, the Nicaraguans were concerned by the fact that the people, even the politically mobilized sectors, appreciate the products of this culture in spite of the analyses of their leaders or intellectuals who speak of cultural alienation and that logically the people ought not to like it.

What separates the classical Marxist texts from the lived reality of these two Latin-American peoples is precisely the fact that, in the most varied forms, mass culture is continually part of everyday consciousness. There was no question, indeed, as in Cuba, of closing the borders and beginning to construct socialism by wiping out all traces of previous media forms. Nor was there any question of condescendingly ignoring the

17. On the experience of the Popular Unity government, see Armand Mattelart, *Mass Media, Ideologies and the Revolutionary Movement*, Sussex, Harvester Press; Atlantic Highlands (N.J.), Humanities Press, 1980, and Michèle Mattelart, *Women, Media and Crisis*, London, Comedia, 1986.

weight of this culture and returning to the predominant conception in the socialist countries where the democratization of culture is above all that of access to high culture such as the opera, ballet, art, classical theatre, and literature. Unlike post-war Eastern Europe, both Chile 1970–73 and revolutionary Nicaragua today are marked by an industrialized audiovisual culture and a model of a market-oriented democratization of cultural goods which have penetrated everyday reflexes, establishing another relation not only to leisure and work but also to education and art.

If the Nicaraguans find themselves in some respects on the same road as that once taken by certain sectors of the Chilean revolution, they do not begin from the same starting point. An important body of studies, research and individual and collective experiences on all these questions in Latin American and elsewhere has accumulated since 1970. In one way or another, the theoretical and practical advances in the domains of the international imbalance of information flow, popular communication, alternative culture, and horizontal communication, among others, are being reinvested in Nicaragua today. Even if the transplant is not always a harmonious one.

WHO CONTROLS WHOM?

Before reviewing the various sectors in which the dialectic between mass culture and the revolutionary project can be observed, we must make four general remarks.

First. Each medium is characterized by unequal development. In television, radio and the press, one finds not only extremely different levels of consciousness on all these problems and their solutions but also practices underlying projects which in the long run are not easily compatible. This became clear when I met future scriptwriters for radio serials during their training course. On the day of my visit, it was the 51st anniversary of the assassination of General Sandino. In his honour a performance of a short play by August Strindberg and a reading of Latin-American poets was organized, which conveyed the vivacity and creativity of these young people, most of whom were no older than 23. The same impression was given during one of the courses when a talk on rock music by a young U.S. musician (the son of the filmmaker Saul Landau) was followed by a debate which lasted late into the night. The homage to Sandino began and ended with a series of slogans and hymns, vigorously chanted or sung in the purest military style, a sign of verticality which makes its presence felt even among those least conscious of the problem. The contrast between the creativity and the ritualism could not have been clearer.

In Nicaragua, there is a very significant popular expression: *"No nos han bajado líneas"* (freely translated "The word hasn't come down"), i.e., those in charge have not given us orders. This expression often crops up and not only among peasants who are much more marked by a submission inherited from decades of dictatorship and authoritarian relations with their bosses. Not having received directives generally serves as an alibi. It justifies the failure to move from word to deed. This wait-and-see attitude scarcely favours the idea that knowledge comes from debate. Without the exchange that comes from discussion, and the sharing of experience, orders parachuted in from above can only reinforce vertical relations.

Admittedly, there is an explanation for this military style. In April 1984 the magazine *Pensamiento propio*, published in Managua and edited by a Panamian Jesuit, the Director of the Instituto de Investigaciones Económicas y Sociales (INIES), asked of the nine Commandants, Bayardo Arce, this question:

There are some people — on the Left as well as on the Right — who think that society is becoming militarized. They refuse, for example, the phrase *"Dirección nacional ... ordene"* ["National Leadership ... Command"].

Arce's reply could not be clearer:

We were born as a political–military organization. We had to accept a vertical discipline in order to survive. This discipline still survives in a certain way with the modalities stamped on it by the new situation. But I should mention that it wasn't the National Leadership that launched this phrase....[18].

Second. Few accounts of the various experiments carried out since the beginning of the revolution have found their way into print. Likewise, there are few texts relating their contradictory nature, the outcome of which is stored in the memory alone. For the most part, the only knowledge one can have of them is by talking to their protagonists, a task which is not always easy as job mobility is very high in the media sector. This absence of a written memory is a real stumbling block when it comes to reinvesting the lessons from these experiences, especially in the training process.

Third. If many Nicaraguans have a heightened consciousness of the deficiencies of their media and a relatively clear idea where they should act to reconcile democracy, popular participation and the war, they have also produced a series of antidotes which prevent them from realizing their ideas. It is here that a system of alibis based on the "war/censorship/lack of resources" syndrome asserts itself: "But the lack of materials/money ... prevents us from doing this or that; correcting this; ... the lack of enough copies of critical texts forces us to make do with what we've got...." The war and censorship are taken in turn as pretexts not to change the course of things. There is a danger that one and the same person criticizes and neutralizes criticism.

Fourth. There is no global communications policy in Nicaragua. There is no overall policy in the sense that each sector is extremely compartmentalized,

each one following its own logic. Sometimes, bilateral relations exist, but rarely anything more. But to speak of the existence of fiefs, however, would also be an exaggeration for this supposes the development and management of a project specific to each preserve and this is clearly not the case. This compartmentalization can be seen between the various media such as the press, radio, television, and cinema as well as between the various sites which produce "communication" such as the state and the administration, the FSLN, and the social movements. The result is that experiences that could have been shared are not. An outside look is needed to cut across the pieces of this mosaic.

Even if this compartmentalization makes it hard to find both primary and secondary axes, there is one advantage. It indicates that the site from which norms will be defined has not been fixed. In other words, there is as yet no way of answering the question *"Quien hegemoniza el sistema?"* ("Who exercises hegemony over the system?") to use the words of Lily Soto, the General Secretary of the UPN.

Who occupies the hegemonic position? This question obviously goes beyond journalists alone and brings us to the nature of the state (under construction) and its links with the party. In the words of the UPN General Secretary:

Above all, it's not a question of transferring the functions of the party to the level of the state.... What is at stake is the notion of pluralism within the state ... [for] the state tends to create controls without creating a policy.

THE MEMORY OF MASS CULTURE

The tearing down of statues has become a clichéd image of revolutions. The Nicaraguans had a lot of tearing down to do, for there were a lot of statues.

In the domain of communication, statues were also torn down. The Nicaraguans wanted to get rid of all U.S. products from one day to the next. They even decided to remove the word *yankees* from the Spanish language. After much debate, the unnatural term *yanques* was preferred to the Spanish term *yankies* in vogue in most Latin American countries. The usefulness of teaching English in schools was questioned, as well as many other things. But this radical period was shortlived, even if the destroyers of statues are longlived. The strategy of encirclement prevailed over that of direct confrontation.

"The electoral campaign has raised consciousness about the need for advertising. But not just any form of advertising; a new concept in which advertising is an instrument of education and training". These are the words of poet Gioconda Belli, who was appointed in 1985 head of a "national advertising system" whose job is to co-ordinate and advise on the different institutional advertising campaigns. Gioconda Belli was trained in the U.S. and worked in an advertising agency before the revolution. Her deputy is a young woman from the Dominican Republic who has worked in the

18. Conversation with Bayardo Arce, *Pensamiento Propio* (Managua), April 1984, p. 15.

field of popular education. Advertising is practically non-existent in Nicaragua today for two reasons. First, the general law on the media has strongly limited its presence on television and has prohibited outright all alcohol and tobacco advertisements as well as those exploiting women and children. Secondly, a large number of consumer goods advertised on television and classified as luxury items using up too much foreign exchange, have been banned from importation. Thus, Nicaraguan television has nothing in common with other South American television systems which are characterized by the massive presence of advertising spots. The subsidiaries of the big U.S. advertising agencies have packed their bags and only a few small private agencies remain.

Gioconda Belli comes straight to the point about the work that needs to be done to change people's attitudes:

There are still too many slogans. What is good in advertising, in the advertising approach, is its capacity for synthesis. Here too much rhetoric is used at the expense of everyday language. There are too many conceptual discourses and not enough reflection on the image. . . . This is a general problem for all communication. It is boring. Thus, when we speak of imperialism, we speak too much and incorrectly. In the end, people get used to it and no longer believe it. It's a bit like the fable: 'The wolf's coming, the wolf's coming. . .'.

Her examples speak for themselves. Concerning a recent experience when she tried to get the army to accept a short film on military service for television:

They wanted the images to be realistic in their representation of imperialist aggression. I emphasized my objections and proposed to stylize the flight of the American eagle. When I showed them the pilot film, they reacted: 'it's too aesthetic. It makes imperialism appear too nice.' It was back to square one. We had to renegotiate everything. . . . Under the need for realism hides an injunctive system: striking instead of trying to convince.

This type of analysis is frequent in Nicaragua. Those who make it generally come from the former advertising industry and are, moreover, long-time Sandinista militants.

This is also the opinion of Bosco Parrales, who also formerly worked in the advertising industry and is now director of CORADEP (People's Radio Broadcasting Corporation) which controls a network of 16 stations, 13 of which are in the provinces:

In Managua, but also elsewhere, competition with commercial stations forces us to fight them with the same weapons: music against music. Obviously, we don't let the private stations have a monopoly over the records of Michael Jackson or Julio Inglesias. Young people like these records. At most, to justify these records we sometimes situate these singers in their context. . . . At the same time, we work with groups of secondary school students. The problem is that we lack qualified personnel. In our regional stations, our announcers have an average of only five or six years of schooling.

For this reason, the training of music programmers and scriptwriters of *radionovelas* (radio serials) has had to be rethought. The popularity of radio serials dates from the beginnings of radio in the 1930s. But instead of reproducing the never-ending threads of the soap operas Nicaragua has begun to work into this tradition while at the same time renewing it. For children, new programmes have been added which make use of the large number of Latin America folk tales. In both cases, people from the theatre have involved themselves totally and many have taken scriptwriting courses.

The development of the only monthly magazine for teenagers has taken the same direction evoked by Gioconda Belli and Bosco Parrales. *Los muchachos* ("The kids") was founded in June 1982 and its editors are on the average no older than 21. After an initial experiment linked to the literacy campaign (*El Brigadista*), they decided to attempt an alternative form of communication with greater emphasis on the daily interests of teenagers:

Our magazine is not a magazine which aims to raise anybody's cultural level. It is a point of contact between teenagers. We are not *consigneros* [sloganeers] because we start from concrete problems. We deal with rock, with Michael Jackson. For us, this music has another significance than it has for a young Mexican. Here, the whole context produces another meaning. For us, dancing and this type of music is not only for Saturday night but also when we go to pick coffee beans.

None of these young editors has had previous journalism experience but their magazine now has a circulation of 45,000 copies and only the shortage of paper prevents it from satisfying the real demand which they estimate at about 100,000. Their opinion on the media of their country:

We must think in terms of media education. This is the only way of not being sucked in by the dynamics of the media which don't agree with our way of looking at life. In our country, there is only a slight tradition of journalism concerning most newspaper columns and subjects. Thus, there is little tradition for cinema or television criticism, and even less for radio and music. In rural areas we have developed a form of theatre which tries to take community life into account. We believe that this approach is essential. For when one sees a film in a cinema one is alone and one often goes home alone.

WHAT FORM OF TELEVISION FICTION?

Even if some sectors of the television have come to similar conclusions, the weight of the television system often prevents them from going beyond pious wishes. The margin of manoeuvre within television policy is extremely tight.

Despite much pressure, the Sandinista Television System refused to suppress from one day to the next the U.S. series and especially *telenovelas* ("soap operas"), the television series produced by other Latin American countries. The latter were reduced from six or seven a day before the revolution to three today. And not just any series; concerning the U.S. series, the most stridently anti-communist ones were banned along with some police series like *Starsky and Hutch* and *Magnum*. To replace them, alternative programme sources were found, first, from the U.S. but not from its stock of prime-time successes; and secondly, from other Latin American countries such as Brazil, Mexico, Venezuela and recently Colombia which have thus become programme suppliers for Nicaragua. But here once again, selections had to be made; the Nicaraguans discovered, for example, that the series produced by the Mexican multimedia conglomerate Televisa were not as good as those produced by the Mexican public channels. In the words of the director of the Sandinista Television System, "Today the situation is difficult. Stocks are beginning to be used up. Lately, Mexico has slowed down its production. We must often resort to re-rebroadcasts. And in addition to this there are third-rate soap operas". A third alternative source is European production, and Nicaraguan television has shown historical series such as *The Legend of King Arthur*, and *Marco Polo* from Italy, Great Britain, France and particularly Spain. Other than films, programmes from Cuba and the Eastern European countries are relatively rare; only the police series produced by the German Democratic Republic seem to interest viewers.

Children's programmes are dominated by Japanese productions. The high-quality programmes from the Eastern European countries are not liked by Nicaraguan children one of whom said: "The characters are a bit silly; they don't hit one another; they don't fight; they don't die". This observation is valid for the children of revolutionary activists as well as other children. It shows, over and above content and genres, how the mass culture consumer has internalized a certain rhythm and narrative mode, a concept of action and televisual time, in short, a concept of "entertainment".

The two television channels produce practically no fiction, and although they produce 37% of their television programming for the most part it is made up of news, children's programmes and games.

News programmes are on 40 minutes a day of which the essential is the evening news bulletin, *Noticiero Sandinista*, at 8.00 p.m. This is the only national programme which is able to compete with the audience success of certain *telenovelas* whose broadcasting causes the people living in popular neighborhoods to desert church meetings or to arrive late for adult education courses[19].

This irrestible attraction for *telenovelas* is a source

of great concern. From time to time, one reads articles in the press asking if there is not a different way of approaching the problem, as for example:

To confront the problem of *telenovelas* which are broadcast at the same time as Sandinista Defense Committee (CDS) meetings and which attract the neighborhood with their alienating content, many CDS have proposed that they be suppressed. Directors of women's organization have demanded the same thing because they feel these programmes have an alienating effect on Nicaraguan women. But why not bring the television set to these meetings to watch the programme together and then analyse it?[20]

It is the Ministry of the Interior which has produced the most original fiction programmes. It is also the audiovisual department of this ministry which produces the programe *Cara al Pueblo* in which Commandants discuss live with the residents of different neighborhoods or villages[21]. Fiction production began in September 1984 and owes its existence to the personal interest of the Minister, Tomás Borge, sole surviving founder of the FSLN. A small team equipped with a Sony camera began producing police series of a particular type reminiscent of the films made by the ICAIC (Cuban Institute of Art and the Film Industry) on the "counter-intelligence" work of the Cuban secret services against counter-revolutionary spies in the 1960s. The success of the first 30 minute programme, *Paso Caballos*, about the infiltration of a double agent into the *Contras*, was unexpected. Two others rapidly followed: *Operación Oro* in two episodes of 30 minutes, which dealt with gold trafficking between Nicaragua and Honduras, and *Nitron*, three episodes of 30 minutes, which was about the dismantling of a CIA network in Nicaragua. The scripts were based on real cases solved by the Nicaraguan secret services during the last five years.

Far from being a self-promotion for the Ministry of the Interior these programmes question the notions of repression, security and surveillance in Nicaragua today. But while watching these programmes in the presence of their two directors, I could not help remarking on the negative impression given by police fictions in which the people (through neighborhood committees) help in the surveillance of traffickers and spies, especially when one is aware of how thin the line is between co-operation with the police and a denunciation mentality encouraged by regimes of exception. After I had expressed my reserves, we discussed the issue for over two hours. It was undoubtedly the first time — and perhaps the last — where I have been able to discuss questions of repression and internal security so seriously with officials from a Ministry of the Interior without hiding my reservations about their project. After I had left the Ministry, I thought why has the U.S. television industry been able to impose on the world market police and spy genres that have become so natural that one forgets to ask the questions about repression, denunciation and delinquency I asked the two Nicaraguan officials? I later reread the interviews by Michèle

19. Michèle Mattelart and Mabel Piccini had made the same observations in the course of their study of television and the popular classes in Santiago, Chile, 1972. For an account of this research in English, see Michèle Mattelart, "Chile: Political Formation and the Reading of Television" in Armand Mattelart and Seth Siegelaub, editors, *Communication and Class Struggle: 2. Liberation, Socialism*, New York, International General, 1983.
20. Luis Serra, *art cit*, p. 24.
21. See the text by Dee Dee Halleck in this volume. See also "Cara al pueblo: Popular Democracy in Practice" in Marlene Dixon and Susan Jonas, editors, *Nicaragua Under Siege*, San Francisco, Synthesis, 1984.

Mattelart and Mabel Piccini of television viewers in the shanty-towns on the outskirts of Santiago, Chile just before the 1973 *coup d'état*. Here is what the *pobladores* said:

It is sufficient to see the character [of these police series]; the hero or good guy is always American while the others, the murderers, in general come from a socialist country. The North-American comes over as being super-brilliant and has all the authority he needs to intervene in the affairs of any country. . . . The detective always appears as a benefactor and the crook almost always repent. The detective is the good guy, very human, while the delinquent is the opposite. But in reality, it's not always like that. Yet it's always justice, "right", "society" that wins. It's propaganda for bourgeois justice[22].

POPULAR CULTURE

Since the end of the 1960s, the notions of popular education and popular culture have profoundly marked both practices and reflections on political activity in Latin America. The question is rooted first in the respect for individuals and their learning capacity: how can one make the elimination of illiteracy and adult education a process in which the learners have a say? Here, the Church sectors have been determinant as one cannot speak of the pedagogy of liberation which emerged at the dawn of the 1960s without also referring to the theology of liberation which appeared at the same time[23]. In the 1970s, the field of communication practices was also affected by this radical questioning. Critical currents from Left political organizations joined forces with radical Christians. The political events in the Southern Cone — particularly in Chile — stimulated an open criticism of the authoritarian models reproduced by the parties in their relations with their own militants and the use of their "communication".

Today one finds throughout Latin America in varying degrees of clarity, the contributions of these two pioneering currents in defining popular communication and popular culture. A definition which is far from being uniform. How could it be otherwise, as these projects of popular communication are undertaken by the most diverse groups from grassroots Church communities in Brazil to miners' radio stations in Bolivia, and the new forms of political and cultural resistance to the military dictatorship in Chile supported by a multiplicity of social movements.

The themes of popular culture and popular communication are obviously present in Nicaragua. In many different ways.

These themes can be found in many concrete experiences in popular communication like that of the weekly of the grassroots Church communities, *El Tayacán*, launched in February 1982. Its aim is to respond to the needs of a recently literate Christian people. Its major concern is to counter the way the Church hierarchy uses religious themes, and beyond that, in a country where there is a permanent exchange between the universe of political symbols and religious symbols, to begin to understand how communication codes function within the popular classes. This has led the editorial team to analyse the photo-novel, comic strips and existing reading modes. The initiative has not always been understood by everyone. Some who are less aware of how religious faith is rooted in everyday life do not hide their reservations about a project they would prefer to be more militant and more directly engaged against the Church hierarchy.

The theme of popular culture has also inspired another look at "popular taste", another approach to what the people like. One important example of this has been the discussions of baseball in *Barricada*. If the Nicaragua of Somoza was not unified through the media, it begun to become so through baseball, introduced into the country by the U.S. Marines. Under the dictatorship, baseball became a form of expression for political confrontations. Even today, the national idols are those who manage to take their "revenge" by playing in the big league in the U.S. After questions on how to deal with the phenomenon of "alienation" or "popular expression" in the sports section of the press, at the end of 1981 discussions began on how to

AMÁ A TU PRÓJIMO
COMO A VOS MISMO

ALFABETIZÁ

Poster, "Love Your Neighbor Like You Love Yourself — [Participate in] the Literacy [Campaign]" (Reprinted from *Vivant Univers* (Namur, Belgium), 333, May–June 1981).

22. Michèle Mattelart, *art cit*, p. 82.
23. The works of the educator Paulo Freire, *Pedagogy of the Oppressed*, and *Cultural Action for Freedom* are typical of this current. On the influence of Freire see the text of Fernando Cardenal and Valerie Miller in this volume.

treat questions of everyday life in other sections of the press. There also began a reflection on the generally neglected sites of popular communication, especially the marketplaces. Enormous and permanent warehouses, similar to the African *souk* and frequented by all social groups, Nicaraguan marketplaces are veritable rumour factories, producing tendentious news as much in favour of the government as against it, during, for example, periods when it was difficult to obtain goods. This return to the popular is an example how the journalists of *Barricada* are trying to do away with verbalism and return to the facts.

The theme of the popular comes up again and again when one tries to go beyond an exclusively media-centred definition of the communication system. No longer the exclusive domain of the radio, press and television, communication becomes a model of social relations and social practices for the transmission and production of knowledge. This is not an easy concept. An idea of communication limited to the media and professional journalism has so impregnated practices that it is difficult for certain sectors to imagine the entry of other social actors in the production of information. The tension is always latent when, for example, anthropologists and educators try to create links with journalists to promote the idea that education, health, agrarian reform and other sectors can also be sites for social communication strategies. Situated at the crossroads of all these tensions, the School of Journalism at the Universidad Centroamericana is trying today to define a new profile wherein communication would no longer be limited only to journalism. Several Latin Americans from the critical school of communication research and members of the Faculty of the Information and Communication Science Department at the Universidad Bellaterra in Barcelona have come to give assistance.

It is also the theme of popular culture which underlies the many popular education initiatives which give priority to the receiver's participation. For as is customary in most revolutionary processes, the great unknown is still the receiver. As there are very few audience ratings, as imperfect as they may be, one must look towards those working in the domain of adult education to find this type of concern within the perspective of research/action or participatory research. These studies throw a particularly harsh light on the difficulties in Nicaragua to repress the memory of vertical communication. A study carried out in the peasant community of *El Regadío* evaluates the impact of adult education:

24. Malena de Montis, *La potencialidad de la educación popular en el proceso de transformación social en las zonas rurales: el caso de El Regadío (Esteli)*, unpublished research report, Managua, December 1982. See also Rosa María Torres, *La post-alfabetización en Nicaragua*, Managua, Publication of the INIES, April 1983.
25. José Luis Coraggio, *Nicaragua, revolución y democracia*, Mexico City, Editorial Linea-Cries, 1985, p. 47.

One has the impression that in this community we are to a certain extent in the process of reproducing the traditional forms of local power. Whereas before power was in the hands of the landowner, the Liberal party delegate or the local judge and was characterized mainly by repression, authoritarianism or more rarely paternalism, today this local power in gestation is essentially manifested by a certain paternalism on the part of outside leaders and delegates who in a certain way maintain the divorce between those below and those above. The latter think they have a monopoly on knowledge, considering that others don't have much to contribute and should be simple receivers of their directions[24].

TOWARDS POPULAR HEGEMONY

Many other examples could be given to show how practices in the domain of popular culture and communication are sometimes the source of tension. Although their supporters are not always fully conscious of this, these concepts of popular culture promote a horizontal communication which is likely to enter into contradiction with the traditional idea of the party as "the vanguard of the masses". This idea of a "vanguard" remains strongly anchored in certain sectors more inclined to consider the problem of plurality of democratic subjects as a tactic rather than an end in itself.

Such ideas expressing antagonistic projects coexist in Nicaragua, and to think that the democratic solution can be found only in one or the other amounts to utopianism. From popular culture, a renewed concept of the party will have to learn to return to everyday life as the terrain for the construction of democracy. From the party, a renewed concept of popular culture will have to learn to be more concerned with organization. This is a central issue for those who refuse to believe that new forms of social organization such as the creation of a national state, the links between the state and civil society, between the party and social movements, and between the party and the state, will be spontaneously created and those who believe, on the contrary, that they will emerge in function of the relations of force. The constitution of popular hegemony is, according to José Luis Coraggio,

the horizontal articulation of specific identities (heterogenous, sexual, cultural, regional, etc.) not only through the exchanges and daily life of social interaction but also explicitly through the exercise of sovereignty by the collective subject, the 'people'[25].

Nicaraguan society has already had many occasions to realize that the project of popular hegemony will not be constructed easily. The evolution of approaches towards the indigenous population on the Atlantic coast is indicative of the different opinions on the question of the plurality of popular interests.

Admittedly, one still meets people in Nicaragua who justify at any price the policy carried out in this domain from the beginning of the revolution. But the vast majority admit that serious errors — and not just unfortunate mistakes — have been made. The most important was to have imposed on the Miskito, Sumo and Rama populations a mode of organization stemming from old mechanical Marxist conceptions whereby one's class position "overdetermined" one's adherence to specific groups and cultures. As Tomás Borge now recognizes:

After the triumph of the revolution, we sent a group of comrades into the region. But they did not understand things properly. Some had a better knowledge of astronomy than anthropology. They committed terrible and alienating errors in the way they treated the Miskitos. For his part, Steadman Fagoth, the leader of the Miskitos and an ex-agent of Somoza's political police, began making tendencious broadcasts in the Miskito language, asserting among other things that our government wanted to exterminate all Miskitos over 30. . . . It's not surprising then that our erroneous policy in combination with this propaganda created suspicion among many Miskitos. A painful situation whose effects are still felt today[26].

67,000 Miskitos, 5,000 Sumos, 1,490 Caribs and 650 Ramas, with their own languages and customs, live in the Atlantic coastal region. Also living there are 26,000 English-speaking Creoles, former black slaves from Africa or the Caribbean, and towards the interior, 182,000 Spanish-speaking Mestizos. The status of the Atlantic coastal area is extremely complex because even though it shelters barely 10% of the population of Nicaragua, it accounts for over 56% of the national territory[27].

On top of the irrefutable errors of the Sandinistas were added a series of circumstances which make the situation even more complex. First, the revolution was thought through and carried out by people on the Pacific coast, whom the inhabitants on the Atlantic coast, colonized and brought over by the British, still refer to as "the Spanish". Secondly, the country itself did not form a true nation-state as the Somoza regime preferred to abandon this area to a marginal status. Less affected by the Somozist exactions, the indigenous populations had less reason than others to see the National Guard and the Somoza regime in a repressive light. This region was so little integrated into national life that the music of the blacks on the Nicaraguan Atlantic coast, which belongs to the same cultural area as Jamaica, was unknown in Managua. It was only in 1979 that the inhabitants of the capital finally danced to this local form of reggae music. The Sandinistas feared that these populations would prefer separatism at the very moment when a project for a nation-state was finally emerging.

Not only were the Miskitos afraid of disappearing as

an ethnic group but also of seeing their community split once again. In 1960, during a border dispute with Honduras, a judgement of the World Court in The Hague had led to a division of the Miskito community, with some installed on the Honduran side of the river (*Rio Coco*) separating Honduras and Nicaragua, and others on the Nicaraguan side. As soon as the first attacks of the FDN began in the region in December 1981, the Sandinist forces moved the Miskitos living along the banks of the river in order to protect them from the fighting without always taking the trouble of explaining the reason behind this forced migration. The real reason was to prevent them from joining the Misura army of Steadman Fagoth, operating from inside Honduras with 2,000 Miskitos. 8,500 Miskitos were thus evacuated and relocated 60 kilometres from the frontier[28].

In 1985, an autonomous status was proposed. It would give the ethnic groups an autonomous government with the power to establish its own policy in the cultural field and become the special representative of the native groups in dealing with the state institutions concerning economic and political decisions affecting the Atlantic region.

This is obviously far less than what is demanded by the leader of Misura, Steadman Fagoth, who wants independence pure and simple. It is also far removed from the propositions of Brooklyn Rivera, leader of the other ethnic political organization, Misurasata, who demands an autonomy recognizing his organization as the sole representative of the peoples of the Atlantic coast, and the expulsion of the Sandinista Popular Army (EPS) from this region and its replacement by the military wing of Misurasata. The Sandinistas replied that these demands posed several problems:

First, these propositions exacerbate the differences between the Atlantic population and the rest of the nation. Secondly, it supposes that the state abandon part of its sovereignty, since what is demanded is that it abandon its rights over natural resources. Finally, the concept of indigenous territory is marked by segregationism and racism, because one seeks the affirmation of an ethnic group exclusively in terms of separation and difference instead of within the framework of a unique national consciousness. If the government accepted this proposition, the next step could be the demand for independence and total separation. Disregarding the fact that the government questions the right of the Misurasata to claim to represent the Miskitos[29].

Apart from the Misurasata and Misura, the Miskitos have another organization, the Misatan, which is close to the Sandinistas.

Irritated by the way the international press has focused on the ethnic problem, the Nicaraguans often respond caustically: "If the European intellectuals who assail us without understanding us mobilized as much energy to defend the autonomy of New Caledonia or the other French overseas territories, perhaps we could begin to understand one another". Without granting any attenuating circumstances to the Sandinistas for their errors, is it not, however, paradoxical, as the Uruguayan writer Eduardo Galeano

26. Interview in *Playboy*, reprinted in *Pensamiento Propio*, January 1984, p. 33.
27. Source. CIDCA (Centro de investigación y documentación de la Costa Atlantica), 1983, quoted in *Pensamiento Propio* (Managua), January 1984, p. 37.
28. See the text by CIDCA in this volume. In 1985, the 37 ethnic communities which were moved to Tasba Pri in February 1982 were authorized to return to Rio Coco.
29. Interview with Luis Carrión, "La costa atlantica vista por el FSLN", *Pensamiento Propio*, January–February 1985, p. 30.

pointed out in a debate in Paris in February 1985:

Those who once killed Indians on the screen as a hero in Westerns poses today as the prime defender of the indigenous minorities in Central America, while at the same time American strategy in this region bathes in the blood of the rebellions of these same minorities — over there majorities — in Guatemala for example.

As the magazine *Pensamiento Propio* pointed out, the paradox is all the more striking in that "the crisis which has exploded on the Atlantic coast and the response to it is, in spite of everything unique in the Latin American continent"[30].

DOUBLE NETWORKS

The Nicaraguan revolution is original in that it is a site where people of many nationalities converge, a site where people belonging to different currents of thought and ways of seeing the world have had little occasion in the past to come together and now find each other face to face with their differences.

Looking at people in the streets of Managua or in other provincial cities already gives one an idea of the originality of the revolution. One meets many young Americans of both sexes. Some are tourists who arrive everyday to observe a revolution unfolding relatively close to their border. Many others have settled in Nicaragua to help in many areas, and especially communication and video. One finds them for example in the *Taller Popular de Video Timoteo Velasquez* which is linked to the Sandinist Workers' Union CST, in the video workshop of the Ministry of Agrarian Reform (Midinra), or in small independent firms like *Tercer Cine* or the state-owned INCINE[31]. One also finds photographers, musicians and, to a much lesser degree, radio technicians.

United States citizens do not need a visa. Despite the belligerent speeches and actions of the U.S. administration, the Managua government has insisted on keeping its borders open as a symbol of its willingness to negotiate. There are also young people from other countries, notably from Scandinavia and particularly Sweden whose foundations and social organizations maintain strong relations with Nicaragua. The Scandinavians are the most easily recognizable in the street: bleached jeans, tee shirts and long bond hair in sharp contrast to the jet black hair of most Nicaraguans. There are young Swiss living in the popular neighborhoods participating in the grassroots Church communities. Young German Christians from Darmstadt have succeeded in making their city the twin city of Ciudad Sandino, several kilometres from Managua.

One should not forget the Chilean, Argentine and Brazilian exiles who have long fought alongside the Sandinistas. The Nicaraguans call this new generation of volunteers *los internacionalistas*. Volunteers from Europe, North America and Latin America rub shoulders daily with other volunteers from Cuba, Bulgaria, the Soviet Union, the German Democratic Republic and Vietnam.

No country has been so closely observed by foreigners. As Bayardo Arce, one of the nine commandants, remarked:

The Sandinista revolution has been scrutinized and examined by all the international human rights organizations, churches, trade unions, minority rights organizations, women's organization, and youth organizations. There has probably never been an election where so many observers, even among our sworn enemies, have been invited with so much insistence to see and criticize. No one was excluded. They were able to analyse this election, the first our country has known, in its virtues and its limitations[32].

For the government, this open welcome is not just a question of principle. Openness is the very foundation of its strategy of international alliances. To those who want to imprison it within a bipolar East–West world, Nicaragua opposes a multiplicity of alliances articulated around other emerging interests:

Faced with the international crisis which persists and deepens, in a world which continues to reproduce hunger and oppression; with the North–South and East–West dialogue being blocked by the new Monroe doctrine, it is vital to recognize the role that can be played by the small countries on the periphery of the system, Third World and Non-Aligned countries. Such as the initiative for nuclear disarmament promoted by Mexico, Argentina, India, Sweden, Greece and Tanzania[33].

The recognition of new historical subjects in international relations is a proposition rarely found in the speeches of other revolutionary governments.

It is urgent to recognize the emergence of new historical subjects which are arising to confront the global crisis: the peace movements, the ecology movement, the churches, the trade unions and their new role, the minorities movement, the black movement, the women's movement, and the youth movement. It is important to analyse the role these new historic subjects could play in a global anti-imperialist project[34].

This vision of the international scene breaks with the tactical, instrumentalist concept which characterizes a good number of initiatives of the international communist movement in its relations with some of these new historical subjects especially the pacifist movement. Nicaragua's reflection on these new subjects accord perfectly with its strategy of pluralist alliances within the country, shown for example by the participation of Christian sectors. We need hardly add that this national project of new social relations within civil society integrating new historical subjects coincides with the ideals of many social movements in the European countries. However, the slow ascension of this new way of envisaging relations between peoples must be analysed within a framework of

---

30. *Ibid*, p. 31.
31. See the text of Dee Dee Halleck in this volume.
32. Bayardo Arce, *La politica de Reagan hacia Nicaragua*, closing speech of the First Congress of Anti-Imperialist Thought, held in Managua in February 1985, p. 12.
33. *Ibid*, p. 13.
34. *Ibid*, p. 13.

relations of force to avoid any idealism.

International aid to Nicaragua comes from multiple sources. It does not necessarily go through the state. Both volunteer groups and funds are international: churches, the Green Movement, foundations, European Social-Democracy, non-governmental organizations and many others. Thanks to this aid, numerous projects in the field of popular communication have seen the light of day. The essential problem in the face of this diversification, which also expresses the diversity of interests and points of view, is that the socialist countries are offering what could be called "ready-to-go" systems. This network of solidarity and aid brings with it specialists who arrive not only with their knowledge but also with a model of social organiza-

35. On the obstacles to a real non-alignment, José Luis Coraggio notes: "Nicaragua is trying to diversify the aid and solidarity it receives from other peoples, However, the East–West confrontation in which it is imprisoned by the Reagan administration means that only the socialist countries are disposed to assist it on a stable basis by supplying the arms which are indispensable to its defense. The diversification of economic relations which have been maintained and even developed during the years of the revolution is impossible in the military field. Not because of a decision by Nicaragua but because of the extremely effective blockade that the U.S. has imposed in this field within the Western countries. The soldiers, the militia and peasants who do the harvest, rifle on the shoulder, understand all too well that only the socialist countries are prepared to give them arms to avoid being killed by the ex-Somozist guards. If non-alignment implies not being the satellite of any superpower, it does not mean that the Nicaraguan people, while keeping its freedom to criticize, cannot tell the difference between the support given by socialism and the permanent aggression from American imperialism." *Op cit*, p. 110.

tion and power which underlies their knowledge. In the face of the availability of a tried-and-tested product other forms of aid from pluralist experiments where contradiction and trial-and-error are basic principles seem somewhat disorganized.

Thus in the communication domain in Nicaragua there is a confrontation between, on the one hand, the well-developed system for the socialization of agitation and propaganda ideas and its related journalism practice from the socialist countries, and on the other, the abundant but unsystematic development of ideas, studies and experiments from a wide range of groups in Latin America, Europe and North America during the past 15 years. Some sectors are obviously tempted to trust the heavy, formalized apparatus of the solidarity network of the socialist countries more than the new hypotheses on popular culture and communication . . . until the day comes when it is realized that a pre-fabricated, standardized product from one reality does not necessarily work in another.

It is fundamental to recognize the existence of the relations of force between these two projects. But this understanding is also essential if one wants to refute the law of the inevitable reproduction of the internationalization of bureaucratic networks. The East–West schema has already done enough damage; it is about time to understand what is happening in Nicaragua with the same analytical *finesse* that one uses to understand the contradictions developing in the Western democracies. If we do not, we run the risk of freezing the cold war and condemning both the East and the West, the North and the South, to stagnation[35].

Managua, February —
Paris, November 1985.

GUILLERMO ROTHSCHUH VILLANUEVA
Notes On the History of
Revolutionary Journalism in Nicaragua

During the liberation process in Nicaragua, the last two years of the revolutionary war, 1977–1979, were the most important historical periods.

During these stages, the guerrilla organization redefined its strategy, introducing as a way of confronting "Somozismo" [the policies of the dictatorship of Anastasio Somoza], the insurectional struggle, by means of which it achieved greater elasticity in the handling of alliances in the political field and established agreements with different social sectors of the country who assumed the revolutionary project of the FSLN as their own.

The FSLN began to give special importance to the organization and mobilization of the masses, capitalizing on armed actions, which lead to the founding of the group "Los Doce" ["The Twelve"] and the "Movimiento Pueblo Unido" (MPU) [the "United People Movement"].

This combination of events began to influence the political actions of the country's existing organizations who had accepted the FSLN's clearly-defined strategic project of struggle. The added participation of the oppositional bourgeois sectors was motivated by a different political project. The polarization of social forces was the most evident sign of these two years of political–military struggle.

Strategic and tactical redefinitions were necessary in order to avoid annihilation by the army of occupation, which had been formed at the end of the 1920s to destroy the "Pequeño Ejercito Loco del General de Hombres Libres, Augusto César Sandino" ["Little Crazy Army of the General of Free Men, Augusto César Sandino"].

It is during this period that certain events occurred in the domain of information which generated a series of historic experiences in the field of social communication. Among the most relevant were:

– The "Sindicato de Radioperiodistas de Managua" (SRPM) [the "Union of Radiojournalists of Managua"] was transformed into one of the most active and belligerent forces in the struggle;

– To be able to confront the regime and its press censorship, the SRPM managed to create one of the most ingenious and fertile forms of communication produced by the struggle: "El Periodismo Catacumbas" ["The Journalism of the Catacombs"];

– Somozismo treacherously assasinated Dr. Pedro Joaquin Chamorro, editor of the daily *La Prensa*, which sharpened the crisis and contributed to radicalizing the masses;

– After ten years of struggle, the journalists went even further, founding the "Union de Periodistas de Nicaragua" (UPN) [the "Union of Nicaraguan Journalists"], taking their greatest step forward in organizing;

– Around mid-1978, the clandestine Radio Sandino went on the air. It later played a strategic role in the agitation, organization, and combat preparation of the people;

– The national cinema was born on the war front. On the Southern Front "Benjamín Zeledón", the Cultural Brigade, "Leonel Rugama", filmed 8,000 feet of film; and

– An entire culture of resistance arose which succeeded in staying alive and reproducing itself.

These notes are a brief account of the principle events in the field of communication during the last two years of the war of liberation. Far from exhausting the subject, it is only a first approach; each event should be studied in depth. We have placed special emphasis on the links between political, military and journalistic events, since the war of liberation was the

This text was first published in *Cuadernos de Periodismo (Revista de la Escuela de Periodismo, Universidad Centroamericana)* (Managua), 1, December 1983 and 2, August 1984. It was translated from the Spanish by Don Clark. English translation Copyright © International General 1986. This is its first English publication.

factor which unleashed these experiences in the field of social communication, and culture in general.

I. THE OCTOBER OFFENSIVE AND PRESS CENSORSHIP

After the first new armed actions of the Sandinista National Liberation Front (FSLN) in October 1977, there began an uninterrupted offensive against the Somoza military dictatorship involving the country's diverse social forces.

The struggle acquired a new character militarily and politically, both nationally and internationally. The FSLN launched a permanent military offensive of insurrectional dimensions, converting the cities for the first time into the main areas of armed struggle, and began to undertake a broad policy of alliances with different sectors of national life.

From the middle of 1977, there was a reactivation of the opposition struggle of the bourgeoisie against Somozismo as a result of the human rights policy of U.S. President Carter. The fundamental reason for the bourgeoisie's contradictions with Somozismo was Somoza's participation in Nicaraguan finance, tacitly reserved in the past for the two most powerful economic groups in the country, the Bank of America and the Banco Nicaragüense.

Somoza broke this formal alliance by founding the Banco de Centroamérica, the Nicaragüense de Ahorro y Préstamo company (NIAPSA), and Interfinanciera, entering with very advantageous conditions into unfair competition with these two economic consortiums.

The first note of discord within the bourgeoisie were translated as a mild questioning of Somoza's management of the state apparatus. His answer to the private sector was categoric. He called them "procesadores de aforos", meaning that they also were benefitting from the economic policies of his government.

The new situation led the FSLN to a new plan of struggle; it decided to take advantage of this favorable opportunity, and try to generate greater contradictions which would weaken Somozismo militarily and politically. The guerrilla attack on the National Guard headquarters in San Carlos on 13 October 1977, inaugurated the insurrectional struggle as a new phase in the revolutionary war in Nicaragua.

These actions were disconcerting to the majority of political sectors in the country, who didn't know how to evaluate the military offensive. But even more surprised was Somoza's military dictatorship, which thought that the FSLN had been completely annihilated as a result of the military ground-razing actions in the north.

We should point out that since December 1974, after the assault on the home of Dr. Jose Maria Castillo Quant, Somozismo imposed martial law, a state of siege and press censorship, in order to create the conditions which would allow them to act with impunity under the supposed veil of legality to repress the guerrilla movement and its logistical support centers in the cities and the mountains. A totally merciless repression was the response to the guerrilla attack.

What surprised Somoza was that, far from having been destroyed, the FSLN reappeared with more strength, openly challenging its military power. The audacious attacks against the Somoza garrisons in San Carlos (13 October 1977), in Monzonte, Nueva Segovia (October 15th), and in Masaya (October 17th), weakened the position of Somoza's political alternative which he was seeking to renovate his regime.

The prolonged state of exception created by Somoza lasted 33 months. This situation forced the Union of Radiojournalists of Managua (SRPM) to rethink their struggle in order to be able to practice their profession. Their very livelihood was in danger. The journalists initiated a new stage marked by two forms of confronting the dictatorship: first, they emphasized their professional work (1975–1976) and demanded the end of press censorship and the abolition of the Radio and TV Code; and secondly, they adopted political forms of struggle against Somozismo (1977).

At its professional stage, the SRPM demanded among other things, that its members were covered by the Social Security system, it initiated a campaign to create its own printed material, and set up seminars on labor unions. Press censorship made them focus their demands on its elimination. Its fundamental activity was directed toward the re-establishment of freedom of the press.

All the initiatives taken by the SRPM to obtain the restitution of freedom of the press and the abolition of the Radio and TV Code were unsuccessful. Yet, these circumstances had positive effects. It served to politicize many of its members leading them to take positions which openly challenged the dynastic power. In June 1977, the SRPM, after two failures successfully led a 24-hour work stoppage, demanding the end of press censorship. Three years of constant struggle had served as a catalyst for their consciousness.

II. THE STRUGGLE TO SUPPRESS THE RADIO AND TV CODE

In this context, the struggle to end the Radio and TV Code eventually was converted into a tactical objective for confronting Somozismo. The different political parties and professional associations opted to include among their demands of the regime the abolition of the Radio and TV Code, finally incorporated into their respective programs a section on the freedom of the press.

The positive reception given by the different political, economic, religious, and professional sectors to the appeal formulated by "Los Doce" ["The Twelve"]

(*La Prensa*, 21 October 1977), to hold a national dialogue to put an end to the violence, legitimized completely the struggle being waged by the FSLN. Once the basis for this dialogue was realized, the suppression of the Radio and TV Code was included in the demands. (Separate paragraph 5.)

The tactical objective had been turned into an important point of discussion on the agenda of the political parties. The lifting of press censorship (19 September 1977) was the result of the pressures by the different sectors of the country. This opportune conjuncture allowed the SRPM to use more pressure and to demand the removal of the Radio and TV Code, not as a professional demand, but rather as part of the struggle for national liberation.

The same crisis in which Somozismo was debated inhibited the Code from being modified or reformed. The Radio and TV Code, promulgated under the presidency of Luis Somoza in July 1962, was created to avoid the increasing propaganda of an armed, political and ideological struggle against Somozismo and, fundamentally, to contain the development of revolutionary ideology.

The Code, in fact, constituted a law of exception against practicing journalism and against the rise of any ideology except extreme liberalism or traditional conservatism. Its exceptional character was that the supposed violations were only known to the director of the Office of Radio and TV who was assigned to the National Guard.

The procedure established for judging the supposed infractions was by means of government order. This kept the courts from knowing about any act or circumstances which apparently violated the Code. In practice, it was converted into an expedient of force which Somozismo used in its duel against the radio and TV journalists (the written press was not covered by the Code).

The fact that the print media remained on the fringe of this judicial statute did not mean that they were outside Somoza's arbitrariness. On 28 January 1967, only six days after the bourgeoisie's "putsch", Somoza enacted a decree which authorized the Executive wing, that is, Somoza, to seize the machines used to print the newspapers. Naturally, only he had the power to determine what constituted a violation.

This decree was directed against the daily *La Prensa*, but it was also aimed at obstructing the circulation of the workers' newspapers at the time. Its purpose was to prevent the professional organizations from counting on their own media to disseminate information. The left parties were practically operating illegally. Bipartisanship was the dominant political

norm in Nicaragua from independence (1821) until 19 July 1979, the year of National Liberation.

The essential content of the Radio and TV Code was oriented to exclude anything except the promotion of the electorial farce in which the two historic traditional parties (liberals and conservatives) participated, and to contain any political ideology founded on other principles, and obviously, to thus impede the growth of left parties. The Code was promulgated in 1962, just a year after the FSLN was founded.

In practice, the Radio and TV Code not only limited the freedom of the press, but also the exercise of political liberties. Its repressive stance forced the FSLN to be constantly creative in order to be able to deliver its message to the masses.

For this reason, no political or professional group remained on the margin of the struggle to have it repealed. Principally, the left groups actively involved themselves since they were fully aware that it was they who were most hurt by it. For the FSLN, it never went beyond a tactical objective in its struggle.

From its clandestine position, it was the FSLN who was in the worst situation. Tacitly or expressly, the social communication media omitted information about their actions, be it because they were distancing themselves from this form of struggle or because they feared Somoza's repression. From its foundation in 1961 until a short time before the triumph, the FSLN had to use their ingenuity to devise their own means of communication. In order to get their message to the people, they had to take over different radio stations by force of arms.

The FSLN was forced to attempt different types of agitation and propaganda among the popular sectors of the country. From the armed incursion of "El Chaparral" (1959), in which the founding members Carlos Fonseca Amador, Tomás Borge, Silvio Mayorga, Victor Manuel Tirado, Germán Pomares, participated, among others, special importance was given to the social communication media, since from that time on it was thought that they should rely on a clandestine radio station[1].

The first experience the leaders had in this field was the control they exercised in directing *El Universitario*, the organ of the University Center of the Autonomous National University of Nicaragua. In order to spread their revolutionary doctrine among the students and the masses, they printed and distributed flyers, leaflets, handouts, and painted "pintas" on the walls, and managed to edit their own media (*El Sandinista, Trinchera, Rojo y Negro, Universidad Revolucionaria*) and their own magazine (*Pensamiento Crítico*).

In the beginning of the war of liberation, they founded their own radio station, "Radio Sandino" (1978), which played a fundamental role in the combat preparation of the Nicaraguan people. The broadcasts fulfilled two basic objectives: the key factor was agitation and mobilization, and the other was to

---

1. Analyzing the capacity for agitation that can be achieved through clandestine broadcasting, Commander Humberto Ortega Saavedra said that the origins of Radio Sandino were connected with a radio which the first antisomozistas had used in 1960. See Humberto Ortega Saavedra, *Sobre la insurrección*, Havana: Editorial de Ciencias Sociales, 1981, p. 79.

transmit political and military watchwords around which the Nicaraguan people should rally their activities.

III. THE ASSASSINATION OF PEDRO JOAQUIN CHAMORRO: THE CATALYST OF THE CRISIS

As we said, in October 1977, the group "Los Doce" ["The Twelve"] came forward as a force for establishing a national dialogue. As a result of its alliances, the FSLN tried to capitalize politically on its military actions. As part of its pre-planned strategy, the FSLN welcomed the dialogue, but warned that Somozismo should not participate. This position was based on the fact that the FSLN thought that the participation of Somoza could lead to an understanding — as had occurred earlier — between the traditional opposition and the dynastic regime.

In this way, the FSLN posed the alternative for Nicaragua: reform or revolution, reiterating a clear preference for the latter.

The possibility to establish a dialogue was eliminated on 10 January 1978, when Dr. Pedro Joaquin Chamorro, the editor of the newspaper *La Prensa*, was assassinated by the Somoza forces. His assassination touched all social sectors of the country. His death served as detonator among the masses. The first abrupt actions took place in the streets during which several properties of the Somozistas were burned. The people were in a state of insurrection during Chamorro's wake and burial.

This led to a deepening of the Somozista crisis. The breaking off of the dialogue meant his total isolation and ruled out any possibility of an understanding between the traditional political sectors and Somozismo.

As a result of the assassination of Dr. Pedro Joaquin Chamorro, a general sit-down strike was begun on 23 January 1978, in which many political, economic, and professional sectors participated. In Managua, the strike spread to business, industry, and the workers' sector of banking. It was supported and sponsored by the traditional opposition and the private sector in an attempt to capitalize on the crisis for their own benefit.

While reporting on the course of these events, the journalists from the different radio and television media in the country again felt the weight of Somozista repression. The newscasters from "Radio Mi Preferida" were the first to be suspended by the Director of the Radio and TV, Col. Alberto Luna. The suspension was due to their reporting on the development of the country's strike. On this occasion, Somozismo sought to frighten the journalists and tried to interfere in the content of their news reports.

The dictatorship's image suffered further deteriora-

tion due to the work stoppage of ten minutes throughout Latin America which was decided by the Federación Latinoamericana de Periodistas [FELAP, the Latinamerican Federation of Journalists] to protest the assassination of the editor of *La Prensa*. The stoppage of the FELAP (which had brought together by its action 60,000 journalists) occurred within the development of the strike in Nicaragua. This further isolated Somozismo internationally while internally it increased the participation of the masses behind the insurrectional focus set out by the FSLN.

The information media lead by *La Prensa* changed and gradually radicalized its offensive against the regime. This situation was a determining factor in the dictatorship's again imposing a state of emergency and press censorship after 28 January 1978.

One of the most important measures adopted by the SRPM was that the communications media wouldn't actively join the work stoppage. Their functioning was vital in order to maintain a state of permanent agitation among the masses. The different media created a unified reporting policy which allowed their reports to be handled by a single editor.

Without necessarily talking on the project of revolution, *La Prensa*, from then on:

spread the clandestine struggles, legal and semi-legal, which our people were developing to confront the dictatorship for the last time. This signified and synthesized the contribution which that newspaper gave to the struggle when all the means of communication were censored, were repressed, when silence was menacing Nicaragua[2].

The attitude of the owners and workers at *La Prensa* had different motivations. Part of its members supported the struggle with the intention of crystalizing the reformist policy of the Frente Amplio Opositor [FAO, the Broad Opposition Front], with which they were affiliated. The other part acted in their capacity as militants or sympathizers of the FSLN. Almost all of the journalists from the social communication media in the country experienced this. The positions taken by many of the journalists put them in open contradiction with the stands taken by the media owners and particularly with the advertising agencies.

At this point, the members of the SRPM understood that the abolition of the Radio and TV Code was not the most important part of the struggle. What was fundamental was to get rid of the dictatorship. In spite of all the risks, the journalists eventually became the principal propagandists for anti-Somoza activities. The new imposition of censorship occurred in a different political context. Far from accepting the orders of the dictatorship, they contravened its orders, going to great lengths to inform the public.

The FSLN has succeeded in transforming the demands of the moment into a total questioning of Somozista power. However, the traditional opposition tried to turn the strike into a means to apply pressure for the resignation of Somoza and present themselves as a legitimate alternative to the crisis. Fundamentally, it attempted to sell that image to the United States

---

2. Carlos Nuñez, "El Debate entre la verdad y la infamia", *Hacia una política cultural de la revolución popular Sandinista*, Managua: Ministerio de Cultura, 1982.

Embassy, who was viewing with growing concern Somozismo's irreversible agony and the necessity of filling the power vacuum with a group who shared their interests in Nicaragua and in the Central American region.

IV. THE SRPM AND "JOURNALISM OF THE CATACOMBS"

Censorship of the press stimulated the creative capacity of national journalism. With the tempestuous closing of the news programs *"Sucesos"* [*"Events"*], *"Mundial"* [*"The World"*], *"Extra"*, and *"Aquí Nicaragua"* [*"Here Nicaragua"*], which broadcast on Radio Corporación, Radio Mundial, Radio Continental, and Radio Preferida, the SRPM created a commission to study a new way to keep the Nicaraguan people informed.

The commission took the name of Comité Popular de Huelga [the Popular Strike Commission]. One of its functions was to establish ties between the sectors involved in the strike and the sectors of the left organically linked to the FSLN who proposed not only the fall of Somoza, but also a radical change in the social, political, and economic structures of the country.

Besides the shutdowns, the Radio and TV Commission imposed considerable fines with the intention of putting the very existence of the information media in danger. During the last two years of the dictatorship there were more than 100 shutdowns. The SRPM proposed that the fines be paid by the people. Bank accounts were opened where people would deposit their help. In this way, the people began to actively participate in the struggle against the repressive laws and earn the right to be independently and freely informed.

With all legal forms of information closed, the sense of invention of Nicaraguan journalism and its commitment to the national liberation cause were put to the test. Leaving behind its traditional professional role of broadcasting on the radio where censorship

prevented reporting, the SRPM sought in interpersonal communication a better way of informing the people. Thus was born what the world would come to know as "Journalism of the Catacombs", a reminder of what had been the persecution of primitive Christians.

Its name was derived from two circumstances: firstly, from the fact that journalism began to be practised almost clandestinely and, secondly, that the journalists found refuge in Catholic churches, where they could bring people together to inform them about the prevailing situation in Nicaragua. Journalism of the Catacombs was begun on 31 January 1978. Participating in this experience were journalism students, editors, photographers, and heads of the different media; an important contribution to national, continental, and world journalism.

Journalism of the Catacombs

can be considered as the most important and most original contribution of Nicaraguan journalists, of those who valiently resisted remaining silent. They were the first paper barricades erected, a parallel to the church naves, which in the dark days of Christian persecution they extended to the eaves like protecting arms and said to the executioners: "You shall not pass"[3].

Journalism of the Catacombs showed, for the first time, that between members of the SRPM there could exist an absolute consensus to challenge the dictatorship and to join in the struggle which would overthrow it. Old academic precepts regarding the supposed nature of professional practice were thrown out. The so-called "objectivity" in the transmission of information, which some schools of social sciences argue, was put to the test and totally defeated. Never before had national journalism been more honest and conscientious in its duty to inform.

These are the periods which crystalize a class consciousness which can go on to become combative positions to question the nature of a profession whose exercise in practice had tended to be corrupted and eroded by those who proclaim that journalism calls for "objectivity". In the field of social science, this "objectivity" does not exist, since in a society divided into antagonistic classes, scientific discourse becomes ideological[4].

Journalism of the Catacombs was a lively, flexible and dynamic journalism. It managed to create a "circuit" of language, or what Pasquali calls a "communicational relation"; transmitter and receiver intimately united, interchangeable. Journalists went to the churches to inform and to gather information. They succeeded in covering 24 churches in Managua and the experience was repeated in León, Matagalpa, Masaya, Granada, and Carazo[5].

This was neither an isolated nor spontaneous action. For its operation, the journalists of the SRPM set up an editor-in-chief, a group of *ad hoc* editors, a distribution department, and group leaders in each church. They transmitted national and international news. La Casa del Periodismo [Journalism House] was

3. Carlos Tünnermann Bernheim, *La contribución del periodismo a la liberación nacional* (Lección inaugural del IV Congreso de la Unión de Periodistas de Nicaragua), Managua: Ministerio de Educación, March 1981.

4. Based on the idea of ideology elaborated by Eliseo Verón, the sociologist José Antonio Alonso says that to relate the ideological with the conditions of production of messages, in the social sciences discourse as any other discourse, is necessarily ideological. "All scientific and non-scientific dialogue which are born in a class society, like capitalist society, are ideological." See José Antonio Alonso, *Metodología*, Mexico City: Editorial Edicol, 1981, p. 20.

5. A detailed study on the experience of Journalism of the Catacombs has been written by journalist María Alicia Chacón Olivas in her thesis for her university degree in journalism, entitled *Refugio de noticieros radiales en las iglesias*. Managua: Universidad Nacional Autonoma de Nicaragua, September 1978.

the epicenter of their work.

In spite of its short duration — this experience ended on February 10th — it had international repercussions. Journalists on this and other continents have harvested this legacy of Nicaraguan journalism. A legacy of liberation for which some Nicaraguan journalists paid for with their lives, such as Walter Mendoza, Aura Ortiz, and Alvaro Montoya Lara, all of whom were organically connected to the FSLN.

The taking of a position against the dictatorship did not come from a specific professional field, but rather it was the result, to a greater or lesser degree, of the level of political consciousness. Periods of revolutionary upsurge are characterized by their being key moments in the clarification of consciousness and in the taking of a position for or against a given class or sector in conflict. The Nicaraguan journalists, joined together in the SRPM, took the side of the people against the regime who, when undergoing a broad crisis showed all its viciousness.

The political consciousness of the journalists was at the same level as the objective crisis which was demolishing the Somozista dictatorship. The subjective factors called for by the country's situation were unleashed by the FSLN offensive. Its constant drive and form of insurrectional struggle radicalized the consciousness of the Nicaraguan people.

A sit-down strike was not a suitable nor sufficient way to topple the Somozista military dictatorship. The reformist sectors, consistent with their traditional way of confronting the regime, never realized that their way of fighting wasn't capable of defeating tyranny. Nevertheless, it served to de-legitimatize Somoza's rule and to isolate it from the rest of Nicaraguan society.

When the bourgeoise sectors backed down from the general strike, the FSLN again began to push forward on the military front in order to make clear that this was the only road which could lead to the defeat of the Somozista military dictatorship. On 2 February 1978, they carried out two very important guerrilla actions in the cities and another in a Somoza counterinsurgency camp in the mountains.

The military takeover of Granada and Rivas, and the attack on the antiguerrilla encampment in Santa Clara, Nueva Segovia were an important step in the Sandinista offensive. From this moment on, the FSLN imposed their form of fighting, while the political parties and traditional movements sought a different way out of the crisis which would allow them to retain power.

V. THE FOUNDING OF THE UPN AND RADIO SANDINO

The journalists' struggle took a qualitative leap forward by founding, on 1 March 1978, a union organization on a national level: la Unión de Periodistas de Nicaragua [UPN, the Union of Nicaraguan Journalists]. The necessities of the struggle had pushed them to create an entity which would permit, under its aegis, the organizing of all the nation's journalists.

The leaders of the SRPM who founded the UPN were the same ones who from 1977 began a movement leading to the creation of a national organizing structure which would involve all of the journalists in the country in the struggle. At that time, the structure of the SRPM was limited to organizing the radio journalists working in Managua. The UPN was founded on the same day that Nicaragua celebrates Journalists' Day. Within the repressive conditions imposed by Somoza, a new institution was born which respected the most honorable tradition of the SRPM's struggle without implying that the journalists had sacrificed the more belligerent objectives of their combative entity.

The events of February and the Journalism of the Catacombs represent two qualitative leaps in the confrontation with the Somoza military dictatorship. The FSLN by its own armed actions had guaranteed its propaganda internally and abroad, and thus succeeded in influencing and enrolling in their ranks numerous journalists attached to the SRPM. In this way, a definitive bridge was built between the journalists and the masses. National journalism presented itself as a permanent frontal attack against the dictatorship, with an important part of its platform being the suppression of the Radio and TV Code.

Afterwards, events would happen one after another with the driving force being the FSLN. Nevertheless, the insurrection of Monimbó (20 February 1978) was a new experience for the guerrilla organization. The struggle proposed by this indigenous community went beyond the intentions of the FSLN, although their leaders were at the forefront of combat. The contact bombs and the native masks formed part of the war arsenal. This form of resistance showed the Nicaraguans they could use rudimentary homemade arms.

Afterwards came the attack on the National Palace (22 August 1978), which would liberate the FSLN prisoners and precipitate a crisis in the dictatorship. Like 1974, Somoza was forced to allow the publication of two communiques which served to propagandize the struggle and to radicalize the masses. With the attack against the National Palace, the FSLN blocked the United States manoeuver to put a civillian–military junta at the head of the government[6].

The evident decomposition of the dictatorship was seen by the United States, who began mediating in 1978 to seek a favorable outcome to the crisis and avoid the triumph of the guerrilla movement. The Broad Opposition Front [Frente Amplio Opositor, FAO] then became the imperialist alternative to fill the power vacuum left by Somozismo.

In the information field, internationally, the FSLN benefitted from a favorable conjuncture. Through the work of the Solidarity Committees, a journalism offen-

6. Humberto Ortega Saavedra, *op. cit.*, p. 83.

sive was kept up which helped to clarify and make understood the struggle taking place in Nicaragua. Foreign correspondents from different news media set themselves up in Managua to transmit to the world the process of the war of liberation.

The evident mediating role of the FAO and its pro-imperialist thesis created a fracture which lead to the rise of the National Patriotic Front [Frente Patriótico Nacional, FPN], in which the United People Movement [Movimiento Pueblo Unido, MPU] played a well-known leadership role as the politcal arm of the FSLN. From this moment on, the two groups represented different options. The FAO turned openly pro-imperialist and the FPN supported the revolutionary project impelled by the guerrilla group.

The Union of Journalists of Nicaragua was active in the ranks of the FPN. With its determination, it confirmed the character of its struggle and the politicizing of national journalism.

During the rest of the year 1978 the FSLN further developed its activity among the masses; in the popular neighborhoods the daily struggle grew more violent with more arms being captured, and the guerrilla force "Pablo Ubeda" attacking many National Guard quarters in the northern and cental mountains.

In April 1979, a guerrilla column took Esteli and defeated the city's military forces, avoiding a double encirclement which Somoza's army had set up in an attempt to annihilate them. This military victory created anticipation nationally and once again demonstrated the vulnerability of the National Guard. It accelerated the final offensive, which was initiated in May 1979.

We should keep in mind that in mid-1978, Radio Sandino had started up, on short wave, with five watts of power and with morning and evening broadcasts, making repeated calls to struggle, teaching the people how to handle all types of arms and to prepare explosives. Radio Sandino was a strategic arm against Somozismo. Journalists of the SRPM and UPN participated in its broadcasts and in preparing its war dispatches and general news.

During the last two months of combat, the communication media began to play a critical role in the development of the war. The newspaper *La Prensa* had been bombed and destroyed by Somoza's airplanes, and the radio stations not connected with Somozismo which were still operating became part of the Radiodifusora Nacional, the official voice of the government. They were forced to rebroadcast information which tended to paralyze the masses and to sow psychological terror especially in the eastern popular neighborhoods of Managua.

As the war fronts of the FSLN reached the cities, a few radio stations began broadcasting messages and war dispatches from the victorious troops. Nicaraguans began to turn their dial to the new stations which were the prelude to the final victory of the

armed population. Radio Insurreción in Matagalpa, Radio Venceremos in León, Radio Liberación in Esteli, Radio Revolución in Juigalpa, all united their voices with broadcasts of clandestine Radio Sandino.

In almost all the radio stations members of the SRPM and UPN were in the forefront. Familiar voices began to spread the good news that the triumph of the people was only a matter of hours.

In the final assessment which Commander Humberto Ortega Saavedra made of the war of liberation, he stated that:

without radio, it would have been difficult to maintain the strike ... [Radio Sandino was] the principal agitational element in the insurrection and the strike.... Without a radio to orient the movement of the masses ... there would not have been a revolutionary triumph[7].

VI. THE COUNTERCULTURE OF THE RESISTANCE

The fundamental forms of communication of the FSLN with the masses were leaflets, flyers, "pintas" [wall graffiti], the seizure of radio stations, its own propaganda linked to each of its battles, and the counterculture which grew throughout the war of liberation.

On the walls in various cities in the country, one can still read the war slogans and the calls to insurrection. Flyers containing the denunciation of assassinations were covertly distributed on the buses, and the messages stuck to the lips of the people.

In the sphere of propaganda the assault of 17 December 1974, had the desired effect. As part of the negotiations, the FSLN made the dictatorship diffuse two communiques on all the radio stations in the country, in all the print media, and on television. This touched everyone and deeply affected the Nicaraguans' sensibilities.

Even more successful was the propaganda repercussions of the assault on the National Palace on 22 August 1978. In addition to forcing Somoza to distribute two communiques to all the news media in the country, this event inspired the publication of a series of books, feature articles and special reports about the audacious guerrilla *coup*. The presence of many journalists in the Cámara de Diputados [House of Representatives] was used advantageously to inform the world of this action via the many news agencies and national news magazines.

In the field of social communication, the war was not only a determining factor in the politization of journalists, but also it was the stage of the struggle during which the Nicaraguan movie industry was born. It was on the southern front "Benjamín Zeledon" where there arose what would later become the Instituto Nicaragüense de Cine [Nicaraguan Film Institute, INCINE], then called the "Brigada Cultural Leonel Rugama", in homage to the militant poet who died in combat against the dictatorship on 15 January

---

7. Humberto Ortega Saavedra, *op. cit.*, pp. 93 and 95.

1970.

The song was a form of struggle and an element in raising consciousness. The appearance of "Guitara Armada" ["Armed Guitar"], by Carlos and Luis Enrique Mejía Godoy, was the result of FSLN's political and cultural work. The content of their songs was an initiation into the struggle showing how to use a gun and how to make explosives. These songs had a widespread national exposure and penetrated profoundly into the popular consciousness. Once again the drums of Subtiava sounded, calling to war.

With good reason, Sergio Ramírez wondered during his speech at the awards for the "Casa de las Américas" prize (22 January 1982), in Havana:

I really don't know how much the revolution owes to the songs of Carlos Mejía Godoy, which organized the collective spirit of the people by extracting the themes and chords from the deepest of our roots, and preparing this feeling for the struggle[8].

"La Misa Campesina" ["The Peasants' Mass"] had a tremendous impact on Catholics. It offered a new version of the Gospel, making it a popular re-creation of the origins of Jesus Christ as His emergence out of the hearts of the oppressed. The Somoza regime became enraged at the authors of "La Misa Campesina" and forbid its public presentation because they understood that its message had penetrated deeply into the Catholic parishioners of Nicaragua. Parallel to the testimonial song introduced by the two Mejía Godoy, other groups of singer-troubadors emerged including the outstanding "Pancasán", whose very name reminds one of the FSLN's guerrilla action of 1967 in the mountains in the north of the country, in the days when the bourgeois opposition tried to overthrow Somoza (22 January 1967) and made martyrs of hundreds of Nicaraguans.

The confrontation with Somozismo, as local representative of imperialism, took on the character not only of military and political resistance, but also of cultural resistance. The FSLN was rooted profoundly in the Nicaraguan nationality and battled in the field of culture with tremendous success.

They were convinced that all the cultural activity sponsored by the Somozista system was designed to justify and legitimize its new existence. The dictatorship had succeeded in elevating:

8. Sergio Ramírez, "La revolución, el hecho cultural mas importante de nuestra historia", *Hacia una política cultural de la revolución popular Sandinista*, Managua: Ministerio de Cultura, 1982. A similar appraisal of the importance of the song of testimony in the struggle for liberation is made by Commander Tomás Borge in his "La Cultura es el pueblo", *Hacia una politica cultural de la revolución popular Sandinista*. Managua: Ministerio de Cultura, 1982.
9. Bayardo Arce, "El dificil terreno de la lucha: el ideologico", *Hacia una politica cultural de la revolución popular Sandinista*, Managua: Ministerio de Cultura, 1982.
10. Bayardo Arce, *op. cit.*, p. 18.
11. Jorge Eduardo Arellano, *Panorama de la literatura Nicaragüense*, Managua: Ediciones Nacionales, 1977.

a whole complex of ideological values which, through the educational system, the communication media, and the culture, in general, were aimed at developing, maintaining, and reproducing the criteria that give rise to economic injustice[9].

In these conditions, the FSLN necessarily had to establish a front of ideological struggle and undertake a confrontation with the country's other currents. Thus a counterculture was elaborated to oppose the ruling culture. In examining this phenomenon, Commander Bayardo Arce explained:

With popular testimonial music, music of protest, we opposed "disco" music, the deformed music which was being fed to our peasantry.

We opposed vapid poetry which entertains itself by shuffling words to make them beautiful with a poetry of revolutionary content.

We opposed the opulent theater with the "sketch" which would reflect the national reality.

We opposed in the ideological field, the backward, antipopular theories of the Church, with theories from the Vatican Council which spoke of the new mentality of the Church.

We opposed the historical lie with the historical truth, we opposed alienated journalism with the leaflets which told the truth about our revolutionary process. And on the same front of ideological struggle, we opened the political front against the institutions and the individuals holding enemy power. We fused together all these battle fronts, the economic, the ideological and the political, with the principal battle front which was the military front[10].

Let us remember that a year after the armed incursion of "El Chaparral" (1959), and the sudden murder of the university students on 23 July 1959, the "Frente Ventana" ["Ventana Front"] arose in 1960 at the National Autonomous University of Nicaragua (UNAN) with the clear political purpose of contributing to the liberation of the country.

During the first roundtable of young Nicaragua poets which was supported by the "Frente Ventana" and held on the 28–29 October 1961 in the city of León, the poets stood out by their literary positions which were "the same as those held on a more combative, political, level, which also was developing in the early sixties"[11].

One of the fundamental tasks of one of the founders of "Frente Ventana", Sergio Ramírez, would be to summarize and spread the thought of Sandino nationally and internationally. Ramírez' work had profound political repercussions. The publication of *El Pensamiento Vivo de Sandino* [*The Living Thought of Sandino*] by the Editorial Universitaria Centroamericana (EDUCA) in 1974, made widely known the political content and doctrine of Augusto César Sandino who was betrayed by the Somoza military dictatorship, and assassinated on 21 February 1934, at the insistence of United States imperialism.

The literary production of two of its founders, Sergio Ramírez and Fernando Gordillo (1940–1967), are permeated with Sandinista thought. Some of their work in poetry and prose revolves around the guerrilla's exploits and, in their political militancy, they were allied with the basic principles of the FSLN.

Literature and art in Nicaragua was always stamped

with political compromise. The guerrilla exploits of Sandino infused generations of writers with his nationalism. Salomón de la Selva was one of the first to sing of the "General de Hombres Libres" ["General of Free Men"], taking his songs into the very heart of the United States. The "Movimiento de Vanguardia" ["Vanguard Movement", 1929] from the very first moment was nourished by the nationalism of the anti-imperialist resistance struggle of Sandino. They hoisted their flag and fought against secular United States intervention in Nicaragua (1926). With a sharp feeling of nationalism, one of its founders, the poet and teacher Luis Alberto Cabrales, expressed clearly that, regarding Nicaragua. "She has only two saving graces in the eyes of the world: Darío and Sandino."

In the north of the country, the scene of the struggle for the defense of national sovereignty, the "Los Romances y Corridos Nicaragüenses" arose which sang of the Sandinista struggle and was transmitted orally and handed down from generation to generation. Initially this material was gathered together and published by Ernesto Mejía Sánchez in Mexico at the Imprenta Universitaria (UNAM) in 1946, and, today, researcher Jorge Eduardo Arellano has again undertaken this project.

Some of the songs of Mejía Godoy are re-creations of the songs which first appeared in the Segovian mountains of Nicaragua. A substantial part of "Guitara Armada" is inspired by these "canciones norteñas" ["northern songs"] and by poems of national writers. "Flor de Pino" ["Pine Flower"], "Allá va el General" ["There Goes the General"], "La Tumba del Guerrillero" ["The Guerrilla Fighter's Tomb"], blend honorably the tradition of song and popular struggle.

A testimony to this permanent confrontation between the creators and the dictatorship is found in the anthology *Poesía Revolucionaria Nicaragüense* [*Nicaraguan Revolutionary Poetry*], whose first edition in 1962 (Talleres B. Costa Amic, México City), prepared by Ernesto Mejía Sánchez and Ernesto Cardenal, was stamped with "Patria y Libertad" ["Homeland and Liberty"], the seal of the Ejército Defensor de la Soberanía Nacional [Defending Army of National Sovereignty].

This anthology:

was re-edited seven times between 1962 and 1973, without counting the offset editions done right in Nicaragua by students at the risk of their lives. In 1973, Ernesto Cardenal himself prepared another anthology, not limited to socio-political themes, with the title *Poesia Nicaragüense* [*Nicaraguan Poetry*] (Habana, Casa de las Américas), which included some of the poems from the earlier collection[12].

12. Gregorio Selser, "Hasta que pudo hacerlo con las armas, el pueblo de Nicaragua peleó con la poesía". *Apuntes sobre Nicaragua*, Mexico City: Centro de Estudios Economicos y Sociales del Tercer Mundo (CEESTEM); Editorial Nueva Imagen, 1981.
13. Jorge Eduardo Arellano, *op. cit.*, p. 115.
14. Leoncio Sáenz, "Breve historia del arte Nicaragüense", *Ventana*, No. 100, *Barricada Cultural*, Vol. III, 18 January 1983.

The anthology *Poesía Política Nicaragüense* [*Nicaraguan Political Poetry*] (Difusión Cultural, UNAM, México City, 1979), put together by Francisco de Asis Fernández, is one of equal political and literary merit. It attempts to show a common denominator between the resistance to cultural colonialism and Somoza's sell out to imperialism, and is focused on showing how creativity takes on a combative character in a country resisting the loss of its personality when faced with foreign subjugation.

The novel *Trágame Tierra* [*Earth Swallow Me*] (1969), by Lizandro Chávez Alfaro, with which Nicaragua definitively became part of the new hispano-american narrative current, is inspired by the nationalism and transcendent anti-imperialism of Sandino.

With a basic use of Nicaraguan history, above all of the first half of the twentieth century, Chávez Alfaro exposes the conflict (between a generation which accepts the intervention of the U.S. Marines and another which rejects it) and succeeds in stamping his work with the concept of the novel as denunciation[13].

The Sandinista militancy of Ernesto Cardenal had its most refined expression in his *Epigramas* (1961) and in *La Hora Cero* (1960) where his blending of political and social themes rose above pamphleteering and produced one of the best political poems from Hispanic America.

In painting, the "Grupo Praxis", during its first period (1962–1967) and its second stage (1971–1972), took a political position similar to that of the "Frente Ventana". In a strictly artistic realm, this gave "rise to the most important and original art movement in Central America and elevated its art to the heights of international renown"[14].

The "Grupo Gradas" (1974), with a more defined militancy, in its short existence generated a movement which was organically tied to the FSLN. Its artistic character was multifaceted, bringing together painters, sculptors, poets, sociologists, journalists, music workshops, and actors, among others. They performed the length and breadth of the country with the development of the popular mobilizations, proposing their message to the people who would then put it into practice.

These different forms of cultural resistance later affected the consciousness of Nicaraguans, helping them to resist the accelerating and continuing transculturation process which Somozismo had forced on the national culture. The masks of Monimbó, the contact bombs, and the drums of Subtiava are indigenous forms of cultural expression whose origins go back to the colonial period. They are cultural forms which could not be destroyed by the implantation of a foreign culture which are alien to our character. The people not only learned to resist, but also to fight, to sing, and most important of all, to triumph.

OMAR CABEZAS
The Voice Of The People Is The Voice Of The "Pintas"

The "pintas" were, at first, the voices of the catacombs. They were the speakers of the clandestine struggle, the spreading of a secret which was beginning. Thus, "la pinta" was a clandestine expression, the surreptitious voice which the country suddenly perceived as an announcement of "clandestinity".

Like the voices from the catacombs, which began to announce the Front, there were walls or isolated "pintas", but they announced a complete act of conspiracy. Like the labor of an ant, secret, solitary, an awareness, an organization beginning to form itself.

I am speaking of, shall we say, from 1965 to 1968 because by 1969 the "pinta" began to become more generalized. From then on, the "pintas" were always keeping the beat, the pulse of what was happening, as much through their range and quantity as through their message. The "pintas" were the stethoscope of the Sandinista Front placed over the political heart of the people. In fact, there began to unfold an entire, yet slow, process of increasing the "pintas" which corresponded to the increase in the political forces of the FSLN, of the people organized at different levels and made into a vanguard by the FSLN. In this way, the "pintas", at one point the voices of political silence became the voice of those who have no voice — the voice of the silenced, of the quiet, of the humiliated, of the hidden, of those who cannot speak.

I remember my first "pinta". The first "pinta" that I put into my life I wrote on the run, out of fear. It was a duty to write this "pinta"; besides, *I* was responsible for it. It was located within the miserable frame of my own neighborhood. What can I tell these people? I asked. They are so alone, so unprotected. So I wrote on the wall, in big letters: "Vivan los pobres, mueran los ricos, FSLN" ["Long live the poor, death to the rich, FSLN"].

The people under the dictatorship didn't have a voice; in appearance they had the vote, but never a voice, and on the walls a process of regaining the word was unfolding, beginning to be expressed. The wall is the voice of a people shouting. Of course, there were different messages, but the important thing is to make clear that it was a process of regaining one's voice on behalf of the people. It was the right of the people to express themselves. The voice of the people is the voice of the "pintas". We took the walls away from the enemy; this was our property. They used the walls before the Front; afterwards, we began to use them and for some time we shared them and there was an equilibrium between "pintas"; and, finally, we displaced them from the walls. Just as we evicted them from power, just as we evicted from the barracks, first, we evicted them from the walls. The "pintas" gave an insurrectional character to the walls. The voice of the silenced ones took the walls by assault. The people let out a shout on the surface of the walls. From then on, the walls bore true witness to what was happening.

I don't know when, historically, the "pintas" first appeared in Nicaragua, but ever since I can remember, in my town there have been "pintas". The political "pintas" which I recall most clearly were those which appeared one day in my neighborhood, "El Laboría", in the town of León: "Viva el Frente de Liberación Nacional" or "Viva el FSLN" ["Long live the National Liberation Front", "Long live the FSLN"]. This was sometime near the end of 1966 or in the beginning of 1967, to the best of my memory. I used to leave for classes at seven in the morning and suddenly I discovered these "pintas" on the wall. My first sensation was one of fear. I felt this because this was something against the government, something dangerous that people painted in darkness, men probably armed with

"Pintas": any painted graffiti, usually containing a socio-political message (Translator's Note).

This text was first published in *La insurrección de las paredes. Píntas y graffiti de Nicaragua*, Managua: Editorial Nueva Nicaragua/Ediciones Monimbó, 1984. It was translated from the Spanish by Don Clark. English translation Copyright © International General 1986. This is its first English publication.

a gun. This is why the "pintas" signified danger. They were people who were doing this at night, unknown people. As to whether or not they would someday win . . . no way; the thought never crossed my mind.

Later, it was different. On the wall it said, "Abajo Somoza" or "Basta ya" ["Down with Somoza", "Enough"]. But also I remember when I saw for the first time the "pintas" "Sandino, Viva Sandino" or "Viva el Frente Sandinista" ["Long live Sandino", "Long live the Sandinista Front"]. That was possibly one of the first times that I felt again close to Sandino. Again, because my grandma used to tell me about Sandino. In Sandino's time, in the north, the Yankees had burnt down my grandfather's ranch, beat him and hung him up from a wooden beam, and then burnt down the farmhouse with him inside. These were the stories that my grandma told me when I was a child, and when I saw those "pintas", I was in my fifth year of my bachelor's degree, and it had been a long time since I had heard anything about Sandino. One morning, I leave my house and there it is, across the street: a large wall with the sign "Viva Sandino", which unexpectedly sends me back to my grandfather, to the stories of my childhood and I feel the presence in red, in red spray paint or in red paint, of Sandino and of my grandfather.

The "pintas" began with the students and afterwards they became more generalized with political work, first in Managua and later throughout the country. But the culture of the "pintas" begins with the university. The "pintas" were always the tasks of the moment. There are "pintas" painted for conjunctural moments, there are "pintas" with tactical and strategic content. There are threatening "pintas", and there are "pintas" which reflect popular humor. There are very direct "pintas", personal ones, as if the people had begun to converse by using the walls as an intermediary. The people began to become conscious of one another; messages began to have a new language all their own. The walls were always announcements.

Here, of course, never appeared: "Mientras más hago el amor, más quiero hacer la revolución, y mientras más hago la revolución, más quiero hacer al amor" ["The more I make love, the more I want to make revolution, and the more I make revolution, the more I want to make love"]. Because this "pinta" belongs in another context, that of May '68 in Paris. The "pintas" in Nicaragua reflect the political content of a concrete event, of a concrete people, of a concrete culture. Because the "pintas" also are a cultural event, a cultural/political phenomenon.

The political phrases appeared on the walls for the masses to interpret. There was, for example, a moment when the bourgeoisie was beginning to prepare a *coup d'Etat* against Somoza, after the tyrant had suffered a heart attack, in order to frustrate the revolution. At that time, this "pinta" came forth: "Golpe Militar No" ["No Military *Coup*"]. There were many preinsurrection "pintas", such as "A desarmar la guardia somocista" [Disarm the Somoza Guard"]. This precise slogan called for the neighborhoods to attack the guard's vehicles and disarm them. If a dumb guard or police watchman is found, he must be disarmed. In order to have weapons, one must take them from the guards; the goal is to get hold of weapons. Each person in his neighborhood, because one has to have weapons for the insurrection, and until now there were few. There are "pintas" which were a very practical example of their use in conjunctural moments.

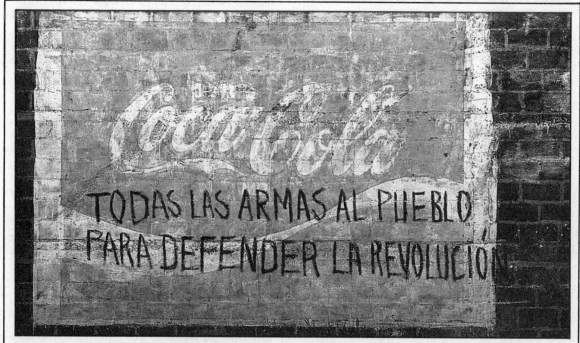

Pinta, "All Arms to the People to Defend the Revolution", photograph by Cordelia Dilg (Reprinted from *La insurrección de las paredes*, Managua: Editorial Nueva Nicaragua/Ediciones Monimbó, 1984).

The 1965 "pinta" "Viva el FSLN" ["Long live the FSLN"] announced the existence of the Front. An entire development was necessary in order for the masses to express "FSLN al poder" ["FSLN to power"]. The "pintas" are the expression of popular ingenuity. There is a saying which goes, "No hay mal que dure cien años ni cuerpo que lo resista" ["There is no illness which lasts one hundred years, nor a body which could stand it"]. Somoza intended his presidential term, which began in 1975, to last until 1981. This lead the people to say on the walls "No hay mal que dure hasta 81 ni pueblo que lo resista" ["There is no illness which lasts until '81, nor a people who could stand it"]. In this one is found the hatred of the people, where insult and obscenity become political: "Somoza hijo de puta" ["Somoza, son of a whore"]. Or this one, after the triumph: "Se fue quien nos jodió" ["The one who screwed us is gone"]. And rhyme is always present; it is one of the characteristics of spontaneous popular expression. Spontaneous rhyme is one of the poetic gifts of this people. It's the presence of Darío[1] in the middle of the insurrection; the existence of Darío in this country.

Other "pintas" give a rallying cry; Somoza must be isolated. For this, it's necessary for the people to gang up on Somoza: "El pueblo se está muriendo por culpa de Somoza" ["The people are dying and it's Somoza's fault"]. This type of "pinta" was a form of propaganda. The "pintas" had to be direct so that the people could grasp them. For that reason, at the same time that the people were acquiring a consciousness, the "pinta" began to acquire different connotations and to reflect the tasks of the moment. If you had written "Todo el poder al FSLN" ["All power to the FSLN"] in the mid-1970s, folks would have looked at you as if you were crazy. But if you wrote it in 1978–79, it is because we were really capable of taking power. That's why the "pintas" of the 1960s and early 1970s, when we were a clandestine few, were different from the "pintas" during the insurrection and the "pintas" after the insurrection. The "pintas" of the revolutionary process reflect the tasks of the class struggle which began after the triumph of the insurrection. Now they have two connotations; some are goals to be worked for — all those dealing with literacy and health — and the others concern ideological debates. Then there are always those defending our sovereignty.

In the beginning, there was very little spray paint with which to make "pintas". We had to use a bucket of paint and a brush. Then, one would always go with one's "compañeros", sometimes with a car, at night or at dawn, in darkness. One of us would stand on one corner and another on the other corner. Then one guy in the middle would paint. When the guardia came we would hide everything in the car and drive off nor-

1. Darío was a Nicaraguan poet of the late 19th and early 20th century, a leader of the Modernist movement and probably Central America's greatest poet (Translator's Note).

Pinta, "The Word is Literacy", photograph by Susan Meiselas (Reprinted from *La insurrección de las paredes*, Managua: Editorial Nueva Nicaragua/Ediciones Monimbó, 1984).

mally. That was the "nocturnal 'pinta'". In the beginning, if they caught you painting "pintas", they would arrest you, convict you and give you six months. Later, when the repression was increasing, if the guards caught you painting, you were a dead man.

But not always. The 15th of September is our traditional patriotic holiday commemorating the battle of San Jacinto against Walker and the independence of Nicaragua, of Central America. The dictatorship always organized events on the 14th or the 15th, I don't remember which, and the mayor or a town representative would speak and a military band would parade playing marches. Well, the night before this, we left the club at the university to "pinta" the streets. We began at about two in the morning. My friend, El Gato Munguia, and I went one way as we were both on foot that night. We painted from two in the morning until dawn when we arrived at the downtown area of the city of León with our "pintas". At 5.30 in the morning we were in the central park in the plaza of León, where the events were going to take place. We did the last "pinta", to finish the job, on the wall of the circular baptismal font in the central park. El Gato and I were completely stained with paint, our hair, our shirts, our pants; everything was red and blue. Those were the only two colors which we had been able to obtain. Our hands, our faces, dripping paint from all sides, with the brushes, were worn out. We did the last "pinta" and we sat down on top of the circular wall of the font, which is across from the cathedral. We were resting there, without speaking, watching the cathedral cutting into the skyline and the large columns holding up the cathedral, when suddenly we heard the sound of a vehicle coming from the street where the National Guard is stationed. We turned our heads around and then said to ourselves, "Damn it, there's the National Guard." We were filthy and besides, in León we were "fingered". We had a certain aura of bravery; how should I know that legends that arise among the people also crop up among the ranks of the enemy. The National Guard's vehicle appeared and parked directly across from where we were sitting. El Gato and I were resolved not to move as long as they didn't approach us. They got out of the vehicle, first one, then another, then afterwards, two others. They stayed there looking at us, and we saw them taking something out. It was the flag of Nicaragua which they put at half mast to be raised for an official ceremony. The guards continued watching us, and we stared back with an air of superiority, just daring them. The best thing is that they didn't dare, and as soon as they left we took off down the street headed for the university. We almost died of fright, but what joy!

There is not only the "nocturnal 'pinta'", when one left the house clandestinely, in darkness, to leave a message for the people via the walls. When the struggle of the masses was reaching a crescendo, they took advantage of the daylight, of the demonstration, to go painting as a group. As such the "pinta" became not the expression of the voice of the silenced, but, rather the expression of the struggle in the streets by the oppressed masses who became active in the streets and regained their voice. In this way, things were said publicly, in demonstrations, by means of the walls. At that time, the guards would throw paint on the "pintas", as a form of drowning out the voice of the people. Another expression of censorship of the media under the dictatorship was throwing black tar over the "pintas". But the people living in the houses became furious because they preferred to put up with the "pintas" rather than the black tar. The walls of the house would really look horrible afterwards. And besides, since the *compañeros* always painted on the recently painted houses, the prettiest ones. . . .

The "pintas" were a voice from darkness, coming from the night, and to tell the truth, the walls were always our accomplices. They were our means of communication with the masses, the means of com-

munication of the masses. The newspaper *Barricada* was born on the walls. The Voice of Nicaragua and Radio Sandino were born on the walls, and the television system in the hands of the people was born on the walls. All those graphic signs, those schemas, those funny drawings, are also the genesis of our means of mass communication.

The "pintas" patiently bore the pain of the masses, the rage, the happiness — I remember a "pinta" after the triumph "Por fin somos libres" ["At last we are free"] — the trust, the poetry, the humor of the masses. The "pintas" are the masses live and in color on the walls. That's why the "pinta" has been the site of a form of culture; the "pintas" were initiated when we were alone and now we even have murals by internationalists who have come to accompany us. This poses a very valid question which is both beautiful and interesting; a very symbolic question. The question of comaraderie. As the culture of the "pinta" has developed, it has given rise to an expression of comaraderie with the Nicaraguan people. We Nicaraguans are not alone and the walls tell us this.

Now that I think about it, creating "pintas" is also an impetus. Someone wrote on a sign under the motto "Una esperanza para Nicaragua — Partido Conservador" ["A Hope for Nicaragua — the Conservative Party"], "Qué clase de esperanza!" ["Some kind of hope!"] This is a great "pinta". This is Nicaraguan humor at its best. There is a sign which inspired me to paint on it. It's on the Northern highway and says, "Con el partido socialdemocrata Nicaragua va a ser república" ["With the Social Democratic Party, Nicaragua is going to be a republic"], and I added underneath, "Banana". I didn't think of this when I was in the mountains because there are no walls, but when we were going back south, it came to me.

JULIANNE BURTON
Filmmaking in Nicaragua
From Insurrection to INCINE:
An Interview with Emilio Rodriguez Vazquez
and Carlos Vicente Ibarra

Q: *Why turn to film in a country like Nicaragua — a country with no film-producing tradition and with limited financial and technical resources, particularly in a time of insurrectionary war?*

CVI: Although there were one or two film production companies in Nicaragua under Somoza, it is true that there was no tradition of national filmmaking. The existence of 150 movie theaters around the country cannot be overlooked, however, since it accounts for a substantial tradition of film viewing — even though we may criticize the kinds of films viewed.

ERV: During the insurrectionary struggle, people from a number of countries came to film in Nicaragua, but the FSLN (Sandinista National Liberation Front) became directly involved in the production of only one of these films, *Patria Libre o Morir (Free Homeland or Death)*. A Costa Rican group called Istmo Films, sympathetic to the cause of Nicaraguan liberation and convinced of the need to create a Central American film industry, began developing a funding structure and presented a film proposal to the FSLN leadership. With a concrete proposal in hand, members of the *Frente* got excited, daring for the first time to believe that it was actually possible to make a film about their struggle. The filming itself took about two

This interview represents the synthesis of separate conversations with two members of INCINE, the newly formed Nicaraguan Film Institute. Emilio Rodriguez Vazquez, on a brief visit to New York, was interviewed by telephone from California in late November. The conversation with Carlos Vicente Ibarra, conducted in person, took place during the First International Festival of the New Latin American Cinema, held in Havana in early December. The combined experience and perspectives of these two individuals — Ibarra a Nicaraguan, Rodriguez a Puerto Rican working in Nicaragua out of an internationalist commitment — offer a richer assessment of the background, nature and goals of the incipient cinematic enterprise in post-Somoza Nicaragua than either could in isolation. I have taken the liberty of structuring the content of the interviews in such a way as to suggest a three-way conversation, taking care not to violate the content or the spirit of either interview. —J.B.

months. Only toward the end of that period did the crew begin to go into combat situations. They wanted to continue filming, but they realized that the film had to come out.

Although no Nicaraguans were members of the production crew, many were involved in writing the screenplay, in the organizing, fundraising, and subsequent distribution. At the time, the utility of such a film was seen primarily in terms of its potential for raising money to purchase arms. The film could not be viewed widely inside Nicaragua until after the liberation, but the process by which it was produced and its effectiveness in generating international solidarity convinced the FSLN leadership of the need to get more directly involved in filmmaking.

The need to document the involvement of the masses during the process of liberation — a mobilization without precedent in Nicaraguan history since Augusto Cesar Sandino's resistance to the U.S.-sponsored invasion in the late 20s and early 30s — suddenly became a priority, although the various uses to which this material might be put could not be fully formulated at that time.

In April 1979, the FSLN decided to develop their own filmmaking and information infrastructure. They organized two offices: the Office for Information to the Exterior, and the War Correspondents Corps, the first composed primarily of journalists, the second of photographers and filmmakers. I joined the Correspondents Corps, working from April to July on the Southern Front which borders on Costa Rica. About nine other people had assignments similar to mine in other parts of the country, including the Northern Front and certain key cities. We came from various parts of Latin America — from Mexico, Colombia, Bolivia, Ecuador, Peru, Uruguay and, in my case, Puerto Rico — in response to an internationalist appeal from the FSLN. The idea was to coalesce the talents, experience and resources that the Nica-

This text was first published in *Cineaste* (New York), X, 2, Spring 1980.

raguans could not assemble by themselves, given the exigencies of the war effort and the fact that media expertise had previously been monopolized by the Somoza government. INCINE has its early roots in that volunteer corps.

Q: *How and why did you initially get involved in film production in Nicaragua?*

ERV: I was working on a film about Puerto Ricans in New York, directed by a North American filmmaker, when I had occasion to see *Patria Libre o Morir*. The film confirmed Cuban theorist Julio Garcia Espinosa's ideas about *imperfect cinema*; despite its technical shortcomings, it moved me deeply. Not too long afterwards, one of the Nicaraguan *companeros* informed me of the search for skilled media people. Two days later, I was on my way to Costa Rica. It was what you'd call a lightning decision, motivated by a unique opportunity to combine my professional interests and my political ideals.

Q: *Would you describe your experience on the Southern Front?*

ERV: Very few of the international volunteers had ever received military training. I had refused to join the U.S. Army. Most of the other *companeros* were also basically pacifists, involved with media rather than armed struggle as the agent of change. Upon arriving in Nicaragua, we all went through two weeks of intense military training.

When we went into the Naranjo offensive on May 20th, things were pretty tense. The whole thing seemed like fiction: 1500 "actors" all landing on the beach, unloaded from cattle trucks at 2 AM. We had to keep very close to the *companero* in front so as not to lose our way in the pitch darkness. For hours an infinite line of invisible bodies moved slowly forward. When day broke, we were spotted by a gunboat offshore which began to attack. A few minutes later, an airplane began firing air-to-land rockets. At first, we didn't know how to react. Those of us who had never been in that kind of spot before stuck very close to those who had. By the end of that first day under fire, we had overcome our panic and learned how to position ourselves so as to avoid being hit.

Q: *What kind of equipment did you carry?*

ERV: My mission was to take both stills and moving footage. I was equipped with two Nikons (with 24mm and 35mm lenses and an 80–200 zoom) as well as a 16mm Bolex.

I was very surprised to see how "objective" one could be, even in the trauma of battle or the exhaustion of its aftermath. I remember a time when we were ambushed. I was part of cadre which was advancing up a hill, down into a valley, and up another incline. As soon as we reached our destination, Somoza's troops opened fire. We rushed to find cover, but even under the onslaught of a surprise attack, I found myself still fully aware of the details of exposure time and composition, able to make sure that the material was professional-looking.

Another time we had been marching for several hours before finally coming to a resting place. The others began to relax, but I had to remain alert — ready to capture spontaneous shots which could not be repeated. We had climbed a steep hill, dodging airplanes, and just as we reached the shelter of the top, it began to rain. Parched and exhausted, all the combatants lay down with their mouths open, trying to catch some drops of water. The rain stopped, but the sky remained dark and low. A young woman suddenly sat up, gazing out into the distance, as if into the future. Behind her, the horizon seemed to open up and the sunlight began to filter through the heavy clouds. In front of her, the sky also began to clear, leaving only a thick blanket of clouds just above her head and producing a rare, magenta-toned light. That photograph later appeared in *Time*.

Comparing experiences and impressions with cameramen and photographers from other fronts after the victory, we remarked on that unexpected sense of clarity which possessd us all, on the drive to survive and to turn that experience into a creative rather than a destructive one.

Q: *Carlos Vicente, what is the history of your involvement with film during the insurrectionary struggle?*

CVI: During the insurrection of September, 1978, I was doing photographic work on the Southern Front. In the final insurrection, I was not working in either film or still photography, but with *Radio Sandino*, a clandestine organization.

When the revolution came to power and we all arrived in Managua, I decided that I wanted to work in the film sector. The leadership of the *Frente* invited me and two other *companeros*, Franklin Caldera and Ramiro Lacayo, to head the newly founded film institute. Calders is an impassioned "film freak"; he is steeped in film history and is a fine critic. Lacayo, who headed the Press and Information Corps (*Equipo de Prensa y Propaganda*) on the Southern Front during the war, is the director of the first INCINE newsreel and president of the Institute.

Q: *Did any of the foreign volunteers remain to become part of INCINE?*

ERV: Only myself and one young Columbian cameraman, Carlos Jimenez. Within a few days of the victory, we all got together and began to confer on what the organization and aims of the Nicaraguan Film Institute would be. The Ministry of Culture, of which we are a part, invited many people to confer with us. Many representatives from international organizations concerned about the country's filmmaking plans were also in Managua during those hectic early days. We spent countless hours in meetings.

We were authorized to set up operations at Somoza's film production company, Producine. We found only an empty shell. We began trying to locate the missing equipment. We managed to retrieve what we found at the airport in crates, ready to leave the country, but a great deal had already left with Somoza.

Q: *Was any of the footage taken by the Somozistas*

retrieved?

CVI: Some 750,000 feet of newsreel footage, equivalent to well over 300 hours of viewing time. Despite the fact that this material was shot by Somozistas, we are confident of being able to put it to good use in future films in which we will explore and assess the long years of rule by the Somoza dynasty.

Q: *How much footage was shot by the liberation forces during the war?*

ERV: We estimate that we produced about 60,000 feet of 16mm color film from 1978 on (no black-and-white film was shot), approximately 4,000 black-and-white still photos and 3,000 color slides. Many of these photographs were distributed to newspapers throughout Latin America and the Caribbean during the war, and we also intend to incorporate them into future films.

Q: *Would you describe the organization and future plans of INCINE?*

CVI: Currently the Film Institute is made up of two departments: Production numbers about 25 people, about half of them technical personnel (including six camera operators, three film editors, a sound technician and a screenwriter), with the remainder in charge of equipment maintenance; another 20 people are working in the Distribution department.

ERV: For its first year, INCINE has a production goal of one 15–20-minute newsreel per month. By July of 1980, we hope to double that output. In addition, we hope to produce four 16mm color feature-length documentaries per year.

We see the newsreel as a way to deepen the news coverage provided by television and newspapers, as well as a means to fill theater time and ease our dependence on some of the alienating material which has up to now formed the bulk of national film programming. Because of the particular discipline required in newsreel production, we also see this undertaking as crucial to the development of technical skills among our filmmakers.

Q: *Is the* Noticiero Latinoamericano, *the weekly newsreel produced in Cuba under the direction of Santiago Alvarez, a potential model for your work?*

CVI: It is to the degree that, like those responsible for the Cuban newsreel, we see the form as more than simply a vehicle for fragments of unconnected information. We conceive of each newsreel as having a unity of theme and structure — more like a documentary film than a standard newsreel.

For example, our first newsreel, which had its international premiere the opening night of the First International Festival of the New Latin American Cinema in Havana in December 1979, deals with nationalization of the Nicaraguan gold mines, but the film is structured around the presence of an old veteran who fought with Sandino in the early 30s. Dressed in the uniform of the original *Sandinistas*, but interviewed and photographed in the context of today's post-Somoza Nicaragua, he symbolically summarizes the evolution of our national history throughout most of this century.

The four projected documentaries, which will be feature-length and in color rather than black-and-white, will take on broader themes than those of the Newsreel. Their development and range, however, will clearly be built upon the experience which we progressively acquire on the Newsreel project, because it must be recognized that our technical preparation as professional filmmakers has barely begun. The wartime experience was just a small introduction — predominantly practical without being totally removed from theoretical considerations — to filmmaking.

Q: *Have you already been approached by people from other countries with proposals for co-productions?*

ERV: Co-productions offer the obvious advantage of additional resources to realize projects which are beyond our current means. The Cuban Film Institute has expressed interest in some kind of co-production. A film on Sandino would be an obvious priority. Diego de La Texera, a Puerto Rican scriptwriter, has been working on such a script for many years. Recently, he has been conferring with Sergio Ramirez, a member of the Provisional Government, and another Nicaraguan, Gregorio Selser.

Peter Lillienthal, who belongs to the group of New German filmmakers, is currently filming a feature on a Nicaraguan family. A Yugoslav crew is also filming now, and Mexican filmmaker Berta Navarro is in Cuba doing post-production on her second documentary about Nicaragua. The Cubans have already produced a short called *Monimbo es Nicaragua*, about a particularly militant population in the Masaya area. Cuban director Jesus Diaz was in the country in November to finish shooting footage for an ambitious four-part, feature-length documentary on Nicaragua. North American filmmaker Barbara Kopple also paid us a visit. It is clear that international interest is high.

In terms of Distribution, our priority is the establishment of an effective mobile cinema program. The idea behind this project is to bring films to the most remote sections of the country, to people who have had little if any prior exposure to the medium. Currently, we are not exactly well-equipped for this undertaking. What is generally involved is a single print of each film, a projector, a take-up reel, and a dedicated *companero* who travels from town to town by bus. This operation will be greatly enhanced when we receive two Land Rovers equipped with projectors, screen and power speakers promised by the Dutch solidarity committees.

Q: *What kind of films are being distributed in this way?*

CVI: Initially, the mobile cinema units had only about five or six titles to work with. Recently, an alternative distribution company called Zafra, with headquarters in Mexico, has begun providing us with a number of Latin American and European films. The donations we received from the participants in the

First International Festival of the New Latin American Cinema will increase our collections manyfold. In addition to a number of Cuban films, we have been given prints of feature-length documentaries like Patricio Guzman's *The Battle of Chile* and Barbara Kopple's *Harlan County, U.S.A.*, as well as documentary shorts from Argentina, Brazil, Colombia, Mexico, Peru and Venezuela. In addition, several European socialist countries have expressed their intention of donating films and equipment.

Commercial theatrical circuits are the other area of concern. Traditionally, only the most alienating and dehumanizing examples of international cinema reached our screens. The task of finding more constructive products for popular entertainment is as difficult as it is urgent. Here again, the Cubans have given us generous assistance, offering 35mm prints of films made in that country and elsewhere.

Q: *What kind of equipment do you currently have to work with?*

CVI: So far, INCINE has only a small studio, an editing room, a darkroom for developing stills, and a recording studio. There is no film laboratory or sound studio because Producine has this kind of work done in Mexico.

ERV: By the middle of next year, we hope to have processing and transfer equipment of our own. Currently, we have to send everything out for processing. It goes either to Mexico or to Cuba, with some peculiar strings attached: namely, that it be done for free since we have no dollars for foreign exchange.

Our cameras consist of two Arriflexes and an old Mitchell and, in 16mm, one CP16 which is in pretty bad shape, since it was used on the front lines, and a Bolex.

I have made two short trips to the United States and Canada recently, with multiple purposes in mind: to organize solidarity groups to channel resources to support our efforts; to approach churches and ecumenical groups; and to contact organized groups like the National Film Board of Canada and individual filmmakers — not only independents but also those who work in "the industry". We are particularly anxious to secure the institutional support of the various film-related technical unions, although we realize that this may not be an easy task. One specific mission was to obtain parts for the 35mm equipment, as well as funds for a synchronous tape recorder and an additional 16mm camera.

Solidarity groups have now been set up in New York, Toronto and Montreal. The New York group, called Comu-Nica (Nicaragua Communicates), is made up primarily of North American and Latin American film workers.

Q: *Have any other films been produced to date by INCINE, in addition to the first newsreel?*

ERV: I wish we had been able to do more filming in the days immediately following the revolutionary takeover, but the planning process required a great deal of attention. We managed to begin shooting the first documentary in early August, despite great difficulties in getting the equipment to work right and a severe shortage of film stock. Consequently, that first documentary was produced in video.

It is a 50-minute film called *La educación no se interrumpio (Education Was Not Interrupted)*. It deals with the six weeks prior to the formal re-opening of the schools, a period when parents, students and teachers met to define their new, post-revolutionary roles, redefine their relationships to one another and come to grips with the fact that they all had more responsibility than ever before. The film records the cultural activities — music, plays — as well as the meetings, conferences and discussions during this period.

Q: *Do you intend to continue work in video even when you have adequate resources for 16mm and 35mm production?*

CVI: No, I think video is more of a short-term strategy. In the early months of the revolutionary government, there was quite a vacuum in television programming. Those in charge sought collaboration from other sectors. Given our shortage of material resources, and our own lack of expertise, even in the film medium, we decided to make the education documentary in video. But I doubt that this will continue, since we prefer to work in 35 or even 16mm.

Q: *You have referred to the alienating nature of the movies traditionally shown in Nicaragua, suggesting that they enforce the passivity rather than the participation of the spectators. It seems to me that the portability and relative inexpensiveness of video might facilitate a more participatory and collaborative kind of filmmaking. The very process of having formative input in a film which depicts one's own situation often provides that person or group of people with the necessary distance or "objectivity" to spark a great leap in awareness and a determination to effect change.*

CVI: I agree that there has to be interaction between the creators themselves and the people, and that everyone should, in fact, participate in the process of creating culture; but that interaction has to be limited to certain moments in the creative process. What I'm unsure about is to what degree filmmaking can offer a continuity of creative process, given the technical requirements of the medium. I see the principal interaction developing in the initial planning stages, as the filmmaker investigates his chosen topic and speaks directly with the people concerned. Afterwards, during the shooting, he records the concerns of those people as faithfully as possible and later, in the finished film, he returns those concerns to the people involved — but in a carefully elaborated, analytical form, with concrete proposals, wherever possible, for resolution of the problems involved. Technical requirements would seem to limit popular participation in any but that early stage of production.

In Nicaragua, as in any revolutionary situation, the expression of individual creativity is always conditioned by the interests of broader sectors of the population since the divorce between the interests of the creative artist and the interests of the people as a whole no longer exists. For one thing, creative artists' membership in political organizations prevents them from losing themselves in idealistic interpretations of reality. I believe that we in Latin America have gone beyond that period where our goal is not merely to demonstrate, to document those problems which plague us. We are now at a stage where events and issues are recorded, reformulated in a revolutionary way, and returned to the people in analytical form, as a project for action and a revolutionary solution.

TOMÁS BORGE MARTINEZ
Marginal Notes On The Propaganda of the FSLN

In order to analyze the history of the various kinds of propaganda and agitation, plus the mediations and institutional supports, by means of which we undertook our ideological struggle, it is necessary to study part of the history of the FSLN — which is part of a given period of our national history — with a certain critical liberty.

According to Gramsci, the history of a party is the monographic study of a country. Within the historical development and evolution of a party gravitate the social, political and ideological variables of a nation. Above all, this history is possible if this party — the FSLN — has given glorious rise to the beginning and continuation of a new history. Without falling prey to either fetishism or the pitfalls of exaggeration, it can be said that each phase in the Sandinista struggle was marked by a specific form of propaganda.

Although we must attempt an introduction to this analysis, obviously it cannot be thoroughly exhausted today. Especially as no one has yet begun this task, which demands both the participation of the FSLN as a party and of each of its members.

It is very important that we examine — in good faith and beyond the limits of political, personal, and sectarian interests — the full spectrum of footprints left by those who took the first steps, the scars, the dialogues, and the monologues misplaced from our history.

Few efforts have been made. Some of the documents such as "An Appraisal of Basic Sources for the Study of the FSLN" by the Institute for Sandinista Studies (IES) are weak, incomplete and full of distortions which, without being carefully considered, could give rise to mistrust.

To continue with this aspect, I would like to make a methodological and political observation. The FSLN and its initial leadership understood reality and the need to transform it with the stubborness of individual suicide and of their historical and collective resurrection. This understanding, frequently empirical but marked by an astute historical intuition, had Carlos Fonseca as its main proponent and architect.

For this reason, rather than covering the entire period, I will begin with the accurate documents prepared by Carlos; that is to say, I will base myself on his texts which refer to the various modes and practices dealing with propaganda. Nothing has been said on this subject, as well as on almost any of the subjects, dealing with the Nicaraguan revolution, and what's more important, nothing new.

I am going to refer to only a limited number of Fonseca's writings; those which express the essence of his thought regarding the strategy and tactics of our struggle.

By comparing what Carlos wrote and the experiences of the FSLN one can deduce that the nature of the propaganda and agitation corresponded to the strategy and the tactics used at each conjuncture, with all its barefoot, sore, ragged solitary accounts.

Our struggle was determined by the logic of taking power through armed struggle. From the beginning, our propaganda efforts were directed toward persuading certain social and political sectors that the only possible alternative for defeating the Somoza dictatorship was by means of a military confrontation. All the tactics and means adopted were subordinated to this strategy.

"Incorporamos al Sandinismo" ["Let us Embody Sandinisim"], which is nothing less than revolutionary scientific theory applied to the concrete reality of Nicaragua, is an essential part of our propaganda. We are Sandinistas because we are Marxist–Leninists in Nicaragua, and we are Marxist–Leninists in Nicaragua because we are Sandinistas. The nature of the early struggle permitted us to be explicit. We were politically but not ideologically clandestine. Even though

This text was first presented as a speech to the Propaganda Department of the FSLN on 1 March 1985. Published by permission of the author. It was translated from the Spanish transcript by Janet Jamieson. English translation Copyright © International General 1986. This is its first publication.

Drawing by Roger Sanchez Flores (Reprinted from *Roger*, **Managua: Committee of U.S. Citizens Living in** *Cartoons from Nicaragua: The Revolutionary Humor of* **Nicaragua, 1984).**

we have political power, today, circumstances ideologically are more complex.

Propaganda formed part of the basis of our strategic concepts. Because our fire power was so insignificant, we were obliged to be abundant with our persuasive power with the different social sectors. The spreading of revolutionary theory and our historical reality formed part of the war and the search for total victory. With this understanding of the organic relationship between strategy and tactics our theoretical ideas were translated into practice for revolutionary transformation.

I do not wish to harp on the essential aspects of our doctrine. It is preferable to underline the connections which exist between propaganda and agitation and their respective material supports. From the beginning, we decided to use the most developed forms available at the moment to spread our message among the masses. The instruments of communication were, as they are today, the technical mediations needed to disseminate our propaganda. For this reason it is not by accident that Carlos Fonseca in 1960 argued that:

Clandestine activity is an important support for armed struggle. This activity organizes sudden surprise demonstrations, pintas on the walls, subversive flyers, etc. We can include in this activity clandestine radio which being in direct contact with the combatants has the ability to communicate the truth to the people, spread the news of the crimes which the dictatorship trys to keep hidden, and refute the measures spread by dictatorial propaganda.

Let us stop to examine the concepts of Carlos Fonseca. In the first place he identifies as the basic instrument for the development of propaganda and agitation the most developed means of mass distribution in the Nicaraguan social formation: the radio. He establishes its importance and outlines the way in which it is needed as a means of information dissemination.

Even before we were born as the Sandinista National Liberation Front we had already stated the importance of the radio. Why were we not able to acquire a radio broadcasting station? Simply because the objective conditions were adverse; the unfavorable internal and external situation. At this time the just idea of armed struggle was questioned by other sectors on the left; it had not become the property of the masses.

We who had lived through the youthful experiences of the publications *Espartaco, Orientación juvenil, Segovia, El Universitario*, and *Juventud revolucionaria* can certainly confirm the need to depend on a radio station as a center for information distribution. Those of us who had already seen the role which the printed media — even with limited circulation — played in the growth of the armed struggle were able to determine which instrument we needed to undertake our ideological struggle under the best possible conditions. But to have a radio station was impossible.

If I insist upon this subject it is so that it will be better understood why we say that Carlos Fonseca both understood and defined with daring and precision the medium we needed to support our struggle. It

was not until 1978 that we could depend on a radio broadcasting station — Radio Sandino — which, under favorable political and military conditions, we could use clandestinely. What Carlos envisioned in the beginning of the 1960s we were able to achieve in practice only toward the dawn of the final offensive.

If we could not depend on our own radio station, this does not mean we lost sight of the sense of history. Although we were objectively limited in our political development because we were a clandestine military organization, this did not prevent our occupying some radio broadcasting stations by force in order to disseminate our messages. The takeover of the radio stations Radio Mundial and Radio Corporación for example, should be understood as a practical application of the theories set forth by Carlos in 1960.

We were permanently involved in the different communication media, *El Sandinista* and *Trinchera* had served as something more than just an exercise in the usefulness of the media. Nevertheless we first had to travel a long and bloody road. We were born as a nucleus of conspirators and conjurers but we never stopped nurturing ourselves with scientific revolutionary ideals.

Two fundamental truths permeated our ideas: the thought and practice of Sandino and the theory of scientific Marxist–Leninist revolution. For us Sandinism was the root. Marxism was the fertilizer which made possible chlorophyll and the rich growth. Without either hiding or contradicting our ideological identity, in our early propaganda we made known the prophetic thinking of Sandino.

Sandinism was outlawed and the Sandinistas were persecuted. Part of our struggle was to persuade the different social sectors that the Sandinista National Liberation Front had deep national roots.

Our flag is red and black. We understand and we sing to the "pocoyo" night bird, our bodies are made of corn, and the milk of the village folk and the honey of wasps runs through our veins.

Our propaganda was — and still is — a combination of revolutionary Marxist–Leninist theory, nationalism and anti-imperialism.

Because of the popular and democratic nature of our struggle it was logical that we would become the heirs of Sandinista thought and action. But Sandinism had been so deformed in the eyes of the Nicaraguans that it became necessary to revive it. This was our first propaganda task.

We began a parallel study of Sandinism and revolutionary theory. This helped us to better understand Sandinism, to understand its national character. As Carlos Fonseca pointed out, the Sandinista resistance had disassociated itself from a bourgeois nationalism which so frequently reduced itself to vulgar nationalism. The religious nationalism of Luis Somoza at the time of Mokorón was nothing other than a repetition of the tricks played by Latin American nationalists to neutralize their countries' popular struggles. The nucleus of the Sandinista resistance was made up of the workers and the peasants.

But in addition, the core of our propaganda was the imposition of armed struggle as the only alternative for national liberation. With aversion, we separated forever from the traditional historical parties and sought the construction of a political–military organization that would not and could not conform to the classical organic forms of Leninism. In other words, I believe that the only form of Leninist organization possible at that moment was the one imposed by historical reality. Wherever possible the principle of democratic centralism was established, but in reality, centralism predominated in spite of the open democratic inclination of Carlos Fonseca.

Our first phase was to seek out and organize our sources for both theory and combat, our errors and successes. Early on, our internationalism was based on a combination of revolutionary experiences related to our own concept of taking power. This is an aspect which is closely related to propaganda.

We considered political practice to be the material expression of ideology. When Carlos wrote the document "Instrucciones a los compañeros" ["Instructions to the *Compañeros*"], he had in mind two things: first, a methodology for carrying out our meetings, and second, to explain in depth the criteria for the information disseminated by the radio and print media.

The militants were directed to pay close attention to the analysis of "the news and its meaning". In the tenth instruction he expressly pointed out "When approaching news topics one must give primary importance to the events in Latin America, Nicaragua, Vietnam, and Cuba".

This insistence on the news was related directly to the necessity for militants to develop the habit of a "concrete analysis of the concrete situation" beginning with whatever appeared in the media and with the practical use of theory analyzing the relations of force. In order to successfully transform our reality, it was necessary to start with an objective understanding of the social, political, and military development of our social formation and the influence of imperialism in the unfolding of our history. The document "Algunos aspectos del trabajo entre las masas" ["Some Aspects of Work Among the Masses"], which I recommend be read by our militants, had the propaganda purpose of organizing and orienting the masses for armed combat. Once again the propaganda supported our basic strategy of struggle.

We are dealing here with a critical text which established a direction for political work at a time when we had undergone the conceptual deviation of making our organization into a primarily military structure. In tackling the need to combine military with political work it clearly stated that one must underline two fundamental political tasks: study and propaganda. These two tasks contribute a great deal toward achieving the third: the contact with and organization of the

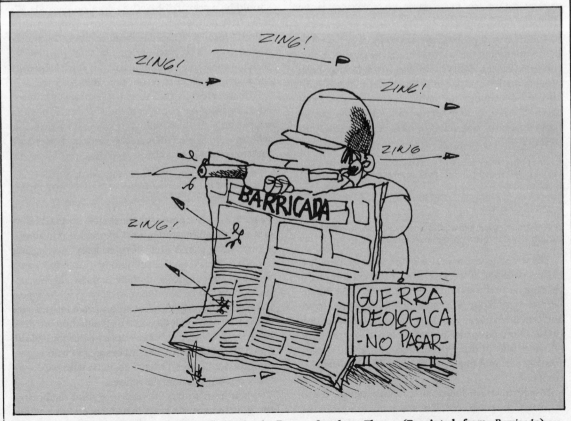

"*Barricada* — Ideological War — Keep Out", drawing by Roger Sanchez Flores (Reprinted from *Barricada*).

popular masses, the exploited and oppressed.

The emphasis in this study was neither bookish, academic, nor generic. Concretely, it was the analysis and study of our national reality. It was a precise, rigorous, scientific understanding of our present and past history in order to incorporate its lessons into our struggle. The emphasis on propaganda was intimately connected with the study of our national reality. Carlos firmly states that:

It will be found very useful for the cadres to pay careful attention to our workers' natural forms of protest in order to develop our plans based not on facile inventions but rather on our own national reality. Related to this are the worker's struggles which have occurred in certain parts of the city and the country, about which the demagogic bourgeois press of this country have not said a word but which our militants have been able to confirm.

More conclusively, Carlos clearly described the type of propaganda that we would have to develop:

Once one has a certain knowledge about a particular place, one can then go on to elaborate relevant demands. We have reached the phase of making our demands known. That is to say, we are taking care of the tasks of propaganda. When talking about propaganda we must make clear that propaganda in general should not always be confused with written propaganda, with newspapers or flyers. Nicaraguan revolutionary propaganda should always keep clearly in mind the high illiteracy rate of the country's population. Also, in addition to this is the irregular reading habits among those who know how to read. This leads one to rely heavily on verbal propaganda which can be transmitted orally. It becomes necessary to create a conversational model by means of which the nature of the tremendous exploitation suffered by workers and the need to act against this exploitation can be explained to the workers in each cell.

Agitation and propaganda are so intimately united in the thought of Carlos Fonseca that he goes from one category to the other with a conviction that both aspects come together in practice and that it is difficult to determine the exact boundaries between them. We are dealing here with a lesson which our party militants and activists must learn to apply in practice.

In the preparatory phase of working among the masses, it is very helpful to keep in mind the repressive extremes of the local tyranny.

He then adds:

It is necessary to eliminate the tendency to abuse what Lenin called "revolutionary phrase-making".

These concepts contain an entire strategy for political propaganda. If we give this document a modern reading, as really should be done, we see that it concerns how to approach the masses in order to attract and win them over to our positions. The consolidation phase of revolutionary power deals with a strategy of alliances and of using persuasion to lead the masses toward our final objective: the building of a socialist society.

Now that we are questioning the language we use to approach the problem and how we should address the masses, it is crucial to stop and examine Carlos' observations on the subject:

When trying to explain the problems to the masses it is necessary while taking into account the experiences which give rise to the rich language of the working masses, to keep clarity and simplicity in mind at all times. Propaganda should never omit concrete examples of the way exploitation is manifested in each locality. This can be done by including names and details about the workers that one knows have suffered the worst consequences of exploitation. If it is true that we must take care to keep our local propaganda serious and objective, we must not forget that in the above-mentioned situations the inevitably low level of ideological preparation makes it impossible to elaborate studies on a high scientific level. It could be said that the objective is to provide a number of worker's cells with a sort of handbook against exploitation, preferably in verbal form.

Is this not our fundamental concern when we have to propagandize and disseminate our decisions? Is this not the kind of problem which we confront in the different production centers? Is it not simple, reiterative, verbal explanations which our workers demand of us? To avoid ambiguity, I should explain the principle that achieving clarity and simplicity does not mean keeping the masses poorly educated. This is at the root of our differences with the exploiters. We aspire to greater and better educational and cultural levels for the people. If we hope to consciously lead our society we must achieve this by means of persuasion and a conscious understanding of our direction.

Lenin was the first to state that it is not a matter of lowering culture to the level of the people but rather one of raising the people to the level of culture. This should be a primary objective of our propaganda. We must have neither a vulgarization nor a lowering of the cultural level. Simplicity is about reaching the people with their own language, relying on their wisdom. We should repeat one more time that one must learn from the masses in order to teach the masses.

This next text by Carlos, which seems to us primary, contains what we consider should be the basis of our propaganda. It deals with a revolutionary principle whose validity and use at the present time seems fundamental. Carlos affirms:

. . . it is not with words but rather through daily activity that members of the organization should know how to express their enthusiasm.

We are dealing here with the reunification of theory and practice. Ernesto Guevara expressed it in similar terms. Che stated that revolutionary propaganda should be based on the strength of example. Ricardo Morales Aviles said something similar: "It was not enough just to be revolutionaries, one had to appear to be one". Here appearance is converted into essence at the root and medulla of our daily situation. In terms of propaganda, one act of exemplary behavior is worth more than ten lectures. If our lives are not marked by a congruence between what we say and what we do, we lose credibility among the masses.

When from within the party and from the heart of the government we insist that our speeches and discourses be congruent, one might think that we are only talking about our public presentations and our appearances before the masses. This congruence is a propaganda necessity which must be complemented by exemplary political behavior. Has it not been our revolutionary consistency which has made our people see us as their true vanguard?

The correspondence between our political discourse — that is, our propaganda — and our daily life is a simple matter. It is not enough to call for austerity and economy, what is important is to practise them. Our behaviors are meaningful deeds subject to the people's scrutiny. Ideology concerns behavior, habits and customs. We must not forget that agitation and propaganda are tributaries of ideology.

Inscribed within that context, the proposals of Carlos were valid forms for propagandizing our struggle, for persuading the masses. The text is rich in ways how propaganda and agitation can be used. In essence, his text is a handbook for organizing propaganda work in the heart of the masses.

One of its singularities is that it regionalizes and focuses the work of propaganda and agitation. The local cadres should take charge of writing on walls and fences. In some circumstances it is useful to write protest letters, in others, to spread information by word of mouth about the nature of the struggle taking place in the factories. This text continues to be valid to the extent that the strengthening of our organization is through our contact with the masses. At present this is essential because of the need to strengthen our propaganda and to attain higher levels in its regionalization. It has been the war itself that has required us to decentralize propaganda and agitation, and take into account local differences and to find support in their most varied manifestations.

I want to make a final remark concerning this document of Fonseca's. It sets forth a concept which is at the base of the direction of Nicaraguan society: the concept of Sandinista hegemony through national unity.

Hegemony supposes the moral and intellectual direction of society. It implies creating a consensus around a political project. It goes much further than simple political legitimation, in the sense that Max Weber gave this concept. It concerns a Leninist principle developed by Gramsci which we must re-assert in the following terms.

The concept of hegemony is linked to social classes and their struggles. Hegemony only becomes unified as an apparatus through reference to a class, and through the mediation of multiple sub-systems: the educational apparatus (from the school to the university), the cultural apparatus (libraries, museums, etc.), the organization of information (newspapers, magazines, radio, television), the union apparatus, the religious apparatus, etc.

1. This speech was presented at the ANDEN (the Asociación Nacional de Educadores de Nicaragua) congress held on 29 June 1984 at the Teatro Gonzales in Managua, to commemorate Nicaraguan Teacher's Day.

This breaks with the concept of an overriding *mass media* in order to express the concept that hegemony is exercised by means of a diversity of mediations each characterized by their material concreteness. They are the centers or institutions of production, dissemination, appropriation and reception of the ideological. They are the centers responsible for the organization and materialization of class hegemony. Consequently, they have the responsibility of obtaining and consolidating the active consensus of the groups and classes which make up civil society.

They are part of the state apparatus; they are the cultural apparatus created by the state in its process of expansion. Each mode of production has had its own dominant cultural apparatus. Under primitive means of production, the oral tradition, rites and the family were the dominant cultural apparatus. Under the feudal mode of production the church exercised this role, and under the capitalist mode of production a dominant cultural apparatus has existed for each distinct phase of its development.

In the mercantile phase of the capitalist mode of production, this role was fulfilled by the police state; in the pre-monopolistic phase it was fulfilled by the school; and during the rise and consolidation of monopolies, the mass communication media took on this role. During the present transnational phase of capitalism, in its most developed centers, it is the new communications technologies which take on the role of the dominant cultural apparatus.

It is necessary to remember that capitalist societies use the most developed cultural apparatus available in each phase. This does not imply that the other apparatuses will disappear. Once displaced, they go on to play a supporting role for the hegemonic apparatus. Nevertheless, one must not forget that these apparatuses are penetrated by class contradictions. In a social formation such as ours, it is necessary to examine the role played by each of these cultural apparatuses and to determine which of them is at the forefront. Although the school still plays a determining role, it is being replaced by the mass communication apparatuses. In its transnational phase, capitalism eliminates ideological boundaries and seeks to articulate its transnational project by basically relying on the organic combination of those communication media with the most highly-developed technologies, such as satellites, computers and data banks.

The creation of our cultural model calls for an organic relationship between the educational school apparatus and the mass communications apparatus which is replacing it. For this reason a national communications policy which harmonizes the operation of both cultural apparatuses is urgently needed. It was with this in mind that during the ANDEN congress we proposed including the study of the communication media as a required subject in their curriculum plans[1]. We suggested a tactical displacement with a view to later proposing the formulation of a national communication policy. Our proposal was like a flight of a firefly under a rain of memoranda.

In this way we can center on a perspective which takes in the entire national ideological system: the Ministries of Education, Culture and Health; the Secretary of Planning; the Political Education Department and the Agitation and Propaganda Department of the FSLN, and the mass communication media. To understand this task in any other way is to believe that the communication media occupy a privileged position in ideological struggle.

What we are trying to resolve are the contradictions between the formal educational model and the informal educational model. We want to overcome their contradictions.

At present, a distinction is made between direct propaganda and indirect propaganda. Up until now I have referred only to indirect propaganda. Since the purpose of this talk is to reclaim a part of our experience, we want to reclaim the propaganda and agitation work developed by Pablo Ubeda in the northern mountains of Nicaragua.

His work was persistent, tenacious and unyielding. He began his work immediately after the guerrilla expeditions of Río Coco and Bocay (1963). He created and established the logistic bases for the guerrillas in Pancasán (1967). Without his organizing work, without his unyielding efforts to persuade and convince the peasants, it would not have been possible for us to have reactivated the armed struggle. Without Pablo Ubeda, Pancasán would never have been possible.

Three consecutive years of underground work visiting everyone, hut by hut, household by household, ravine by ravine, from Pancasán passing through Peñas Blancas in Jinotega and following the Tuma River until he arrived on the Atlantic Coast where he traveled the long footpaths through the mining areas. This feat, unequalled to date, has made him a paradigm of what present party activists should aspire to become.

Before concluding, we are going to formulate some ideas how our current forms of propaganda and agitation can be improved. First I wish to refer to the propaganda which we express through *murals*. I think the adoption of this type of propaganda has been simply a mechanical transfer of other countries' experiences without asking the reasons which motivated those countries to give such importance to murals in the first place. The limited development of their mass distribution apparatuses and, often, the absence of a popular mass culture were determining factors in using this form of propaganda.

Secondly, I want to rethink the problem which I noted concerning *slogans*. I think that they are repetitive, mechanical and boring. The masses do not have the possibility of developing their capacity for creation. Slogans are imposed on them. We must let the creative torrent of the masses overflow and launch its own slogans according to the circumstances of the moment. Admittedly, the war imposes centralization,

however, democratization within the party is also a strategic necessity. The basis of its democratization must be established as an unavoidable goal. Culture is "the artistic arm of the revolution".

Thirdly, I believe we should break with a way of writing, painting, and composing songs and anthems as if they were made to order.

Finally, I am going to make certain marginal remarks. The ideology embodied in the Sandinista Popular Revolution is universal and at the same time, particular. Our ideology is universal because it is Marxism–Leninism which gives coherence to our historical project, and particular because without taking into consideration our Nicaraguan reality this universal theory would become a sterile litany.

Our ideology is Marxist because we base ourselves on the scientific analysis of society; because historical materialism permits us to understand our past and to illuminate the future; because dialectic materialism forces us to reject an idealist concept of the world. It is Leninist because it recognizes that a human being, as a social being and as a member of a social class, can — even in the era of capitalism — participate in the building of a superior society, of a socialist society.

Therefore, to be a Marxist–Leninist is not only to understand the contradictions of this society but to be engaged in its transformation as well. It is to understand the importance of the vanguard, of the party, as a light and guide in this process of transformation.

But to be a Marxist–Leninist in Nicaragua is to understand the specificities of class struggle in our reality and our history. How can a revolutionary Nicaraguan ignore the heroic, anti-imperialist deeds of Sandino? How can one negate that our principal enemy has been and continues to be North American imperialism? How can a Nicaraguan revolutionary forget our geo-political reality? Political pluralism is a specificity, a historic necessity of this revolution, of this moment, of the geography. It is not simply a strategic concept.

It is precisely because we have investigated our reality and because we are Marxists that we accept, at this historic juncture, the existence of a mixed economy and its synthesis, political pluralism. Both constitute a reality and not an aspiration. We live with political and economic pluralism, as a part of a reality imposed by history. It is inevitable that we will overcome them for biological reasons. Political pluralism and a mixed economy will undoubtedly die a natural death just as imperialism will eventually be buried without honors, no matter how distant the day. Our realities form a part of our historical project, which is without doubt, the correct one and the shortest one for the construction of paradise in our own land.

Historical experience itself has demonstrated the nefarious consequences for the revolutionary movement of having a mechanical, sclerotic interpretation of Marxism.

For many years the Third International of the Communist movement was dominated by dogmatism;

dogma and sacraments were the order of the day. Strategy and tactics were the same for all countries, i.e., the strategy and tactics of the Communist movement would be the same in Mexico, Holland or India, for example.

This generalization, so remote from Marxism, created serious difficulties in understanding what was happening in Latin America. Sandino, while he was defending the dignity of Latin America in Segovias, was attacked by textbook Marxists as "a petty bourgeois boss", whom the Mexican Communists said was incapable of "carrying the fight against imperialism through to the end, which could only be done consistently by the International Communist movement".

It is not accidental that two of the principal revolutionary exponents of this era, two of the greatest Marxists produced by Latin America, the Peruvian José Carlos Mariátegui[2], and the Cuban Julio Antonio Mella[3], both completely understood the struggle of Sandino. It is not by chance because they saw that our specific historical formation, with the squalid nature of the national bourgeoisies and the subordination of capitalist penetration to pre-capitalist forms, created a situation in which nationalism was the way to oppose imperialism.

The Third International condemned nationalism, but in Latin America nationalistic feeling gave rise to huge mass revolutionary movements. The Third Internationalists were unable to understand that if European nationalism had a counterrevolutionary character, Latin American nationalism had a revolutionary character.

National affirmation was a grass-roots action and by definition an anti-imperialistic act. An anti-imperialistic act in Latin America is inevitably a popular action of the workers and peasants.

Consequently, to be a Marxist in Latin America is to be a nationalist, to be an anti-imperialist. Obviously we are not speaking of the narrow chauvinistic nationalism of the dominant classes but rather of a revolutionary nationalism which is sweeping Latin America from top to bottom uniting our peoples. The peasants of the Andes, the oil field workers, the Latin American worker, the committed intellectual, the millions of dispossessed, the poor and unemployed of Latin America all speak the same language, have the same problems, the same aspirations, and the same oppressors.

The Sandinista Popular Revolution signifies a massive participation on the part of Christians in the struggle for power and the radical transformation of society. Does this mean that our ideology sacrificed materialism in order to incorporate idealism and that

the idealism of the Christians has been converted into a type of idealistic materialism?

It is necessary for us to deal however briefly with this subject. With Christians committed to the cause of the poor there is a political communion, a political concurrence with many common values and aspirations; but there is no common body of ideology.

Our affinities are political. Our concurrences are political. We are committed to the same historical project while mutually respecting each other's philosophical concepts. Each one acts out of their own cosmic view of the world. Besides, it must be understood that the Sandinista National Liberation Front is not a confessional party.

We have a community of political interests that should be stimulated and deepened.

But there are many Christians who have come to our Sandinista Popular Revolution and have adopted

Photograph by Cordelia Dilg (Reprinted from *La insurrección de las paredes*, Managua: Editorial Nueva Nicaragua/Ediciones Monimbó, 1984).

2. José Carlos Mariátegui, one of the first and most important Latin American Marxist theoreticians, died in 1930. He is the author of *Siete ensayos de interpretación de la realidad peruana*, Lima, 1928.
3. Julio Antonio Mella (1903–1929) was a Cuban Communist leader murdered in Mexico City by the agents of the Cuban dictator Gerardo Machado.

principles from our ideological concept and who have fully identified with the revolution in political terms. They have contributed by their undeniable courage and by the spreading of some practical principles, revolutionary mysticism, daily behavior and in the development of the state apparatus.

It would not surprise us, therefore, that in the ranks of the FSLN there are many Christians who, starting with this political communion, engage in revolutionary practice along with the Marxist Sandinista militants. The ideological development of our party has taken place during a long historical period, but we have always kept our guiding principle of Marxism–Leninism.

And what party are we speaking of? A party which rejects dogma and recipes, which is continuously nurtured on theory and fed by reality, an FSLN which is clear about its ideological foundations, a strong party which leads the people and its revolution, an FSLN which knows how to communicate its ideology to the masses in their own language, and which combines the national character with pleasure, with simplicity; this is the party we must develop.

DAVID KUNZLE
Nicaragua's *La Prensa*:
Capitalist Thorn in Socialist Flesh

The Sandinistas overthrew Somoza on 19 July 1979 in alliance with certain bourgeois forces, and on the promise to preserve pluralism in politics, the economy and the media. The private sector (which accounts for about three-fifths of the economy) in order to recover the political and military advantage it has lost, is engaged in an ideological battle, a "war of nerves" at once fierce and devious. Its representative is the daily newspaper *La Prensa*, which is hailed by itself and the U.S. mainstream media (henceforth, U.S. media) as a great symbol and martyr of the freedom of the press, "proudly independent"[1], "the most conspicuous adornment of the regime"[2], the mouthpiece of unpleasant truths the Revolution seeks to hide, the impartial "outspoken critic" whose purpose is to "chronicle (d) the Revolution's mounting failures" at a time of "plummeting popularity" and when the "economy [is] in a tailspin and public restiveness [is] on the rise"[3]. Yet one has only to look carefully at *La Prensa* to find incontrovertible evidence that it is not concerned with the "truth" as such, but rather that it twists facts, slants stories, and peddles lies and half truths, in order to undermine the government and make it look bad at home and abroad. In short, it promotes the very appearance of economic failure and public dissatisfaction that it pretends to deplore. Its tactics are in many respects similar to those of the U.S. media, which are its model, and which, under a more or less openly anti-communist banner, also seek to make socialist revolutions look bad, and give ideological underpinnings to the various political and military strategies the U.S. government undertakes against them. Similar tactics are also used by the press in other

Third World countries where capitalism is in any way threatened by popular or socialist demands, and the media are vulnerable to CIA manipulations. The particular similarity between the role of *La Prensa* in Nicaragua today and *El Mercurio* in Allende's Chile will be discussed below.

In this article, based on a systematic, day-to-day examination of the content of the three Nicaraguan dailies over a six week period in 1981[4], we shall see how *La Prensa* exploits, manipulates and seeks to exacerbate some of the basic problems faced by Nicaragua today. We shall also discover how closely *La Prensa* hews to the foreign policy interests of the current U.S. administration and the transnational corporations. Far from being a symbol of national independence, it seeks to restore the full influence of U.S. capital. Although it pays lip-service and pretends to be advocating a "third way" between capitalism and communism, it would surely welcome a restoration of capitalist relations, some kind of return to the past, Somocism without Somoza. The *Time* magazine article cited above is subheaded, "Like Somoza, the Sandinistas crack down on a dissenting family", and the view that the Sandinista government is now behaving in many respects like the defeated Nicaraguan tyrant (or Fidel Castro, deemed his Cuban equivalent), is shared by both U.S. press and *Prensa*.

HISTORY

La Prensa's success in maintaining a duplicitous posture has much to do with the popularity and credibility it inherited from pre-revolutionary days when it was in the forefront of the opposition to Somoza. Many Nicaraguans fail to realize that conditions now, determined by the difficulties of extricating a society from capitalist relations in a world still dominated by capitalism, are very different from those in which the

1. "Nine Little Castros", *Newsweek*, 16 November 1981, p. 59.
2. "As Goes *La Prensa*", Editorial, *Washington Post*, 19 July 1981, p. C6.
3. "Broken Promises in Nicaragua", *Time*, 26 October 1981, p. 97.
4. 10 July to 20 August.

This text was first published in *Media, Culture and Society* (London), 6, 1984. Reprinted by permission of the author.

struggle was waged against Somoza; and that *La Prensa* is now staffed by different people with different ideas. Some history of *La Prensa* is necessary here[5].

The descendant of four Conservative Presidents of Nicaragua, Pedro Jaoquín Chamorro Cardenal took over *La Prensa* (founded in 1926) at the death of his father in 1952. He was many times arrested, exiled and imprisoned for revolutionary activities. He was unjustly accused of complicity in the assassination of President Anastasio Somoza García in 1956, and was personally tortured by both his son and his successor, Somoza Debayle, a former school classmate[6]. Courageous and tactically astute, Chamorro Cardenal turned his paper into a forum for anti-Somoza forces which Somoza was never able entirely to suppress, as he did all the other opposition media. Somoza's inability to win complete control of the media was

"pivotal in his downfall" (Nichols, p. 187).

When Pedro Joaquín Chamorro Cardenal was murdered by Somoza in January 1978, national and international protest fanned the fire of Revolution into a roaring conflagration[7]. The offices of *La Prensa* became a strategic and even military headquarters for anti-Somoza forces, with top Sandinista leaders doubling as reporters for the newspaper, until it was finally bombed and shelled out of production in June 1979.

After the triumph of the Sandinistas, counsels within *La Prensa* were divided on what policy the paper should pursue. Chamorro Cardenal's elder son Pedro Joaquín Chamorro Barrios, his widow Violeta (for some months in the government) and his old collaborator Pablo Antonio Cuadra wanted to defend the private sector and "moderate" the course of the Revolution; the slain editor's brother Xavier and most of the staff wanted to give total support to the Revolution and help to make it a truly socialist one. In April 1980 moves were made to remove Xavier Chamorro, to counter which the paper was closed down by the government-supported (and supporting) union of journalists, which is represented in the Council of State. Relations between the government and the Superior Council of Private Enterprise (COSEP) which saw *La Prensa* as a major weapon in the struggle, had meanwhile deteriorated, until an agreement was reached which would allow *La Prensa* to continue criticizing the government, while Xavier Chamorro, with 25 per cent of La Prensa's assets and the majority of the paper's editorial and technical staff, was allowed to start a new daily, called just that, *El Nuevo Diario*[8].

El Nuevo Diario has thrived, attaining a circulation of around 35,000, equal to that of the official government (FSLN, Sandinista) newspaper, *Barricada*, edited by another son of Chamorro Cardenal, Carlos Chamorro. The circulation of *La Prensa* remains around 65,000[9]. The fact that *La Prensa* commands a circulation so much higher than either of the pro-government papers worries the Sandinistas and might, superficially, confirm the view (which is, I believe, mistaken) that the opposition in Nicaragua has a firm popular base. But *La Prensa* can, and does at every opportunity in the most strident fashion, call upon its pre-Revolutionary history as the scourge of government abuses, defender of the rights of the people, and heir to the ideals of the martyred former editor Chamorro Cardenal, who is constantly quoted on the subject of freedom of the press. The mere fact of being in opposition in a country which has only just emerged from 44 years of dictatorship and a life-long habit of distrust of government is in *La Prensa*'s favour; and one may assume, as a fundamental of political psychology, that *La Prensa* can count on a number of readers who are not unsympathetic to the regime but enjoy seeing it sniped at. The figure of *La Prensa* sales would also be swollen by the ranks of those who buy the paper in order to find out what the opposition is saying, without agreeing with it. The

5. In this historical review I rely heavily on the excellent article by John Spicer Nichols, "News Media in the Nicaraguan Revolution", in Thomas Walker, ed., *The Nicaraguan Revolution*, pp. 187–205, imminent from Praeger, New York. My thanks to the publishers for providing me with an advance copy of this important book. I have also benefited from Nichols' paper presented to the Latin American Studies Association meeting in Washington, DC, March 1982, "The Principle and Realities of Press Freedom in Nicaragua and Beyond", and a private conversation with the author on that occasion. For a richly anecdotal history of the Chamorro publishing family, with photographs by Susan Meiselas, see Lawrence Wright, "War of Words", *Mother Jones*, June 1983, pp. 26–28 and 37–40. Cf. also "Why the Sandinistas censor La Prensa", *Guardian* (New York), August 10, 1983, p. 19, and letter from C. Pazera and M. Freeman, *In These Times*, 19–25 January 1983, p. 10.

6. Epic Task Force, *Nicaragua, A People's Revolution*, Washington, 1980, p. 18.

7. The commonly held view that the assassination was "the spark that touched off the fires of revolution in Nicaragua" (Nichols, p. 192), or that it was the "catalyst" of the Revolution (*Washington Post*, loc. cit.) tends to ignore or minimize the 18-year history of continuous, ever-intensifying struggle led by the FSLN. The assassination certainly served to generalize revolutionary feeling in the cities and among the bourgeoisie.

8. Cf. Alan Riding, "Newspaper Family Typifies Nicaragua's Division", *New York Times*, 24 May 1980. One wonders whether there was any discussion as to who should keep the name of *La Prensa*, which was probably the most important property of all. If the majority which left to form *El Nuevo Diario* had been able to take the name with them, they would have benefited from its established popular reputation, and prevented the minority from exploiting it in order to further very different editorial policies. To the above question, raised by John Nichols, may be added another: was the split also an occasion for the CIA to infiltrate its own people onto the *La Prensa* staff? P. J. Chamorro told Nichols that *La Prensa* was not faced with the immediate necessity of hiring a number of new hands, since the paper had previously been much overstaffed.

9. These figures are not audited, but represent a consensus. After closures, *La Prensa*'s circulation tends to rise: according to an editorial of 17 July, up to 80,000. The claim of four readers per copy of the paper seems exaggerated (cf. below). The figure given by Riding, op, cit., at the time of the family dispute in May 1980, was 55,000.

newspaper vendor who touted his wares with the loud cry "Reacción", as I heard on one occasion, was certainly not planning to sell *La Prensa* only to its supporters. The superior sales of *La Prensa* may not, moreover, reflect a proportionately greater readership, for *La Prensa* readers, being by and large better educated and more monied, can more easily afford to buy the paper individually, whereas the poorer readers of *El Nuevo Diario* and *Barricada* would be more inclined to share and borrow.

La Prensa also retains a wide, pre-conditioned audience by means of a traditional "bourgeois" emphasis on spectator sport, local crimes, sensations, and gossip about U.S. entertainers. Below, we analyse the nature and political effect of this emphasis. *Barricada*, recognizing *La Prensa*'s advantage, places the problem in the wider perspective: "The ideological area is objectively the only one in which the residue of the classes displaced from political power (i.e. the bourgeoisie) can move with any ease, thanks to the deformations which they have been inflicting for centuries in the mind of the exploited classes[10]. In the words of a former *La Prensa* reporter now with *Barricada*, "large sectors of the population are politically backward and don't understand the way *La Prensa* is manipulating them"[11].

In comparison with the flashy *La Prensa, El Nuevo Diario* and *Barricada* seem monotonously enthusiastic and dogmatic. (*Barricada* has actually much improved in popular appeal since it was started just after the revolution, but remains very much the official newspaper of the Sandinist National Liberation Front.) Many Sandinista sympathizers, no doubt, find it easier to get the official version of the news from the government-owned TV stations (both channels are controlled by the Sandinistas, who took them over from Somoza), and the radio (where 34 of the 51 stations remain, however, in private hands).

Barricada, incidentally, gives a greater cut of its cover price (at two córdobas, indentical to the other papers) to its vendors, poor and often barefoot small boys who brave dangerous flows of traffic in order to sell to people in cars. Their trade is regarded by the Sandinistas as a degrading and exploitative form of child-labour, as a pathetic symptom of under-development and social inequity; it is depicted as such in a mural on a Ministry of Education building, contrasting with the happy, carefree play of luckier children. (There are no such vendors in Cuba.)

"FREEDOM OF THE PRESS"

10. Onofre Guevara L., "Las Razones de la Provocación", *Barricada*, 31 July.
11. Interview (filmed by Carol Wells and Ted Hajjar) with Emilio Barreto.
12. David Wood, "Nicaraguan exile training may be exercise in futility", *Los Angeles Times*, 19 January 1982, p. 1, col. 5.

Drawing by Roger Sanchez Flores (Reprinted from *Cartoons from Nicaragua: The Revolutionary Humor of Roger*, Managua: Committee of U.S. Citizens Living in Nicaragua, 1984).

Nichols (p. 188) compares the "collaborative" function of the Latin American press, its commitment to political advocacy and parties, with the U.S. ideal of "balanced, dispassionate reporting". This distinction, however theoretically important, fosters the widespread and carefully inculcated illusion that U.S. media are generally concerned with "balanced and dispassionate" reporting, and that they are relatively unresponsive to government and partisan propaganda pressure. Yet one has only to consider the reporting on Central America today, as on Vietnam yesterday, to see how biased it is in favour of Washington's world view. Just recently, for instance, the *Los Angeles Times*[12] carried a long article on ex-Somocista National Guardsmen in exile training, illegally, in California, for invasion of Nicaragua; they are presented as bizarre adventurers on a quixotic quest to liberate their homeland, with no mention of the dreadful and well documented crimes committed by the National Guard under Somoza.

La Prensa, like the U.S. media, pretends to impartiality in presenting the news. Its only admitted advocacy is for "Truth and Justice" as abstracts (and emblazoned thus on the masthead: "al Servicio de la Verdad y la Justicia"). The word "freedom" is similarly used in the abstract; to close down *La Prensa* for lying is to close down Freedom of the Press (the fact that "Prensa" means "Press" helps the ploy); to close down *La Prensa*, says *La Prensa*, is to close down Freedom. The freedom asserted instrumentally under Somoza, to defend popular interests, is now asserted in the abstract.

True, *La Prensa* will occasionally reveal that it is primarily defending the interests of those it calls the "economically active", that is, the owners of business. But by and large, *La Prensa* pretends that it is "the daily of the Nicaraguans" (as it puts on the masthead) in general, the protagonist of a classless society where social divisions were swept away once and for all by the overthrow of Somoza. And then came the Sandinistas "creating" social divisions and class warfare. So that now, says *La Prensa*, Nicaragua is divided between the government, its militants and its armed mobs on the one side, and the people, backed by the Church and *La Prensa*, on the other.

Whenever it is suspended *La Prensa* appeals to "the people" for a verdict, by means of street interviews of groups of selected individuals usually representing service and petty bourgeois professions, and students, often female ("Pretty Miss So and So . . ."), and always with photographs to enhance their particularity. *Barricada* and *El Nuevo Diario*, on the other hand, seek to confirm the popularity and correctness of controversial measures (notably, *La Prensa* suspensions) less by means of individual testimonials (although there are some of these) than through representatives of the various mass organizations who appear to (and probably do to a degree) write spontaneously, often to demand greater sanctions than the government is prepared to apply.

La Prensa also establishes grandiose historical analogies. On the one hand, it purports to stand in the line of true Christianity, the Gospel of Love resisting the heathen (atheistic communist) avatars of hate; on the other hand it stands for the Voice of Dissent from "religious" political (Marxist) orthodoxy. In overt allusion to the public burnings of the paper and the threats of the "mobs" (turbas) after two suspensions in quick succession, the newspaper compared itself to no less a hero and martyr than the Bohemian religious reformer John Huss. Reproductions from a 15th-century mansucript showing Huss being led away by soldiers, and being burned at the stake, carry this commentary:

Why is John Huss being taken bound, why do the masses [masas, with reference to Sandinist mass organizations] beat him with sticks and spit on him? Why is his sad thinker's face the cause of mockery and the blows of the monks? We are horrified to think there was once a time when a heresy, a divergence, a critical position gave rise not to dialogue and discussion, but aggression, the stake. John Huss interpreted the Bible in his own way, he was labelled a heretic and despite the safe conduct of the Emperor Sigismund [despite this "constitutional" guarantee] his tormentors whipped up fanatical monks against him, and what is more shameful and contradictory, Christian monks [reference to the numerous

Christians and priests in and supporting the government]; and judged by popular tribunals, he was taken to the stake.

It was 1415. We thought this human epoch was over . . . but no . . . once again fanaticism is reborn, and yet again thought is being burned, as the paper on which this is written is burned — burning newspapers — *La Prensa* to the stake, and once again appears the Inquisition of Liberty and the censorshp of expression and opinion [13].

The government papers do not claim to be impartial. *Barricada* sees itself, in terms similar to those enunciated by Lenin, as the "organizer, agitator, guide, and educator" of the working masses. "News is not simply news. Just as a reactionary daily (i.e. *La Prensa*) seeks its angle of narrow class vision, we see news as a means of minute examination from the perspective of the Revolution, a means of deepening the process and the interests of the people (which are) the *raison d'être* of revolutionary journalism". ("Barricada desde adentro", 25 July.) The same article goes on to affirm the necessity of "autocritica revolucionaria" (revolutionary self-criticism) to fight bureaucratic corruption, rigidity and chaos.

The Office of Communications Media[14] basing itself on a Provisional General Law Regarding Communications Media passed 13 September 1979 defines freedom of the press not as an absolute, not in terms of the rights of the editors or owners but in terms of the rights of the readers to be truthfully informed, and in terms of social responsibility. *La Prensa* denies that these are primary criteria. After the first suspension over the religious billboards (cf. below) *La Prensa* editor P. J. Chamorro Barrios was given the opportunity to defend his position orally in public, and under questioning, at the Foro Nacional (ongoing "parliament" where government and opposition debate), and on a government-owned radio station. According to the complete transcription published the following day, Chamorro defined freedom of the press as a matter of individual conscience, including the "right" to lie (or more precisely, with the claim that lying — to which he did not admit — would not be a reason to suspend the paper), and the right to commit errors, to which he did admit. On the latter topic, when confronted with the figure of 28 "distorted news items" in the period January–June 1981, he excused himself on the grounds that all humans are subject to error, that *La Prensa* suffers unfair discrimination ("a Sherlock Holmes or Agatha Christie-like scrutiny") from the government which allows the errors of its own newspapers to go unsanctioned (which is not true; cf. below). To the charge that he was trying to undermine the government, he responded elliptically by saying that it was not the attacks by *La Prensa* but the attacks *on La Prensa* which were endangering the security of the state[15].

Attacks on *La Prensa* have not succeeded in weakening substantially the credibility it enjoys; nor have they strengthened the credibility of the officialist papers. In an interview, Emilio Barreto, a foremost reporter for *Barricada*, admitted that the paper had

13. "Meditación ante un manuscrito iluminado", *Prensa Literaria* (literary supplement to *La Prensa*), 9 August, p. 1. All translations in this article are my own, except those transcribed from the interviews, which are by Karin Pally.
14. Dirección de Medios de Comunicación. Now directly responsible to the Ministry of the Interior, it was formerly under the Ministry of Culture.
15. "Si el comunismo es dictadura, somos anticommunistas", *La Prensa*, 12 July, p. 11.

failed to reach the public. *Barricada*, conceived according to principles entirely new to Nicaragua, rejecting yellow journalism — the journalism of so-called entertainment which is actually a means of moral corruption — had not yet found the way to convince the people at their present level of comprehension.

Self-criticism is a notable feature of Sandinista government. Foreign observers generally have been struck by the readiness with which the youthful Sandinista leadership will admit to errors attributable to lack of experience and excess of revolutionary zeal. They have been accessible to criticism from the base, and the pro-government newspapers have extensive letter columns, which often lead to investigation, and correction of the reader's complaint.

This is done, of course, within the framework of revolutionary ideals. The right to criticize bureaucracy is usually allowed in socialist countries, and the example of Cuba is probably present in the minds of the Sandinistas. In Cuba, where anti-Castro media had been "starved out of business" by the end of 1960, the government came, eventually, to recognize the press as a useful avenue for dissent "within the Revolution"[16]. In 1974 the two dailies *Granma* and especially *Juventud Rebelde* inaugurated "consumer action" columns, which became very popular indeed. This was done at a time when transmission of ideas from the base, public debate on certain domestic issues, and a system of local elections called "Poder Popular", was being developed. Another means by which the Nicaraguan government takes criticism is in *Cara al Pueblo* (Face the People), a weekly television programme where government officials field some quite tough questioning from members of the public. Both *Barricada* and *El Nuevo Diario*, moreover, have been "admonished" by the government Office of Communications Media for inaccuracy and improper reporting (appearing to endorse, for instance, the popular takeover of land without pointing out that the crime was illegal (14 August), or for giving the name of a minor involved in crime)[17]. The Office of Communications Media, moreover, is capable of its own "self-criticism", having on one occasion seen fit to retract an order to withdraw a (mildly) sexist advertisement published in *La Prensa*, after protests from the paper. (Advertising of a sexist nature, like that for alcohol and tobacco, is prohibited by law.)

16. John Spicer Nichols, "Cuba: Right Arm of Revolution" in Robert N. Pierce, *Keeping the Flame, Media and Government in Latin America*, Hastings House, New York, 1979, pp. 80–96.
17. Interview with Martinez Caldera, cf. below. *El Nuevo Diario* has been "repeatedly" admonished. According to a report from KPFK radio on the State of National Emergency just declared in Nicaragua as a result of internal sabotage (17 March), and necessitating the imposition of press censorship, *El Nuevo Diario* was suspended.

"*La Prensa*: 'Oh horror! I am surrounded by a "small group of excitable people" demanding that I be confiscated!!!'". The "small group of excitable people" is *La Prensa's* phrase for the hundreds of militants who called for *La Prensa's* confiscation during the 19 July 1981 celebrations. Drawing by Roger Sanchez Flores (Reprinted from *Barricada* (Managua)).

SUSPENSIONS OF *LA PRENSA*: THE RELIGIOUS BILLBOARD

The billboards of opposition parties in Managua, which are numerous and prominent but aesthetically negligible compared with those of the government, are occasionally defaced. One put up by the Conservative Democratic Party, whose motto is "Dios, Orden, Justicia", had "Entreguistas, Vendepatria" (traitors, sell-out capitulators) spray-painted on it. Another CDP billboard which I saw had been partly burned. One put up by *La Prensa* itself, saying "Pesa mas el amor que odio" (love counts more than hatred, a phrase attributed to P. J. Chamorro Cardenal in an editorial of 1965) showed signs of having been trashed. And it was the defacement of a religious billboard, saying "No Hay que un solo dios" (there is only one God — which was generally understood as opposing the "deification" of revolutionary heroes) which led to the first suspension of *La Prensa*.

The billboard stood outside a radio station which had suffered government sanction for telling lies about the government's attitude to religious matters. Front and back-page photographs in *La Prensa* (7 July) showed this billboard in a completely broken state, with a caption implicating Sandinist vandals inspired by a government "anti-religious escalation". Investigation by the police, reported in *Barricada* (11 & 12 July) revealed the responsibility of a nun who confessed to having ordered the billboard dismantled, for purposes of restoration after its defacement. *Barricada* furthermore denounced *La Prensa* for using the issue of the broken billboard in its own "sinister campaign to promote a climate of chaos, anxiety and anguish, manipulating the religious sentiments of the people".

The issue was inflamed by the fact that the church hierarchy, in the person of Archbishop Miguel Obando y Bravo, had taken a position hostile to the government, and prohibited the four priests in the government from functioning as priests as long as they held ministerial posts. When *La Prensa* reappeared on Sunday 12 July, the Archbishop was quoted as saying, in a banner front-page headline, "they may erase the name of Christ from the billboards, but never from the heart of the Nicaraguan people". The pre-headline "the people with the bishops" which suggested that the people were against the government, and the photograph of the "thousands" who came to hear the Archbishop's "impromptu" speech, were designed to affirm popular support for *La Prensa*'s position. The mid-page headline stigmatized the government's action as that of a Communist dictatorship.

"The people" support the Bishops, who support *La Prensa*; so apparently, do the poor, as represented by the little newspaper vendors, 30 of whom demonstrated outside the Casa de Gobierno. Questioned by *Barricada* reporters, the children admitted that their demonstration was not spontaneous, that it had been organized by *La Prensa* itself, who provided the placards. Thus, noted *Barricada* (14 August, p. 3), does the paper have the "infamy" to exploit the poverty and economic necessity of the poor.

Barricada calls *La Prensa* "La voz del amo" (his master's voice). And the master was quick to spring to the defence of an injured disciple. An editorial in *The Washington Post* of 19 July was reprinted in translation on the front page of the 23 July issue of *La Prensa*, praising the paper as "conspicuous adornment of the regime", as noted above. The *Post*'s summary of the "problem" which caused the closure does not even mention that *La Prensa* was accused of having lied, let alone that it was proved to have done so, but only that it "reported on government[18] destruction of billboards bearing religious themes, (and) official efforts to keep a critical (*La Prensa* translation, "independent") radio station off the air . . .".

This closure heralds the slide into "Cuban-style Somocism". "It is not easy to foretell whether Nicaragua in Sandinista hands will take the Cuban way (*La Prensa* translation: "be another Cuba") which is not so difficult in many respects from the Somoza way, or

18. The Spanish translation omits the word "government" so as to exculpate the *Post* from its own twisted reporting of what not even *La Prensa* claimed was a direct government action.

whether it will find its path to respectable and enduring pluralism" based on the institutional pillars of independence, the private economic sector, the Church, and *La Prensa*.

A FITTING GIFT FOR THE ROYAL WEDDING: "A WELL-BOUND COPY OF THE WORKS OF CARLOS FONSECA"

After weathering the heavy storms of the first suspension and the celebrations of 17–19 July which affirmed the massive popularity of the Sandinistas, *La Prensa* found the British Royal Wedding a most fortunately timed diversion. While the pro-government press noted the bitter irony of plans for the nuptial extravaganza coinciding with riots in Britain against unemployment, racism and police repression, and the fact that a lavish firework display in Hyde Park was followed immediately by "another kind of fireworks" — the explosion of the petrol bombs in Toxteth, Liverpool, *La Prensa* (27 July) indulged its fantasies of the fairyland escape from horrid realities:

After this wedding, the world will continue the same; the Palestinians will continue to fight the Jews, the Afghan guerrillas will continue to try to throw out Soviet soldiers from their country, the Polish workers will go on wanting a better life. . . . Why this tremendous publicity . . . why spend millions of dollars on a wedding lasting a few hours? The reply may be dramatic. . . . The world we live in each day becomes heavier, with its war, its violence, its natural disasters, its poverty, its tyrannies. . . . Suddenly, in England, a Prince and a Lady marry; all the latent romanticism, the idealism of young and old in all the world place their hopes, their dreams on (this) event. . . . When all is said and done, all girls have something of Lady Diana and all boys something of Charles.

The priority given to Royalty over Reality is graphically reinforced by the extent of the headline and story, with its six pictures of Diana in a variety of poses, plus one of Miss Universe 1981 (a Venezuelan), dominating "lesser" political stories, such as the announcement of a political amnesty in Uruguay, and Fidel Castro's (always presented as absurd) denunciations of possible U.S. responsibility for the virus (dengue) which was causing havoc in Cuba.

Two days later (29 July) the wedding itself dominated the whole front page, with a story which wrapped round to the back page under the headline "Nicaragua absent at the wedding" and a pre-headline, "We might have given them a hammock". *La Prensa* expressed shock at the government's failure to secure representation at the "incredible fairy-tale dream" which "fascinates millions", and to offer an appropriate gift. Nicaragua's new ambassador, Francisco d'Escoto Brockmann (brother of Chancellor Miguel, cf. below) had not yet presented his credentials and was therefore ineligible to attend. It was left open whether this was due to negligence or intended as a rebuff to the notoriously anti-communist, anti-popular and pro-U.S. Thatcher regime, which unlike most other major

European powers, had offered little or no help to Nicaragua. *La Prensa* goes on to cite a spokesman for the Chancellery who said that whatever gift Nicaragua might have been able to make, could not compare with the Steben (*sic*) vase valued at $70,000, for which Mrs Reagan boasted having paid only $8,000. The scorn surely intended by the foreign ministry official for Mrs Reagan's commercial degradation of the diplomatic gift, is turned in *La Prensa* to a note of national self-deprecation: "Where could we find money like that?" he said, and somewhat in jest added that "we could have sent them a traditional hammock (one of Nicaragua's native crafts) for their delectation".

Then comes the clincher: "Finally, someone proposed that also for the delectation of the noble newly-weds, we should have sent as gift for the royal wedding a volume of the Works of Carlos Fonseca, well-bound."

Citing article 3, paragraph (g) of the General Law of Communications Media which prohibits the publication of writings "which outrage Nicaraguan national feeling, language and cultural values", the Office of Communications Media interpreted the comment as a "clear lack of respect" (*franco irrespeto*) for compañero Carlos Fonseca (*El Nuevo Diario*, 30 July. Fonseca is revered in Nicaragua rather as Che is in Cuba). "Lack of respect" was the official, but mildest term used; more typical of the hail of protest from individuals and popular organizations channeled through *Barricada* and *El Nuevo Diario* as soon as *La Prensa* hit the streets, were such phrases as "outrage", "incredible vulgarity", "cynical and dirty satire", "the work of treacherous minds accustomed to trafficking in the most sacred values of the nation" (*Barricada*, 3 August).

In the United States we might be tempted to write off the allusion as a silly joke (which in form it was), hardly deserving sanction and uproar. To understand the situation, we would have to imagine ourselves as patriots defending the American Revolution (during which George Washington has died in battle) against the threat of a return of the British army, and confronted with the suggestion that the new Revolutionary government send a copy of Washington's speeches as a gift to the wedding of the Prussian Crown Prince (Prussia then standing, as an ally in Britain's war against the American colony, as Britain does to the U.S. today in its "war" against Nicaragua).

La Prensa's defense did not, however, take the line that it was all intended as a joke. The offending comment was, incredibly, a "mistake", an "oversight", "an error of transcription" (whatever that might mean), an "ill-turned phrase", born, so *La Prensa* alleged, of a conversation overheard in a ministry. *Barricada*'s response (3 August) to this weak defense was scathing, deriding *La Prensa* for its hypocrisy and pusillanimity in not declaring outright its class-ridden contempt for the values of the people, and reminding readers of the journal's "rage" at witnessing the popu-

lar enthusiasm when the remains of Carlos Fonseca were recoverd and placed in the Plaza Revolución, thereupon renamed Plaza Carlos Fonseca.

La Prensa wants its readers to identify with Carlos the princeling of a distant hostile capitalist country, rather than Carlos the leader and martyr of the great local struggle against Somoza. It holds up personal models which are diametrically opposed to revolutionary or socialist ideals. Bourgeois to the core, it peddles the most trivial gossip about U.S. movie and rock stars and the "beautiful" and super-rich, in a way more reminiscent of the most reactionary and vulgar of the Euro–American tabloids, than any "responsible" press. On 28 July (thus between stories of the Royal Wedding) "Jacqueline al estilo Nica", that is, Barbara Carrera, and her romance with shipping millionaire Philippe Niarchos, become the cynosure of the editorial eye. Born in poverty on a river barge in Nicaragua, now living in Beverly Hills, this model and actress proudly proclaims herself, with implicit editorial endorsement, totally selfish, living only for herself and the present moment, hating politics, rejecting her country of origin. To this may be contrasted the story run by *Barricada* on another Nicaraguan who succeeded in the U.S. as Bianca Jagger (Blanca Perez) but who is admired in Nicaragua and by the U.S. Left for her vociferous support of the Revolution, and recent activity in helping save the lives of Salvadoran refugees in Honduras[19].

"THE ARCHBISHOP THE DRIVING FORCE BEHIND THE COUNTERREVOLUTION"

Another suspension followed the publication by *La Prensa* on 18 August of a declaration, attributed to Chancellor (Foreign Minister) Miguel d'Escoto, that Archbishop Obando y Bravo was "the driving force (el principal impulsor) behind the counterrevolution in Nicaragua". The declaration was published despite the fact that *La Prensa* had been warned in advance by Sergio Ramirez, member of the Junta de Gobierno, and d'Escoto himself, that it was false: d'Escoto denied having made it, and said he disagreed with it. *La Prensa* had also been informed that the proof it alleged — a tape-recording made by a Mexican journalist six months before in New Delhi — was not forthcoming. The publication of the declaration notwithstanding, was taken as a premeditated affront, "an open defiance of the law", and punished with a heavier sanction than before, a 78-hour closure.

A CASE OF DECAPITALIZATION

On 28 September, a 48-hour suspension was followed by another of the same duration on 1 October for recidivism. *La Prensa* had been unable to prove the accusations against the government contained in an interview with Alberto Mantilla, former head of

19. *Barricada Internacional* (English-language monthly published by the FSLN), 5 December 1981, p. 5.

LAMSA laboratories, who disappeared following an indictment for having defrauded the Treasury of $1,200,000. Under his direction LAMSA had operated for some time using an unregistered "ghost" firm, which avoided paying taxes. He was denounced by the workers who discovered he was decapitalizing (taking machinery and raw materials to Costa Rica), and who demanded the government take the firm over. In violation of Article 3, paragraph (e) of the Communications Media Law, which prohibts defense of persons engaged in illegal activities, La Prensa eulogized Mantilla as a true patriot victimized by government oppression. It also failed to give the reasons for the government intervention, and attacked the Vice-Minister of Industry responsible for it[20].

UNDERMINING GOVERNMENT POLICY

These examples of tactics which the government has found offensive enough to warrant suspensions, represent not aberrations, but the common stuff of La Prensa's discourse, the hostility and dishonesty which is manifested daily and in countless ways.

La Prensa inflates the trivial and trivializes the important, in any way that will seem to discredit the government. Minor traffic accidents, for instance, involving government vehicles (the reckless driving of which has been also, but discreetly, criticized by Sandinista papers) are treated like major atrocities. The minor failure of an engine on a national airline plane, causing a perfectly safe emergency landing, became the front page scare headline of the day: "54 endangered in Lanica" (18 August).

But the main concern of La Prensa is to attack major government programmes. Amid the manifold indications of its determination to undermine Sandinista economic and social reforms we will single out just two articles, both on subjects about which one would have thought people of goodwill might agree: the literacy campaign and the right of self-defense.

At the time it was underway, La Prensa opposed the literacy "crusade", the merit of which has been recognized world-wide, and which won last year a special and prestigious prize from the UN. The campaign was undertaken immediately after the Revolution in July 1979, in the worst circumstances, when the Nicaraguan economy was much damaged and the social fabric still raw. But in a period of five months, volunteer workers, many of them mere children, managed to reduce illiteracy from 50 per cent to 10 per cent. La

20. According to George Black in *Nicaragua*, published by the National Network in Solidarity with the Nicaraguan People in Washington, March–April 1982, p. 3, *La Prensa* was an active collaborator in the decapitalization. LAMSA workers he interviewed told him "that Mantilla had threatened in advance to go to *La Prensa* 'in order to cause the workers here as much trouble as possible, knowing that the paper wouldn't check the truth of his allegations before publishing'".

21. "Crece analfabetismo en el mundo", 17 July, p. 5.

Prensa objected to the campaign's openly declared function to politicize the people, that is teach them in a positive way about the Revolution of recent history. *La Prensa* wanted literacy books containing only "neutral" words and phrases, rather than the names of revolutionary heroes like Sandino, Fonseca and the very words "La Revolución", which have the incidental merit of containing all the vowels. *La Prensa's* continuing effort to deny the merit of the literacy crusade is exemplified in an article headed "Illiteracy increases throughout the world", purportedly based on a UNESCO report[21]. *La Prensa* pinpoints success in China, failures in Africa, "good results" in Cuba (surprise) and "other nations". Which "other nations"? Nicaragua is not even mentioned. The article also manages to distort the nature of the methods now almost universally recognized as most apposite to the Third World, successfully applied in Cuba immediately after their Revolution, and based on the writings of Paolo Freire. These methods are characterized by *La Prensa* as a type of "practical education" which sounds not dissimilar to that satirized by Dickens in Dotheboys Hall (*Nicholas Nickleby*). There is no mention of Freire's essential prerequisite, that any literacy campaign be tied to demands for social and political reforms or revolution.

The Sandinistas defeated Somoza by force of arms and by mobilizing the masses. *La Prensa* likes to pretend that it was its own, that is, the bourgeois opposition to Somoza, which was the critical factor of bringing down the dictator. Notwithstanding all Reagan's threats to destabilize, blockade, and even invade the country, the ex-Somocista guards openly in training in Honduras and the U.S. for invasion, the ever-escalating threat from the U.S. military commitment to crush the Salvadorean insurrection, the continuous acts of counterrevolutionary terrorism within Nicaragua, *La Prensa* feels more threatened by the Sandinista army than the counterrevolutionary terrorists, whom it refers to as the "armed opposition" and whom it portrays as the victims of government repression. The Sandinista army and militia are viewed as threats to "liberty", potential instruments of totalitarian rule, and an unnecessary provocation of neighboring countries.

An article entitled "Youth and Violence" by a Salesian Rector Mayor, occupying the best part of a page, is backed (literally: on the back of the same page, in a typical coincidence) by the sensational story of the (non-political) murder of a bolsista (money-changer) and a gory photograph of his bloody handmark on the wall. The article laments world-wide terrorism and in particular common juvenile violence (the distinction is not made) as structurally endemic to both the two major "liberty-denying" systems, capitalism and socialism ("that prefabricated plan with merely rational categories"), and proposes to eliminate violence by establishing a realm based on the spirit alone, and the Gospel: a "Civilization of Love". This and much more of a very portentous nature ("this is a new historic moment, as at the end of the Dark Ages, when all civilization must be rebuilt", etc.), is conspicuously illustrated by means of two photographs of Sandinista children engaged in militia training, and handling rifles. This juxtaposition preys upon prevalent fears, which are to a degree legitimate, and common among older people confronted with an extremely juvenile army (the average age is 20; a high proportion of the revolutionary combatants were teenagers and some even younger), and a militia who certainly were and perhaps still are insufficiently disciplined in the handling of weapons in public[22]. Fear of such a militia could only be increased by exercises, which one would have thought it imprudent to publicize, such as the (mock) seizure by a children's commando group, masked and armed, of Radio Sandino, reported by *Barricada* complete with a provocative photograph (11 July).

That armed self-defense is a downright unChristian concept, that Sandinismo and Christianity have nothing in common, is the theme running through an extensive series of articles called "The Gospel Upside Down or The Gospel of Judas" (*El Evangelio al Revés o el Evangelio de Judas*), extracted from the work of "the great Latin American Writer" Guillermo Blanco. This posits Christian duty as that of "struggle against (class) struggle", in favour of (class) harmony and peace. The Sandinistas are accused of trying to erect the Kingdom of Heaven with bullets, and turning Nicaragua into a battleground of vice, hatred and envy. "Hate one another" is the true Sandinist slogan. The series as a whole is straight, familiar ideology of *La Prensa* and the bourgeois opposition and remarkably lacking in Biblical reference; but at one point at least it becomes a curious study in the manipulation of history. The article entitled "The swastika in the churches" (2 August) contains a contradiction in much right-wing, anti-communist rhetoric which tries to hide its historical alignment with Nazism by equating Nazism with Communism. The Sandinista attempt to create a "Christian Revolutionary culture" (incarnated, of course, in priests like poet and Minister of Culture Ernesto Cardenal) is likened to the Nazi's co-optation of the Christian churches. The Christian duty in Nazi Germany was not to oppose Nazism but to keep clear of it: "The evil thing was not so much to have believed in Nazism, as to have used Christian arguments to support it". Amid such sophistries the rise of Nazism is likened, implicitly, to the rise of Sandinism, and the tactics of the Sandinists are likened, implicitly, to those of the Nazis. In order to gain popular support, warns the writer, a government promises as the Nazis to reinvigorate industry, improve the

An illustration for a series of *La Prensa* articles entitled "The Gospel Upside Down, or The Gospel of Judas" attacking the idea of the Christian Sandinista militant.

standard of living, and recover national dignity; but in order to preserve itself, it also creates a powerful army, and seeks forcibly to destroy its enemies.

La Prensa blames the problems of the Nicaraguan economy not on the legacy of Somoza, or the difficulties of transition from one kind of economy to another (from feudal-capitalist to mixed private-socialized). Blame falls upon the "exaggeraged zeal" and "fanaticism" of a "sectarian" government which deliberately creates a climate of enmity, anarchy, bureaucracy and dependence on Socialist countries[23]. *La Prensa* derides the name given to the current year, "Year of Defense and Production", since production, in the "straitjacket" of absurd economic plans hatched out by "foreign" advisors, is catastrophically low and the economy "almost bankrupt". This is the familiar refrain of the U.S. media, which like *La Prensa* ignore figures which already indicate a substantial increase in production since the 1970s. The litany of the "climate of chaos and instability" allegedly induced by Sandinista economic planning, is of course intended to bring on the very conditions it pretends to deplore. In character and function it is remarkably similar to the attacks of *El Mercurio* on the Allende government in Chile (cf. below).

FOREIGN POLICY: CUBA, EL SALVADOR

The foreign policy alignment of *La Prensa* is

22. 9 August, p. 2. Cf. also an article "Children in Nicaraguan society" (*Prensa*, 27 March 1981) illustrated with a conspicuous photograph of a child aiming an automatic weapon at the reader, to which *Barricada* drew attention 15 July.

23. "Para una efermeride gloriosa", 28 July, and "balances y perspctives de la Gestion Sandinista, 5 August.

squarely with the U.S. The paper applauds the latest developments in U.S. armaments and arms exports: the sending of a new batch of "Fast and Accurate F.16s" (headline, 20 July) to Israel, praised for its attacks on Lebanon and Iraq; the decision to build the neutron bomb (with no mention of the world-wide revulsion it generated) and the general strategy of obtaining (further) military superiority over the USSR. *La Prensa*'s foreign policy is of as simple-minded an anti-communism as is to be found in the average conservative U.S. paper. The small economic aid given by the Soviet Union, and the (proportionately) bigger aid given by East European countries, are taken as evidence of rampant Sovietization. *La Prensa* ran a campaign of villification against the Eastern European countries, and especially the German Democratic Republic, at the very moment when the GDR was sending massive amounts of wheat to Nicaragua to replace the shipments denied by Reagan (*El Nuevo Diario*, 17 July).

In Latin America, Chile is, for *La Prensa* citing Jeane Kirkpatrick, the model of a proper liberal economy. Cuba, on the other hand, is the model of the totalitarian Marxist state. *La Prensa*'s fear and hatred of Cuba is fed by the massive aid which that country, out of all proportion to its resources, has given in the educational, medical, cultural and technical fields. *La Prensa*, like the U.S. government, sees this aid as the "Cubanizing" of Nicaragua, and leading it down the slippery path to totalitarianism.

An arena of particular sensitivity to the newspaper, and one on which it bases much of its popular appeal, is that of sport: and here the internationally as well as regionally self-evident distinction of Cuba is taken as an insufferable humiliation of Nicaragua. *La Prensa* coined this bitter parody of a favourite Sandinista slogan, with particular reference to Cuba's sporting achievements, but also as a general indictment of Nicaragua's "self-abasement" before a country the Sandinistas gratefully acknowledge as the "Sister Republic": "Cuba ayer, Cuba hoy, y Cuba siempre" (Cuba yesterday, Cuba today, Cuba forever — the parody substitutes the name of Cuba, of course, for that of Sandino in the original; cf. *Barricada*, 13 July).

Cuba can give rise to satirical flights of fancy in the outraged breast of *La Prensa*. "Rionsito", the regular satirical columnist who writes under a "logo" of a grinning negro head (the kind of racist caricature which would not be tolerated in most U.S. papers), addresses this letter to the Minister of Economic Planning, Comandante Jaime Wheelock (11 August):

Dear Commander Jaime:
I am excited to read in BarriKGBa of Friday that on the Island (Cuba) there are cows which give 100 litres a day, or 200 pounds in weight, some five times the weight of the entire blood of the cow in pure milk.

I am asking you not to take any notice of the CIA to deprive us of the meat market if we import Cuban cattle, and that you ask compañero Fidel (Castro) to send us some five hundred of these little cows and problem solved, we will have milk enough to put in a milk fountain.

I am moreover sure, Compañero Ministro, that in Cuba they are already so advanced that they must doubtless already have cows programmed to produce instant flavored milk. Perhaps you could arrange that those sent here should come in raspberry, cocoa, jícaro seed or banana flavor, the latter being, by the way, my favorite flavor.

Finally, the struggle in neighbouring El Salvador, when it cannot be ignored, is disguised and distorted. *La Prensa* never complains about lack of press freedom there, or under other Latin American dictatorships. U.S. government officials are cited as if they represented the impartial truth; *La Prensa* editorials simply repeat sources such as the (then) U.S. ambassador to Nicaragua, Lawrence Pezzullo, who, in an interview filling most of a page (5 August) said, incredibly, that the "U.S. in giving help to El Salvador which is solely economic and is four or five times greater than any military aid ... we are not interested in the war". The Salvadorean guerrillas are labelled "leftists and extremists" who are primarily responsible for all the chaos and killing. In a cameo of twisted news reporting, *La Prensa* carried (17 August) an account of FMLN (Salvadoran guerrilla) acts of sabotage, followed by a statement of progressive Salvadoran Archbishop Arturo Rivera y Damas, giving recent statistics of victims of violence and murders (23 persons in Armenia alone on 30 July). These are clearly implied to be the work of the guerrillas, not the army, whose operations are not even mentioned. The Nicaraguan pro-government press, meanwhile, was emphasizing ex-ambassador to El Salvador Robert White's condemnation of Reagan's policy, which *La Prensa* completely ignored.

COMICS: POLIDECTO AND AGENT XZ

The dependency of La Prensa on the U.S. is visually self-evident in its choice of comics, which are generally of an old-fashioned and non-critical kind and obviously cater to bourgeois interests and fantasies: *Popeye, Bringing up Father, Blondie* ("Pepita") and of course Disney's *Donald Duck*. In a Third World context, Blondie's compulsive consumerism seems a cruel mockery of an impoverished people; whereas the character of Donald, presented again and again as lazy, sleepy and incompetent worker, fits all too well the degrading stereotype of the Latin American manufactured in the U.S. (The reasons for his particular appeal in Latin America, *vis-à-vis* that of other Disney characters, have been analysed by Dorfman and Mattelart[24].) *La Prensa* also carries Ripley's *Believe It Or Not*, to which pot pourri of senseless information the Sandinista papers like to consign analogically any *Prensa* item of self-justification which strikes them as

24. Ariel Dorfman and Armand Mattelart. *How to Read Donald Duck*, International General, 1975, etc. The Donald Duck strip was however dropped from *La Prensa* shortly after 7 August, in favour of *Olaf* by Dik Browne.

particularly absurd.

El Nuevo Diario has two U.S. strips, *Mutt and Jeff* and *Mandrake the Magician*, one Cuban strip called *El Capitan Blood* about 18th century pirates credited to the Cuban comics magazine and agency *C Linea*, and a native production called *Welfare of Childhood* (Bienestar da la Niñez), by "MLM". The drawing here, usually of two babies in conversation, could not be more primitive, the work as it were of babies themselves, and the subject is as important as it is limited: the human, medical and political virtues of breast-feeding (the incidence of which has fallen dramatically since the 1960s; Nestlé baby formula is sold unhindered in the supermarkets). *El Nuevo Diario* also carries regular strips on the theme "Jornadas Populares de Salud", about various aspects of personal and social hygiene.

Barricada carries only one comic strip: *Polidecto*, very much a native production, occasionally signed by the 22-year-old Roger. Polidecto, representative of the revolutionary working class, maintains a daily dialogue with a representative of the bourgeoisie who speaks with the voice of *La Prensa*, and sometimes is identified as *La Prensa*. The strip encapsulates the continuous ideological duel between the two papers, but here there is never any question as to who is right, and who is winning. Roger also commands the back page of the *Semana Comica*, the humorous supplement of *Barricada*, which carries the paradoxical motto: "humor is always a bit bourgeois, even if the true bourgeois is incapable of understanding it". This back page recounts the adventures of a CIA spy called Agente XZ who, like *La Prensa*, declares himself "in the service of truth and justice". XZ is a squat, rain-coated figure with a fierce scowl and burning eyes in a black, choleric face which radiates hostility.

We may single out an episode run through two successive issues[25] called "El Observador", which is itself a self-conscious comment on the power of the press (and CIA agents within it) to make and unmake images. Agent XZ receives orders, which emanate magically from a Coca Cola bottle marked "La Chispa de la Vida" (the spark of life), to break up the Foro Nacional, the debating arena for government and opposition. He gets into the Foro armed with press credentials fixed for him by CIA agents in the Venezuelan embassy, and observes the opposition parties being defeated, amid humorous asides (the speaker for the "pseudo-Christian party" causes XZ's pocket lie detector to go off; another opposition speaker offers to "prove" his Marxism by cutting off his right hand). XZ accomplishes his mission by literally breaking up the Foro, or rather, the image the reader receives of it, tearing down the box of the comic strip

25. Año 1, vol. 2, nos. 46 and 47, 10–17 and 17–24 July 1981.

26. Fred Landis. Cf. Donald Freed, with Fred Landis, *Death in Washington, The Murder of Orlando Letelier*, Lawrence Hill, Westport, Conn. 1980, pp. 84–93.

as if it were a poster on the wall — an eloquent metaphor for CIA interference in the media-which-represent-the-event (or media-as-event) and, at another level, for CIA tactics in dividing opponents and breaking up their unity. (XZ also does literal breaking-in of the Watergate burglar kind). By a twist at the end, however, Agent XZ is shown to have failed, for the broken fragments of the Foro (or its media image) carry portraits of the opposition party leaders he is supposed to be helping and whose defeat he has clumsily precipitated.

"ARGUCIAS SICOLOGICAS": PSYCHOLOGICAL TERRORISM AND SUBLIMINAL MANIPULATION

The striking similarity between *La Prensa*'s tactics and those used by the CIA-financed Chilean reactionary paper *El Mercurio* under Allende (1970–73), is the topic of a series of highly detailed articles in *Barricada* (10 July ff.) by one *La Prensa* scornfully identified as "some Chilean advisor to the Sandinista government"[26]. *El Mercurio* also engaged in psychological terrorism, scare-mongering, and every kind of ideological subversion of government programmes. Strikes, sabotage and hoarding were dramatized, often out of all proportion, and blamed on the government's economic policies, when in fact it was the bourgeoisie, egged on by *El Mercurio*, which was doing everything to obstruct Allende's attempts at social re-distribution. *El Mercurio* and *La Prensa* alike were also shown to be engaged in more subtle, subliminal psychological manipulation, whereby natural disasters and horrible personal crimes were juxtaposed, by means of crafty front-page layouts, with photographs and stories of government leaders and actions. Fires, plagues, accidental deaths, and even mutilated corpses (a speciality of *La Prensa*), with appropriate photographs and dramatized headlines, came to be associated with the government, as if the government (or Cuba, or the Soviet Union) were either directly or, more subliminally, indirectly in some way responsible for them.

Some of the juxtapositions and graphic manipulations cited seem of dubious intentionality, and one may legitimately wonder whether Landis, the author of the articles, is not giving too much credit to the deviousness and ingenuity of the layout people at *La Prensa*. Daily newspapers are put together at great speed, and given *La Prensa*'s predilection for accidents, disaster, etc. on the one hand, and any sign of government misbehaviour on the other, "subliminal juxtapositions" need not be deliberate, but arise of their own accord. Once alerted to this effect, however, one can easily find examples of one's own: I was personally much struck by the placing of what have become *La Prensa* slogans whenever it is shut down: "Closing the *Prensa* is like killing Liberty" ("cerrar a *la Prensa* es como matar la Libertad") and "Closing *La*

Prensa is an assault on the People" (Cerrar a *La Prensa* es atentar contra el pueblo) as major headlines next to photographs of the Mysterious Sleeping Man, an unidentified man found in a coma, appearing as if dead (9 August).

As *Barricada* remarked (22 July), "A society fed with heavy doses of cannibalism (reference to *La Prensa*'s story of Vietnamese refugees eating each other), mutilation, decomposed human flesh, plagues, exotic diseases, will lose confidence not only in the government, but also in itself". The Sandinistas know what happens when the CIA is unleashed upon the media in an embattled country: "The Chileans were first destroyed psychologically and then physically; they were made first mad and then blind"[27]. The Sandinistas response is unequivocal: "No seremos otro Chile" (We shall not be another Chile).

PRENCIA

Over the last decade, the activity of the CIA in assassination, subversion, destabilization and media manipulation in foreign countries has become all too well documented. There can be no doubt that the CIA is now engaged in, and has plans to increase, a destabilization programme in Nicaragua akin to that which helped topple Allende in 1973. *The Washington Post* for 14 February 1982 reported on CIA plans for a 19 million dollar covert operation programme against Nicaragua, in concert with a similar programme against Cuba and Grenada, and the Salvadoran and Guatemalan insurgents. In a recent article, Saul Landau and Craig Nelson have documented the CIA plans to foment counterrevolutionary activities in Nicaragua, especially in the inaccessible and vulnerable northeastern region, where 45 Nicaraguan soldiers were killed by former Somocistas in December alone. Landau and Nelson do not however mention *La Prensa* or plans for direct intervention in the Nicaraguan media[28].

To judge by La Prensa's policies, as we have analysed them, such intervention would appear unnecessary. But Fred Landis implies that is already present. In a recent article he has argued that when the CIA intervenes in a newspaper it does so massively in terms of layout and content, firing typesetters and staff. He does not indicate, however, when this happened with *El Mercurio* (or the CIA-funded Jamaican *Daily Gleaner*), or adduce examples contrasting the appearance of these papers before and after the CIA

27. Freed and Landis, p. 93.
28. "The CIA rides again", *The Nation*, 6 March 1982, pp. 257, 274–5.
29. See *Covert Action Information Bulletin No. 1*, "The CIA and the Media" in December 1979–January 1980, pp. 10–12. Edward Seaga, the present Jamaican prime minister who defeated his left-leaning predecessor Michael Manley with the help of the U.S. is popularly known as "CIAGA".

"takeover". His analysis of *La Prensa* also lacks this "before and after" methodology. It seems to me more likely that CIA infiltration is more of an indirect, gradual and even "subliminal" nature, in so far as the *Prensa* staff themselves may not be fully aware of the extent to which they are playing the CIA's game, and duplicating *El Mercurio* tactics. It is reasonable to assume that conservative papers in the Third World, with their close links to the U.S., are sophisticated enough to evolve tactics similar to those of the CIA, without being directly funded and influenced by the agency, as were *El Mercurio* and the *Daily Gleaner*. "Disinformation" may be a new word, but it is an old concept; and the use of the graphics of natural disaster, freak and gruesome crime to vilify the enemy and create an apocalyptic atmosphere in the public psyche was a characteristic of the great pamphlet and broadsheet war between Luther and the Pope.

A famous ditty seems appropriate here:

> You cannot hope to bribe or twist
> The honest British journalist
> But seeing what the man will do
> Unbribed, there's no occasion to.

While direct links between the CIA and *La Prensa* have yet to be proven or divulged, as they have between the CIA and *El Mercurio*, sentiment in Nicaragua — manifested in the newspapers and journals, in the shouts of militants, in mural graffiti, in carnival floats — has pre-empted the question by turning the very name of the paper into *PRENCIA*. (*La Prensa* responds by referring to the Sandinista paper as *BARRIKGBA* — a formula which is not of course vocalizable.)

The indirect links are there for all to see. *La Prensa* adds to its masthead (unlike *El Mercurio* or the Jamaican *Daily Gleaner*, another recipient of CIA funds[29]) "Miembro de la Sociedad Interamericana de Prensa" (SIP). The SIP was originally promoted and financed by the U.S., after a 1950 meeting in New York of continental journalists; leftists were denied visas by the State Department. It has been described as the "axis of CIA operations in Latin America" with the "names of its ex-Presidents and directors . . . (reading) like a list of key CIA agents in Latin American communications media" (*Barricada* 13 July). It represents some 1,000 journals throughout the hemisphere. The SIP orchestrated the news media campaign against Allende, through *El Mercurio*, many of whose officers worked with the CIA and are now in the Pinochet government. Pedro Joaquín Chamorro Barrios, co-Director of *La Prensa*, is now on the Board of Directors of the SIP; he was given a special prize for defense of freedom of the press at a SIP conference in San Diego, October 1980, where Nicaragua was denounced for violations of press freedom.

There are moreover many indirect links between *La Prensa*, right-wing Nicaraguan unions, Somocistas, the CIA and the American Institute for Free Labor

Development (AIFLD), the U.S. based AFL–CIO affiliated and CIA-financed enterprise which organized economic sabotage leading to the downfall of Salvador Allende in Chile. *La Prensa* correspondent Felix Pedro Espinoza, President of the Democratic Conservative Party and President of the Association of Ranchers in Estelí, was condemned after a two month investigation for crimes committed in association with the Somocist National Guard in 1978 (*Barricada* 11 August). One of *La Prensa*'s "persecuted martyrs", an opposition trade union (CTN) leader was identified as an individual implicated in the assassination of former *La Prensa* editor P. J. Chamorro and condemned in his absence to 18 years in jail. *El Nuevo Diario*, noting the irony of this ("fit for Ripley's Believe it or Not" — 11 August) attached to a photograph of this person the very same slogan *La Prensa* likes to put in the mouth of the individuals it canvasses in the street: "This man also thinks: 'Closing the *Prensa* is like killing Pedro all over again'" (Cerrar la *Prensa* es como volver a matar a Pedro)[30]. One of *La Prensa*'s connections with the AIFLD would be through the opposition labor union, the Confederación de Unificación Sindical (CUS), which is a major supporter of the paper and has free access to it. The CUS is AIFLD financed and its officials have received training in the U.S. (*Barricada*, 11 August, citing *AFL–CIO Free Trade Union News*, November 1980). According to *El Nuevo Diario* (10 August), the right wing unions such as the CUS have "daily meetings" with CIA agents.

In its defense, *La Prensa* points out (14 July) that it is wholly a Nicaraguan enterprise, which has belonged to the Chamorro family for 55 years, and is not a transnational, because it does not have offices or staff in other countries. The argument is disingenuous, for the paper is sustained by advertising of firms which do have transnational connections and its defence of the Nicaraguan private sector can only be to the benefit of the U.S. business invested in that sector. This is the point of departure of an exemplary analysis of the role of the "peripheral" and "less than transnational" company with all the appearance of a local, family firm:[31]

The *Prensa* is not a transnational in the traditional and conventional sense of the word; but to be rigorous and just, it is less than this, scarcely a peripheral and dependent branch of the imperialist transnationals of disinformation, whose function is to produce organized lies against the interests of the popular classes, and disinformation which will then be

fed into the international wire services and published in the news media of the capitalist countries of which the *Prensa* is a part. The *Prensa* also reproduces in its pages the point of view of U.S. imperialist capital and the creole capital of the periphery, about the danger to its interests represented by a Democratic Popular Revolution firmly fixed in the heart of imperialism's area of continental geopolitical influence.

CONCLUSION:
A "GENEROUS REVOLUTION":
FOR HOW LONG?

The question whether *La Prensa* is actually CIA infiltrated like Chile's *El Mercurio*, or whether it merely does the CIA's job of its own accord, is succinctly resolved in a Polidecto cartoon (*Barricada* 15 July), in which a figure representing *La Prensa* says "We wish to deny tendentious rumors that claim we are copying the *Mercurio* ... we copy directly from the (CIA) manual" (with reference to the books he carries under his arm, entitled Destabilization Techniques, made in USA).

Financially, *La Prensa* at present has no need of outside funds[32], and could probably survive with less commercial advertising, of which it has a virtual

"**We want to deny tendentious rumors that claim we are copying** *El Mercurio* [Chile] — We copy directly from the Manual — CIA Destabilization Techniques", drawing by Roger Sanchez Flores (Reprinted from *Barricada* (Managua)).

30. This formula-become-cliché, *La Prensa*'s own knee-jerk reaction to sanctions, appears as the "most poignant statement on the fate of the troubled newspaper ... from a youth in the barrios of Managua", in the *Time* magazine article cited at the beginning.
31. "*La Prensa*, es una Transnacional", *Barricada*, 27 July, p. 3.
32. According to George Black, *Nicaragua*, op. cit. p. 2. However, "The West German Friedrich Naumann Foundation has reportedly made *La Prensa* a grant of $500,000".
33. "Nicaragua: familiar trumpet", *The Nation*, 30 May 1981, p. 657.

monopoly. It boasts of being well capitalized, and of reinvesting profits which are presumably unaffected by the periodic suspensions. And the Chamorro family is certainly one of the richest in the land.

There is strong pressure from the mass organizations to close down the newspaper for good. "Confiscate the *Prensa*, mouthpiece of the CIA" was the organized chant of a 100 or so (by my own reckoning — the figure was reduced in the *La Prensa* report to "a little group of a dozen persons") during the second anniverary celebrations of 19 July, at the moment when Tomás Borge announced the confiscation of firms discovered to be guilty of decapitalization *La Prensa* is accused of "ideological decapitalization".

The principal mass organization of the base, the Sandinist Committees for Defense (CDS) have found various ways to dramatize their contempt for *La Prensa*. They organized public bonfires of the newspaper. They made a caroza or float for a new festival, launched by the Ministry of Culture, to celebrate the flight of Somoza, the "Day of Joy" on 17 July. This float was quite an elaborate affair showing the PRENCIA as a grotesque head, hatted with the Stars and Stripes, with a huge tongue lolling out, marked *El Mercurio*, UPI, AP, VOA (two news agencies and Voice of America) and representing the imperialist, Somocist and mendacious nature of the paper. The float also condemned Alfonso Robelo, leader of the small opposition Nicaraguan Democratic Movement, and major spokesman for Nicaraguan big business, who has said, "The U.S. must move now to directly aid newspapers, radio stations, unions and private sector groups that are opposing the Sandinists.[33]. Ironically, Robelo was, with *La Prensa* co-owner Violeta Chamorro, one of the five-member government Junta which signed the Communications Law into effect on 13 September 1979. (He is now working for violent overthrow of the government from Costa Rica).

La Prensa is courting, and may be deliberately provoking serious physical confrontations with government supporters. On 13 January a demonstration of about 500 small merchants from the principal market of Managua, protesting the newspaper's editorial line, particuarly with respect to counterrevolutionary terrorism was shot at by *La Prensa* guards, who wounded a leader of a Sandinist Defense Committee, and a cameraman from the Sandinist Television System. While thousands of workers registered their protest, *La Prensa* premises were closed down for three days "under the protection of the military authorities"[34].

There is a strong undercurrent of resentment against the government for being too lenient towards *La Prensa*. Even U.S. liberals admit that, considering the circumstances in which they took power, and the

34. *Barricada Internacional*, 30 January 1982, p. 6.
35. Cf. *Envío*, no. 9, 17 February 1982, of the Instituto Historico Centroamericano, Managua, p. 2. This envío gives excerpts from the Provisional General Law Regarding Communications Media, and a summary of the problems relating to its application.

fearful record of criminality left by the Somocistas, the Sandinistas have been generous towards their enemies. There were a few spontaneous popular executions of the most hated National Guardsmen, but no judicial killing (there is no death penalty in Nicaragua). The cries of repression and denial of human rights orchestrated from the U.S. have not been justified by the UN Commissions on Human Rights, or Amnesty International.

The theme of the Revolution's generosity to its opponents was expressed in the interview I had with Martino Martinez Caldera of the Office of Communications Media (Dirección de Medios de Comunicación) in Managua. He emphasized that the suspensions of *La Prensa* were provoked by a long "accumulation of lies" and after the failure of attempts at amicable "dialogue" conducted in "the spirit of generosity and tolerance" which was the hallmark of revolutionary law. Since *La Prensa* took no heed, the government had no choice but to apply the law, which prohibits lying and deliberate distortion of news. Constant "admonitions" (amonestaciones) had no effect on the incidence of "errors" or the failure to compensate them by means of properly emphasized rectifications, which were moreover ignored by the international wire services who had seized upon the original "misinformation". "This policy of information is turning into a policy of lies. We are worried because this appears to be a policy of information taken out of the Nazi books of Hitler's propaganda minister (Goebbels), that is: a lie repeated often enough ends up by being considered a truth. This is really dangerous."

It should be noted that *La Prensa* has never been subject to prior censorship. Nor has it ever been sanctioned for its editorial line, but only for its news reporting. Here it has been deemed a threat to national security, but always within the framework of the UN Universal Declaration of Human Rights, as well as the Nicaraguan law we have cited[35]. Minister of the Interior Tomás Borge has called for "patience" with *La Prensa*; but the paper seems determined to test that patience to the limit. To the question whether *La Prensa* was following a deliberately suicidal course, Martinez Caldera replied that neither his office nor the government wanted to close down the paper for good. "To the contrary, we would like to see the *Prensa* maintain itself, as long as it is able to exercise freedom of expression responsibly. But where we see it destroying itself is in the conscience, in the awareness of the Nicaraguan people. To the extent that it hides information from the people, to the extent that it lies to the people, to that extent the *Prensa* is destroyed in the mind (conciencia) of the people. We consider that it isn't necessary to physically close the *Prensa*, it will be enough that it is closed in the minds of the Nicaraguans."

As it trumpets forth the periodic suspensions of *La Prensa* as signs of creeping totalitarianism, the U.S.

Drawing by Roger Sanchez Flores (Reprinted from *Para una lectura crítica del diario "La Prensa"*, **Managua:** **Escuela de Periodismo, Universidad Centroamericana, 1985).**

media ignore the fact that hitherto the government has chosen to exercise its power to suppress a newspaper altogether, not against the Right but the Left. In January 1980 it closed down permanently *El Pueblo*, the daily of the Worker's Front, a radical/ultra-left organization which had called for active sabotage of the government's economic plan in order to bring power back "into the hands of the people". The editors were jailed on a variety of charges, including subversion and storing of illegal arms[36]. In a more recent media-related incident, it was both Left and Right who were punished; members of the Nicaraguan Communist Party, who accused the government of selling out to imperialism, and at the same time, members of COSEP, the primary big businessmen's organization, who published in *La Prensa* a letter alleging that Nicaragua was on the verge of economic collapse and that the government was preparing genocide. These attacks on the government coincided with the murder of two Cuban schoolteachers in the latest counterrevolutionary escalation[37].

If the Sandinist Revolution is determined to build socialism, it is hard to see *La Prensa* surviving in its present course. There is simply no precedent for the existence of a capitalist press in a socialist society, even if such a society is committed to a degree of economic pluralism. If *La Prensa*, emboldened as it demonstrably is by the attitude of Washington, continues on its path of confrontation, and if the internal

opposition, led by *La Prensa*, succeeds in mounting a serious challenge to the political hegemony of the Sandinistas, the Revolution must harden in order to survive. If it does, the private sector will suffer, and *La Prensa* will suffer. But to close *La Prensa* for good, and silence the primary voice of the private sector, is to risk losing much important social-democratic support on an international scale, and to fuel Washington's accusations of totalitarianism. Will the Sandinista Revolution be forced to pluck out the capitalist thorn in its socialist flesh?

POSTSCRIPT

Since the above was written, the $19 million CIA campaign to "destabilize" (i.e. overthrow) the Nicaraguan government has been made public, and the military threat has escalated dramatically. Nicaragua is now effectively at war with thousands of U.S.-financed, trained and armed Honduran regulars and ex-Somocista guardsmen, who have killed and assassinated hundreds of Nicaraguan civilians on Nicaraguan soil, and committed extensive sabotage inside the country. In this state of war, the Sandinista government has imposed prior censorship with respect to news coverage on all three dailies, which has resulted in the temporary suspension of the pro-government *El Nuevo Diario*. *La Prensa* continues to attack and undermine the government, in a way which would not have been tolerated by the governments of democratic countries during the Second World War.

36. Nichols in Walker, op. cit. pp. 198–9.
37. Larry Boyd, "Nicaragua cracks down on Critics", *Guardian*, 4 November 1981, p. 13.

HOWARD H. FREDERICK
The Radio War Against Nicaragua[1]

"In effect, the human being should be considered the priority objective in a political war. And conceived as the military target of a guerrilla war, the human being has his most critical point in his mind. Once his mind has been reached, the 'political animal' has been defeated, without necessarily receiving bullets.[2]"

INTRODUCTION

Nicaragua is suffering a veritable torrent of foreign radio signals penetrating its borders. This ideological war of ideas against Nicaragua is as incessant and damaging to morale as the military raids by the CIA-financed counterrevolutionaries based in Honduras and Costa Rica. It is as destabilizing as the economic blockade imposed by the United States government. In a world linked by instantaneous electronic and broadcast communication, Nicaragua is caught up in a radio war with foreign powers possessing superior broadcast resources and bent on winning the hearts and minds of the Nicaraguan population. The struggle in Nicaragua between the Sandinista government and foreign-backed counterrevolutionaries (known as *Contras*)[3] is more than a war over mere territory. It is fundamentally a war between competing conceptions of how the country should be governed. These competing conceptions clash on many fronts, including a daily battle throughout the Central American radio spectrum.

On one side is the present Sandinista pluralist democracy, with deep roots in Latin American socialism and liberation theology. With just six years of consolidating its gains, the Sandinista revolution is the product of popular revulsion against the horrors of the Somoza dictatorship and of a need to make a better life for the majority of its people[4]. That revolutionary ideology now finds itself pitted against an array of foreign and domestic enemies, each with powerful broadcast voices inundating the country with disinformation and propaganda. The Nicaraguan government is hard pressed to respond to these external radio signals. Indeed, the 16-station, state-run CORADEP (Corporación de Radiodifusión del Pueblo — People's Radio Broadcasting Corporation) network is beset on all sides by broadcasters with far more resources and signal strength. CORADEP's signals, unlike those of a number of its foreign competitors, do not even reach the entire country.

BACKGROUND

Radio broadcasting plays an important role in con-

1. The author gratefully acknowledges the assistance of Robert Merlino, graduate student in the School of Telecommunications, Ohio University, for his help in this study.

2. Tayacán, *Psychological Operations in Guerrilla Warfare: The CIA's Nicaragua Manual.* With essays by Joanne Omang and Aryeh Neier. New York: Vintage Books, 1985, p. 33.
3. Following the 1979 revolution, several thousand National Guardsmen fled to Honduras. Initally these former Guardsmen formed small bands to raid peasant communities and attack literacy campaign workers. But Ronald Reagan's election assured them of training, weapons and supplies. Their political leadership was organized as the Nicaraguan Democratic Front (FDN), led by former officers of the National Guard. During 1982 a new counterrevolutionary organization headed by former Sandinista military hero Eden Pastora was formed in Costa Rica. Called the Democratic Revolutionary Alliance (ARDE), this new organization, like the FDN, was supported by the CIA. Pastora insisted that he would not unite his organization with the FDN as long as former Guardsmen remained in the leadership of that organization. Operating in close association with Pastora is the Miskito organization Misurasata, led by Brooklyn Rivera. A larger Miskito organization, Misura, led by Steadman Fagoth, is co-ordinated in Honduras with the FDN.
4. A unique overview of the Nicaraguan revolutionary ideology can be found in Xavier Gorostiaga, S.J. "The Logic of the Majority" *Southern Changes* 6 (1, 1984), pp. 6–10.

This text is published for the first time by permission of the author.

temporary international relations. Throughout the world's radio spectrum, ardent opponents battle for the hearts and minds of attentive publics. This international war of ideas shows no sign of abating. Indeed, 129 stations in over 80 countries daily broadcast some 21,200 hours of international programming in 125 languages to over 250 million listeners thoughout the world[5].

History is replete with examples of the effectiveness of transborder radio broadcasting[6]. The Caribbean/Central American region, although not as prominent on the world stage as Europe or the Middle East, for years has been the target of a radio war of ideas[7]. Some brief historical incidents might be illustrative. At the beginning of World War II, Radio Zeesen, the Nazi External Service, tried to woo Mexicans to the Axis cause by calling them "fellow Nordics". By July 1941, NBC, CBS, Westinghouse and others had established WRUL, broadcasting with 50,000 watts to Latin America to counteract the deluge of shortwave propaganda emanating from Europe. Before the Cuban revolution, Che Guevara saw the utility of clandestine broadcasting and established Rebel Radio in the Sierra Maestra mountains of Cuba. In 1960, the Voice of America stepped up its broadcasts in Spanish with an eye toward Cuba. The CIA operated a clandestine transmitter called Radio Swan, which used "Havana Rose" to broadcast gray and black propaganda from a barren island off Honduras.

As a result of this twin U.S. radio penetration, in 1961 Cuba launched its own service, Radio Havana Cuba, in eight languages. Cuba later allowed the Voice of Vietnam and Radio Free Dixie to broadcast from its shores to the United States. Today's 50,000 watt Radio Marti, broadcasting the Reagan administration's version of the truth from Florida to Cuba, is a direct descendent of this earlier engagement. At this writing, Cuba's radio response to Radio Marti has not been officially announced. But Cuban sources confirm that "Radio Lincoln" is ready to broadcast "the truth" to the United States and will go on the air at a suitable occasion.

Located in the heart of the region, Nicaragua is the largest nation in Central America. Due to strict control by the Somoza dictatorship, Nicaragua for many years was a backwater in this war of ideas. Today, however, Nicaragua is a society in transition and revolution, caught among the legacy of a brutal dictatorship, the pain of violent armed struggle and the travails of a wrenching and continuing social upheaval. Central to this process is radio, the great mobilizer, agitator and propagandizer of change.

Nicaragua is really two countries, a Spanish-speaking Pacific coast and an English- and Miskito-speaking Atlantic coast. Separated by jungles and mountains, this topography has created a difficult situation for radio engineers, who for years have hoped to unite the country electronically. In the pre-revolutionary period, only one station (Radio Nacional) could reach the East coast from Managua, and then only at night[8].

In Nicaragua and the rest of Central America, sovereign nations, clandestine organizations, private institutions, churches and peoples are fighting as much for cherished ideals and values as for national territory. Radio is one of the most effective weapons in this struggle. It can reach people in rural hinterlands as well as urban areas. It requires no literacy and it has the impact and immediacy of electronic communication. In an insurgency environment, radio hardware can be moved quickly to new locations and the broadcast frequency can be changed often to avoid electronic countermeasures such as jamming.

Radio plays a strategic role in Nicaragua's fight against its foreign enemies. It mobilizes the people to resist external and internal threats and it agitates in support of national goals. The importance of radio in Nicaragua was cruelly demonstrated in June 1984. Counterrevolutionary fighters attacked the town of Ocotal and burned down the town's only radio station, Radio Segovia, one of the 15 government-operated CORADEP stations. In the process they killed eight members of the station's staff and knocked the station off the air. Within 24 hours the station found temporary quarters and was back on the air in a mood of defiance.

Nicaragua's present radio infrastructure has its roots in the history of repression by U.S. forces and the Somoza dictatorship. Radio broadcasting began in 1931, during the occupation by U.S. Marines, as a means of fighting insurgent guerrillas. Frustrated by poor telecommunications, the Marines set up Radio Nacional to assist their efforts at routing Augusto César Sandino and his troops, who were fighting a

5. U.S. House of Representatives, Committee on Foreign Affairs, *Authorizing Appropriations for Fiscal Years 1984–85 for the Department of State, the U.S. Information Agency, the Board for International Broadcasting, the Inter-American Foundation, the Asia Foundation, to Establish the National Endowment for Democracy*. Washington: Government Printing Office, 1983, p. 1110.
6. See for example: David M. Abshire, *International Broadcasting: A New Dimension in Western Diplomacy*, (The Washington Papers, Vol. 4, No. 35), Beverly Hills, CA: Sage Publications, 1976; A. Panifilov, *Broadcasting Pirates*, Moscow: n.p.; Julian A. Hale, *Radio Power: Propaganda and International Broadcasting*, Philadelphia: Temple University Press, 1976; Donald R. Browne, *International Broadcasting: The Limits of the Limitless Medium*, New York: Praeger, 1982; James O. H. Nason, "International Broadcasting as an Instrument of Foreign Policy", *Millenium* (London) 6 (2, 1977), pp. 128–45; Bernard Bumpus, *Seventy Years of International Broadcasting*, Paris: UNESCO, 1985.
7. For a detailed history of the Cuban–American radio war, see Howard H. Frederick, *Cuban–American Radio Wars: Ideology in International Telecommunications*, Norwood, NJ: Ablex Publishing Corporation, 1985.
8. Bonnie J. Brownlee, "Broadcasting in Nicaragua", in *Broadcasting in Latin America*, edited by Joseph Straubhaar and Elizabeth Mahan, Philadelphia: Temple University Press, forthcoming 1986.

guerrilla war against U.S. occupation[9]. The Somoza family maintained control over Radio Nacional until the 1979 Sandinista revolution. Throughout this period, numerous independent commercial and religious stations were active.

In 1979, Somoza controlled approximately 35% of the national economy. This included numerous radio and television transmitters, which immediately became property of the new government. The Nicaraguan revolution never had to seize its media of mass communication. When Somoza collapsed, the government inherited 16 radio stations, two TV stations and one newspaper. In 1979, some 48 radio stations were operating in the country[10].

In 1985, 48 radio stations are still operating in Nicaragua, of which 32 are in private hands and 16 belong to the Corporación de Radiodifusión del Pueblo (CORADEP), the People's Radio Broadcasting Corporation, which inherited Somoza's radio assets[11]. According to CORADEP, the network hopes to expand to 20 stations by the end of 1985. The Sandinista response to outside radio aggression depends largely on CORADEP.

METHODOLOGY

This study was made possible by a grant from the Ohio University Research Council. With the assistance of the Nicaraguan Confederation of Professionals (Confediraciòn Nicaraguënse de Profesionales — CONAPRO) and the People's Radio Broadcasting Corporation in July 1985 the author was able to monitor the source, content and signal strength of foreign radio broadcasts in central Nicaragua and along the northern border with Honduras.

Recordings and transcripts were made of radio programs penetrating the country from a variety of regional AM, FM, and shortwave stations. Data compiled by CORADEP in November 1984 on penetration of foreign AM and FM radio were verified and corrected. Interviews with Nicaraguan radio managers complemented this monitoring process. Transcripts of the Foreign Broadcasts Information Service, operated by the Central Intelligence Agency for the U.S. Department of Commerce, were examined for the period January 1 to June 11, 1985. Verification and confirmation with other sources have corroborated these data.

This study focuses on AM and FM signals, easily heard on the estimated 500,000 radio receivers in Nicaragua[12]. Reference is also made to regional shortwave broadcasts heard in the country, but the broadcasts of international shortwave stations, such as the BBC and the Voice of Germany, are excluded from this study. Data were correlated by the regions and special zones that comprise the Nicaraguan state[13]. Power

9. Richard Millett, Guardians of the Dynasty, Maryknoll, NY: Orbis Books, 1977, p. 76.
10. Carlos F. Chamorro, "Experiencias de la Comunicación Revolucionaria en Nicaragua," paper presented at the International Forum on Social Communication, Mexico City, June 1982, quoted in Bonnie J. Brownlee, "Broadcasting in Nicaragua", in Broadcasting in Latin America, op. cit.
11. Interview with Oscar Oviedo Mosquera, Vice Director, Corporación de Radiodifusión del Pueblo, Managua, Nicaragua, 4 June 1984. Please note that Centro de Investigaciones y Estudios de la Reforma Agraria, Participatory Democracy in Nicaragua, Managua: CIERA, c1984, p. 120 indicates 27 private and 19 official stations, for a total of 46. Oveido told the author in July 1985 that CORADEP hopes to expand to 20 stations soon.
12. Stephen M. Gorman, "Nicaragua", in Jack W. Hopkins, editor, Latin American and Caribbean Contemporary Record, Vol. II, 1982–1983, New York: Holmes and Meier, 1984, p. 568. Note: World Radio TV Handbook (1985) reports only 200,000.
13. These correlations were made in accordance with the new Regions and Special Zones in Nicaragua set up in 1982 for all governmental functions. Six Regions were made up of two to four of the old departments. Three Special Zones were formed on the Atlantic Coast, two corresponding to northern and southern Zelaya

TABLE I.
Foreign AM and FM Radio Penetrating Nicaraguan Territory

Originating Country	Nicaraguan Region							Total Number of Stations
	I	II	IV	V	VI	ZE 2	ZE 3	
Belize	1	0	0	0	0	0	0	1
Colombia	3	1	0	1	1	3	0	7
Costa Rica	6	6	6	6	9	18	16	26
Cuba	3	0	0	2	2	5	0	5
El Salvador	2	3	0	0	2	0	0	4
Guatemala	0	1	1	0	3	0	0	5
Honduras	12	7	2	2	10	1	0	18
Mexico	2	2	0	1	0	0	0	3
Neth Antilles	2	1	0	0	0	0	0	2
Panama	0	0	1	0	0	0	0	1
USA	1	1	1	1	1	1	1	1
USSR	1	0	0	0	0	0	0	1
Venezuela	0	1	0	0	0	0	0	1
Totals	33	23	11	13	27	28	16	76

calculations in kilowatts were made based on listings in the *World Radio TV Handbook*[14].

RESULTS

Source, Power and Signal Quality

In 1985, 76 foreign AM and FM radio stations penetrate Nicaraguan territory (see Table 1). One-third of these foreign stations emanate from Costa Rica, while another one-fifth come from Honduras. Other regional broadcasts from Belize, Colombia, Cuba, El Salvador, Guatemala, Mexico, Netherlands Antilles, Panama, the United States, the USSR (Cuban relay) and Venezuela are heard in the country.

Because of the characteristics of AM and FM radio signal propagation, reception is not uniform throughout the country (see Map 1). Region I, site of intense insurgent action from counterrevolutionary troops

> department and one to the department of Rio San Juan. No data were reported for Region III (Managua) and Special Zone I (Puerto Cabezas). See Charles Downs, "Local and Regional Government", in *Nicaragua: The First Five Years*, edited by Thomas W. Walker, New York: Praeger, 1985, p. 57. *Caveat lector*: Downs' map has mislabelled three of the regions. Region IV should be VI. Region V should be IV. Region VI should be V.
>
> 14. J. M. Frost, editor-in-chief, *World Radio TV Handbook*, Vol. 39, New York: Billboard Publications, 1984. For purposes of this calculation, the 500 kw transmitter of Trans World Radio in the Netherlands Antilles was changed to 100 kw so as not to skew this admittedly rough measure. For stations with no power listed in WRTH, the author arbitrarily assigned 10,000 watts.

based in Honduras, can hear 33 foreign stations. Only two Nicaraguan government stations broadcast in this region. Region I's neighbor, mountainous Region VI comprising the departments of Matagalpa and Jinotega, also the site of devastating *Contra* actions, is penetrated by 27 stations. Special Zones 2 and 3 on the Atlantic are especially susceptible to foreign radio penetration due to their low-lying topography and proximity to the saline coast. For example, Special Zone 2, also the scene of numerous counterrevolutionary actions from troops based in Costa Rica, is second in penetration of foreign radio, with 27 non-Nicaraguan stations available on the ordinary radio. There is only one Nicaraguan station in that zone.

In contrast, the government-owned and operated CORADEP network has only 15 stations with signals of varying qualities to cover the entire country. They have primary responsibility for responding to the 76 external stations penetrating Nicaragua (see Map 2). Formed on 26 April 1981 by Decree 109 of the Junta of National Reconstruction, the People's Broadcasting Corporation currently operates its stations with old, poorly maintained equipment of North American manufacture. (This presents a critical problem today because of the U.S. trade embargo.) Everything from tape to microphones is in short supply. Transmitter capacities range from 1 kilowatt to 10 kilowatts. CORADEP counts two stations in Region I (Esteli and Ocotal); two in Region II (Chinandega and León); three small stations in Region III (Managua); two in Region IV (Granada and Rivas); one in Region V (Juigalpa); and two stations in Region VI (Matagalpa

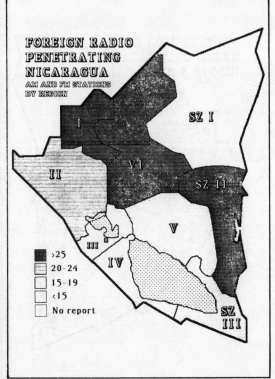

Map 1

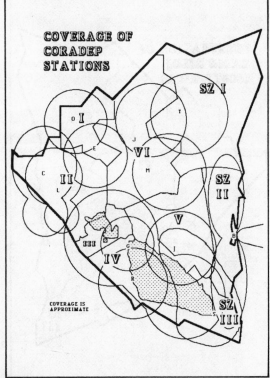

Map 2

and Jinotega). CORADEP has one station in each of the Special Zones (Tasba Pri, Bluefields and San Carlos).

In opposition to the CORADEP coverage, five foreign AM stations are clearly the radio superpowers in Nicaragua, with coverage far superior to any Nicaraguan station. These include four Costa Rican stations (TIHB Reloj, TILX Columbia, TIRI Impacto and TITNT Monumental) and the Voice of America. Three other stations (TISCL Santa Clara from Costa Rica, YSS Radio El Salvador and HRN Voice of Honduras) can also be heard widely in parts of the country. (See maps.)

Seventy-six exterior stations heard in Nicaragua were correlated by region, power and signal quality. (Region III and Special Zone 1 were not reported in the original CORADEP data.) Region I and Special Zone II, where terrorist action by counterrevolutionaries is greatest, receives a flood of high quality signals. In Region I, which comprises the departments of Esteli, Madriz and Nuevo Segovia, 17 stations from Honduras, 2 from El Salvador, 2 from Costa Rica, and one each from Mexico and Colombia and Cuba enter with a "good" signal. Fourteen stations penetrate this region with a "fair" signal, while 2 stations enter with a "poor" signal. The equivalent figures for Special Zone 2, containing the Bluefields area of Zelaya department, are 20 "good", 4 "fair", and 5 "poor". For Region VI (Matagalpa and Jinotega), those figures are 10 "good", 11 "fair", and 6 "poor".

Another rough measure of radio infiltration is total kilowatts entering the region. By this tally, Region I again leads with 2001 kilowatts of radiated power externally directed at its territory. Special Zone 2 finds itself in second place with 743.5 kilowatts, followed by Region II (710.5 kw) and Region VI (534.5 kw).

Correlating total kilowatts with each region's population, the same pattern emerges. Special Zone III on the Costa Rican border is subjected 8.0 watts of foreign radio per capita. Region I on the Honduran border receives 6.67 watts per capita, while Special Zone 2, containing the strategic city of Bluefields, is subject to 6.65 watts per capita. Region IV, in contrast, receives only 0.79 watts per capita.

Of interest also are stations poorly heard in Nicaragua. For example, our findings show that five Cuban radio stations on the AM dial are received poorly and erratically in Nicaragua. Radio Reloj, Cuba's 24-hour all news station, is heard in Regions I and VI and Special Zone 3, with a fair to good signal. This is better than the Voice of Cuba, ostensibly the station with the greatest regional coverage and emphasis of the Cuban stations.

Shortwave stations, of course, have a far greater international reach. Though they are not included in this study, all of the major international broadcasters have servicable signals throughout Nicaragua and Central America. A U.S. Congress study during the debate on Radio Martí claimed that foreign international broadcasters had far more hours of Spanish programs directed at the Caribbean/Central American region than U.S. stations. Religious station HCJB, the Voice of the Andes, leads the list with 427 hours per week, followed by Cuba, 280; BBC, 186; Soviet Union, 133; Federal Germany, 98; Voice of America, 84; China, 67; Albania, 56; South Korea, 56; and German

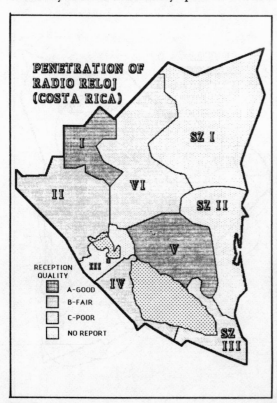

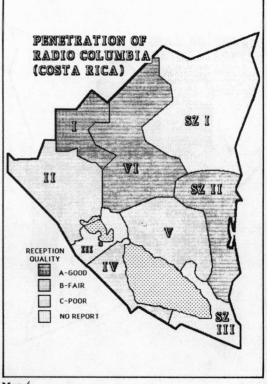

Map 3

Map 4

Democratic Republic, 54[15].

In addition to these strong international voices, numerous regional shortwave broadcasters direct their beams to include Nicaragua. In Region II, the author was able to pick up signals from nine regional shortwave stations. These stations were particularly interesting because they include two clandestine stations, and three religious stations as well as commercial stations.

Content and Ideological Perspectives

The following remarks on these stations' ideological perspectives are based on transcripts of non-music content made from recordings in Chinandega (Region II), Nicaragua during July 1985 as well as transcripts of the *Foreign Broadcasts Information Service* from 1 January to 11 June 1985.

The war of ideas against Nicaragua has three main orientations. Perhaps the most pervasive penetration of alien values comes from commercial stations in the exterior. Not only are their economic messages often at odds with the goals of Nicaraguan government, but their overall ideological line is markedly anti-Sandinista and pro-*Contra*. Several clandestine/ insurgent stations have language and content that is so at variance with normal radio programming that all but the most committed listener may tune them out. Similarly, religious stations from the exterior are

15. Howard H. Frederick, *Cuban–American Radio Wars*, Norwood, NJ: Ablex Publishing Corporation, 1985.

generally of the evangelical/proselytizing variety that many devout Nicaraguan Catholics may diregard.

Despite disinformation to the contrary, Nicaragua is itself largely a capitalist country, with about 60 per cent of the economy in private hands. Today, consumer goods are in short supply because of the U.S. program of economic destabilization which began in 1981, the economic embargo of 1984, and the necessity of directing available resources to repulse an external threat. Foreign commercial advertising and market-orientated news must be seen in the light of severe economic deprivation at home.

Typical of the orientation of many small stations penetrating Nicaraguan air space is Radio Valle, broadcasting from Choluteca, Honduras, to Region I and II. Advertising dominates the non-music content of the station. Headache medicine and youth potions ("for bad moods and good figures") appeal to the symptoms of life's stresses while automobile ads appeal to the desire for physical and psychic mobility. Eye drops, nail polish, numerous brands of coffee, and appliances: all may contribute to an impression in the mind of the average Nicaraguan that life may be better in the exterior. Particularly susceptible to this subtext message are the disaffected people in rural Nicaragua. Despite numerous efforts by a resource-strapped government in Managua, their lives have improved only slightly since the revolution in 1979.

Radio Valle is typical of the many small-market stations run by the petty bourgeois class and aimed at the incipent middle class. The true superstations of commercialism, on the other hand, serve as market

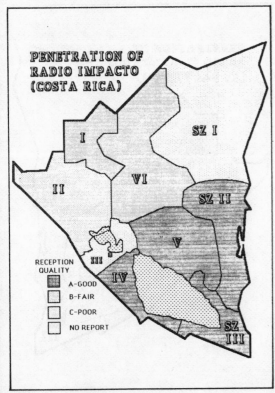

Map 5

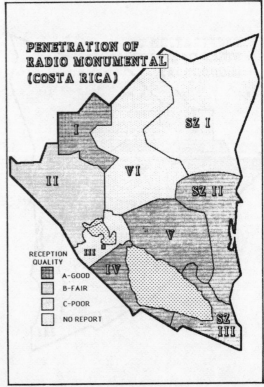

Map 6

thermometers and drivers for the capitalist elite. For example, the evening news from Costa Rica's Radio Columbia includes stock reports from foreign capitals, bank advertisements announcing new loans, travel offers to Miami and other elements of market-dominated content. Regarding Nicaragua, Radio Columbia is quick to point out the apparent violations of Costa Rican territorial integrity by the Sandinista Popular Army but does not mention Costa Rican aid to the counterrevolutionaries operating inside its territory. One civic affairs announcement on Radio Columbia, sponsored by the Costa Rica Institute for the Entrepreneurial Sector, summarizes the perspective in favor of bourgeois democracy that this station projects:

Costa Rica is a free, independent and sovereign country. Costa Ricans know what this means because they live it daily. You don't fear persecution or unjust imprisonment. Because you, Costa Rican, are a citizen in a free country. Costa Rican democracy is a model for the world.

Such announcements, laden with ideological content, are the heavy artillery in the international war of ideas.

Even more biased against the Nicaragua revolution is Radio Impacto, heard throughout Nicaragua. Broad-

16. *Foreign Broadcast Information Service*, 8 January 1985, p. P21.
17. *Foreign Broadcast Information Service*, 9 May 1985, p. P19.
18. *Foreign Broadcast Information Service*, 9 May 1985, p. P18.
19. *Foreign Broadcast Information Service*, 10 May 1985, p. P3.

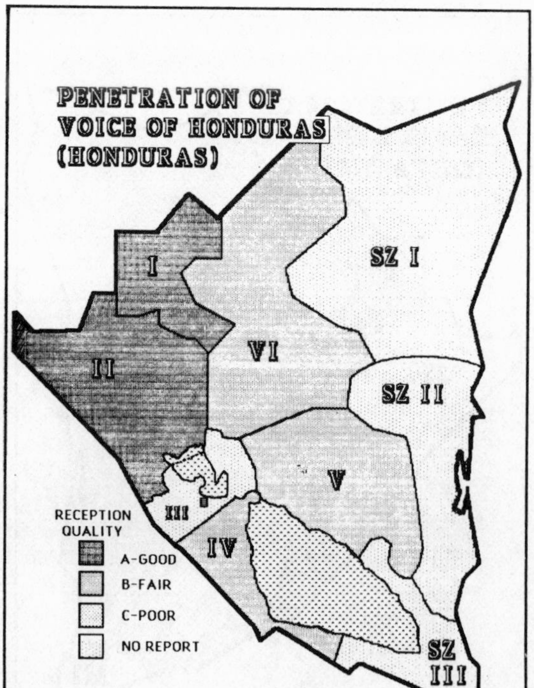

casting with 50,000 watts from San Pedro de Montes de Oca, Costa Rica, Impacto is widely suspected by Sandinista supporters for its *Contra* orientation. Its station I.D. states its perceived self-image: ". . . from San José, Costa Rica, capital of Latin American democracy."

Radio Impacto can be counted on to carry the news and views of the counterrevolutionary as well as the legitimate opposition forces in Managua. A sampling of some of these *Contra* statements on the station is indicative of its orientation:

3 January 1985: Miskito Indian *Contra* leader Steadman Fagoth stated that "his forces that fight the infamous and bloodthirsty Nicaraguan communist regime have always maintained Christian feelings, even when we have been at a disadvantage against the Soviet empire[16]."

3 May 1985: Augustín Jarquin, leader of the Nicaraguan Social Christian Party [which joined the forces of abstention during the November 1984 elections — HF] told Impacto he was a victim of the Sandinista police who attacked a demonstration[17].

4 May 1985: Alfonso Robelo, "leader of the Nicaraguan resistance, told Impacto news that the impact of Ortega's visit to the Soviet bloc countries is so great that a new bill to aid the *Contras* would easily be approved by Congress[18]."

8 May 1985: Nicaraguan draft resister José Urbina Lara, whose case was covered heavily thoughout 1985, said "he will continue to support the Democratic Revolutionary Alliance [a *Contra* group] while urging the Nicaraguan people to resist[19]."

5 June 1985: Fernando Chamorro, *Contra* leader in southern Nicaragua sent a "solidarity message to the Costa Rican people" stating that the *Contra* forces "are fighting to free Nicaragua from the claws of the international terrorism that

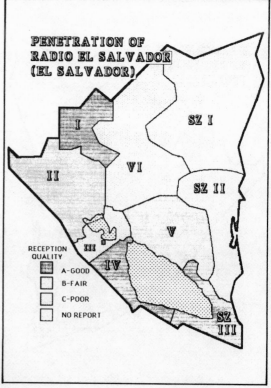

Map 7

Map 8

has plunged our people into a situation of barbarism and terror[20]."

Occasional references lead one to believe that Impacto's newswriters may be impatient with official Costa Rican news sources regarding Nicaraguan activities. In a 1 July news item about the disappearance of a Costa Rican citizen near the border, Impacto described "the case of an apparent kidnapping [by] elements of the Sandinista Popular Army, *but this was not the official version.*" [Emphasis added.]

In the author's monitoring, about one-quarter of the items on a typical Impacto newscast deal with Nicaragua. Thus, Radio Impacto is much like Radio Free Europe and Radio Liberty, stations that broadcast only to the socialist countries of Eastern Europe and bill themselves as alternative home services. For example, during the Nicaraguan elections in November 1984, the author heard Impacto warning its listeners on the Atlantic coast that *Contra* attacks were likely and that people should stay away from the polls for their own safety.

Impacto's continual *Contra* orientation is not lost on the Nicaraguan authorities. On 29 December 1984, Sandinista security officers arrested Impacto's correspondent in Managua, Salomon Calvo Arrieta. According to Managua's Radio Noticias, he had:

disseminated ... reportage that distorts Nicaraguan reality, threatens the country's security, and is aimed at causing Nicaragua's relations with neighboring countries to deteriorate. Calvo keeps in touch with counterrevolutionary leaders who have assigned to him the role of provocateur and propagandist in following instructions in the CIA manual[21].

Calvo also was accused of giving news and information to the *Contra* station 15 de Septiembre. Radio Noticias reported that he would be turned over to popular courts to be tried. This was the second reported incident of harrassment of Impacto reporters. In 1984, the Anti-Somozist People's Tribunals, a quasi-official people's judiciary, arrested, tried and convicted Luis Manuel Mora Sanchez to nine years imprisonment. He received a pardon after six months[22].

The most blatant incident of overt disinformation during the author's monitoring was done by HRN, the Voice of Honduras, broadcasting at 10 kilowatts from Tegucigalpa. As the self-proclaimed "voice of the Honduran government and people", HRN crosses that gray boundary dividing commercial from governmental broadcasters. On 4 July 1985, the station broadcast the following report during a morning talk show:

We interrupt this program with the latest news. Attention friends of HRN in the entire country. The Nicaraguan People's Army is currently bombarding the village of Alauca.

This morning at 7 in the morning the bombardments began in this village on the Nicaraguan border.

We are informed that a great number of the residents of this village have abandoned their houses. For that reason, Alauca, which has about 1,500 people, remains totally isolated. A great number of people have arrived at El Paraiso and others have left their homes to find refuge in other locales in the region. We want to point out that this is another violation of our country's integrity on the part of the Nicaraguan People's Army.

The broadcast continued with a report of an attack by the Nicaraguan army on Honduran territory. Subsequent checking revealed *no other mention* of the attack in the Honduran or U.S. press. The Nicaraguan press denied the charge.

In the author's opinion, one of two things is true. Either the attack did not take place and the report was a total prefabrication by HRN or the attack was the work of counterrevolutionries dressed as Nicaraguan army regulars against a defenseless Honduran village. Especially suspicious was the fact that correspondents were already in the field interviewing eyewitnesses at the time of the alleged attack. Either way, the report leaves little doubt that the HRN broadcast was a provocation against Nicaragua. The intent of this prefabricated broadcast was to push the government of Honduras into the position of declaring an emergency and requesting military aid from the United States to drive out the supposed Nicaraguan aggressor.

No review of Central America broadcasting would be complete without mention of clandestine stations active in the radio wars. At least four stations have a direct bearing on events in Nicaragua: Radio Venceremos, la Voz de Sandino, Radio 15 de Septiembre and Radio Miskus. All but the first are intransigently opposed to the Nicaraguan government.

Radio 15 de Septiembre is thought to be located in Valle de Andeles, 30 kilometers northeast of Tegucigalpa, though the station claims that it broadcasts from within Honduras. The director is Frank Arana, a Nicaraguan expatriate[23]. It is the official voice of the Nicaraguan Democratic Front, the *Contra* organization operating in Honduras. Its orientation is vehemently anti-Sandinista and its broadcast content includes virtually nothing that is not propaganda. (Interestingly, the *Foreign Broadcast Information Service*, operated by the Central Intelligence Agency for the U.S. Department of Commerce, never includes transcripts of this station's broadcasts.)

Broadcasts monitored in July 1985 contained interviews with FDN commanders and Nicaraguan peasants, who revealed details of Sandinista repression and harrassment. They also included statements by FDN leaders about battles, death counts and promises of further violence, military music, coded messages and announcements. One interview with "Johnny" and "Henry", both instructors of a regional command, boasted that:

One day we will walk freely in Nicaragua. Don't worry, we will be in the cities. We will kill the contemptuous Sandinista army that is killing our women and children. We don't want a

20. *Foreign Broadcast Information Service*, 7 June 1985, p. P17.

21. *Foreign Broadcast Information Service*, 7 January 1985, p. P18.

22. *Foreign Broadcast Information Service*, 3 January 1985, p. P20.

23. "War of the Airwaves", *Latin America Regional Reports*, 16 August 1985, p. 6.

communist regime. We are commandos for freedom and democracy.

To the sounds of martial music, the announcer proclaims Radio 15 de Septiembre, "Voice of the Christian freedom commandos.... The puppets of Castro will be destroyed."

Many claims are made about the support of the Nicaraguan people for the *Contra* forces. Commander "Dennis" said "about 80% of the people are on our side. About 40% in the cities are on our side." The Nicaraguan people, it is claimed, are against the "Sandino-communists". "The number of tanks makes no difference because the people support us.... We have about 20,000 commandos." Announcers excoriate the Sandinista Defense Committee and the so-called divine mobs allegedly operated by the government.

FDN leader Adolfo Calero Portocarrero is often at the microphone exhorting his supporters and trying to win converts:

With God and patriotism we will destroy communism. Our forces are growing each day.... Our people should not believe what *Nuevo Diario* and *Barricada* [Managua newspapers that support the Sandinistas] are saying. Radio Sandino and Radio Nacional [sic] are full of lies. Soon we will be in Managua. They are not capable of confronting our troops. This is the reality.

Radio 15 de Septiembre features statements by ordinary Nicaraguans who have "escaped Sandinista tyranny." One woman complained of the Sandinista militiamen raping women and oppressing Nicaraguan peasants. "You have two small meals a day to keep the Sandinistas in power. Young Nicaraguans, your families are experiencing hunger. 1985 will be the year of victory."

At the opposite side of the country, broadcasting from northern Costa Rica, is the Voice of Sandino, the official station of the Democratic Revolutionary Alliance. Ex-Sandinista Eden Pastora is often heard conducting lessons in guerrilla warfare for Nicaraguans who oppose the government.

A beehive — at night you cut a hole in the beehive, place it at the edge of the road, tie a 50-meter rope to it, and pull on the rope when the enemy is close — becomes a weapon.... A nail sticking out of a piece of wood covered with mud becomes a powerful weapon, especially if you smear horse or human manure on the tip. This immediately becomes a mortal weapon. When the nail penetrates a shoe it punctures the sole of the soldier's foot and causes gangrene or tetanus.

The peasants who are living in the jungle are persecuted by the foreign forces and by the occupation troops, and are always in danger of being captured, tortured and killed.... The traitors, those who defend foreign intervention, should be shot in the back with a well-aimed shot.

The FSLN manipulates information but does not realize that actions in the heart of Managua will follow shortly. There in the heart of the FSLN; there where they plot repressive actions, where they plan their servile policy, where they plot mass murders and people's genocide.... Let us fight those communist-Marxist troops, those that imported pre-

24. *Foreign Broadcast Information Service*, 9 May 1985, p. P7.

conceived schemes; those who deceived Sandinism; those who in the name of Sandinism are establishing a Stalinist revolution, a Leninist revolution, a communist revolution in Nicaragua.

Fight, fight, fight is our war slogan! Our slogan is no longer "Free Homeland or Death" because we no longer want to die. Our slogan is now: Free Homeland or Kill!

The Misura organization, run by Miskito Indian *Contra* Steadman Fagoth, is operating Radio Miskut in the Honduran town of Rus Rus, close to Fagoth's house. The station broadcasts in Miskito to the indigenous population along the Atlantic coast region of Nicaragua. No transcripts or recordings of this station were available for this study.

Finally, mention must be made of one clandestine station that supports the Sandinista revolution. Radio Venceremos broadcasts from mobile studios somewhere in eastern El Salvador. Dedicated to setting up a worker/peasant state in El Salvador by overthrowing the Duarte government, Venceremos occasionally makes reference also to Nicaragua:

Radio Venceremos sends a fraternal and revolutionary greeting to the Nicaraguan people at the time when the modern Hitler, whose planes and cannons kill women and children throughout the world, and warmonger Ronald Reagan is launching new attacks on Nicaragua through an immoral blackmail called an economic embargo.... Nicaraguan brothers, with Sandino you expelled the Yankee Marines. You with your vanguard the FSLN defeated the gringos' Somozist project. You will again defeat the Somozist beasts and all the aggressions orchestrated by the new crime boss Ronald Reagan. Neither mercenary bands nor economic embargoes will diminish the will of the Central American peoples, they will to be free and independent. We will win! [Venceremos! — HF][24]

The Voice of America has been heard for years throughout Nicaragua from transmitters in the Caribbean. But the VOA has just launched a new AM transmitter in Costa Rica (see below), so the signal quality is among the best heard in Nicaragua. These facilities retransmit the VOA's Spanish service, directed at all of Central and South America. Though it is a hemispheric, and therefore generalist, news and information service, numerous news items focus on Nicaragua. Here, for example, is sample of VOA's coverage during the sixth anniversary of the Nicaraguan revolution:

18 July 1985: The Sandinista government tomorrow commemorates the sixth anniversary of its revolution at a time when the country is confronting serious economic problems and a guerrilla war of four year's duration. Sandinista leaders say 400,000 people will attend the cermonies but among the mass media covering the event will not be an American, Spanish-speaking crew that was deported.

July 18 1985: In interviews published on the evening of the celebrations, President Daniel Ortega reiterated his belief that the United States is planning to invade his country.... In Washington, President Reagan's security advisor Robert MacFarland repeated that the U.S. has no intention of invading Nicaragua.

19 July 1985: The United States has offered a reward of $100,000 for information leading to the arrest of the murderers of six Americans in El Salvador last month.... The reward was offered after an accusation by the U.S. govern-

ment that Nicaragua could be directly involved in terrorist plans against Americans in Honduras.

20 July 1985: ... the Nicaraguan government aided the terrorist attack carried out last month in El Salvador.

No mention is made of Nicaragua's progress in six years, nor its ongoing struggle against external military threat. The reports clearly insinuate that Nicaragua is responsible for the deaths of six Americans in El Salvador. This reinforces a constant propaganda theme, that Nicaragua is trying to foment revolution elsewhere in the region.

The VOA, like the clandestine *Contra* stations, gives ample coverage to Nicaragua's enemies. When Eden Pastora's helicopter crashed, daily news items followed his rescue and recovery. The hierarchy of the Nicaraguan Catholic Church is especially highlighted:

24 July 1985: Nicaraguan Catholic bishops oppose a national fast by the so-called liberation theology in support of Foreign Relations Minister Miguel D'Escoto's hunger fast.... It warned that only the bishops have the authority to envoke a religious act.... Father D'Escoto is protesting U.S. support of Nicaraguan rebels trying to overthrow the government.

The "so-called" liberation theology movement, the VOA fails to inform, makes up a large part of Nicaragua's churchgoers. The report legitimizes the minority hierarchy's absolute powers. The item also calls the *Contras* "rebels" and labels their aims as mere overthrow. In this way, the Voice of America's ideological orientation puts it in the same camp with other destabilizing stations such as Radio Impacto and the Voice of Honduras.

Finally, some brief mention must be made of the religious stations broadcasting to Nicaragua. More than 90 percent of Nicaraguans are practising Catholics; many find themselves, as indicated above, in opposition to the Catholic hierarchy, which supports Nicaragua's enemies. Several religious stations send evangelical Protestant signals to the country. The Lighthouse of the Caribbean (Faro del Caribe) from Costa Rica has North American preachers who insist that "God helps only those who use the Bible". The Evangelical Voice from Honduras is owned by the Conservative Home Baptist Mission Society in Wheaton, Illinois. It blames the region's problems on lack of faith: "Souls are dying today because Christians are not preaching the word of God. Christians are sleeping." External religious stations oppose both the Catholic hierarchy and the liberation theology movement.

OTHER DEVELOPMENTS

One of the most interesting recent developments is

25. Maureen Meehan, "Briefing: U.S. Pre-Empts Costa Rican Airwaves", *In These Times*, 31 October 1986, p. 5.
26. *Ibid*.
27. Walter Pincus, "U.S. Enhances VOA, Sets Pact in Costa Rica, *Washington Post*, 11 September 1984, p. 1.
28. "War of the Airwaves", *Latin America Regional Reports*, 16 August 1985, p. 6.

the Voice of America's overt attempts to circumvent Costa Rican law. Costa Rican laws prohibit foreign nationals (individuals or corporations) from operating a radio station there. But the law does not prohibit the Voice of America from operating a *Costa Rican owned* transmitter facility. After learning that the VOA would be violating Costa Rica neutrality by setting up a repeater facility, a group of conservative Costa Rican media executives, journalists and politicians set up the Costa Rican Association for Information and Culture. One of the leaders of this group was Lilia Berrocal, owner of seven other stations, three of which are already penetrating Nicaraguan territory. Sra. Berrocal has defended the move, saying that "the people of northern Costa Rica have been exposed to extensive propaganda from the Nicaraguan communication system[25]."

The Voice of America, through formal agreements with Costa Rican citizens, installed a repeater station at Ciudad Quesada, in north-central Costa Rica and began broadcasting on 19 January 1985. In addition to VOA broadcasts, the transmitter makes a semblance of being a local station by sending out locally produced material of the Costa Rican Association for Information and Culture. The installations are made up of four 70 meter towers, directional at 100,000 watts. In addition to the $3.2 million authorized to build the facility, the VOA will send $168,000 each year to the private association that controls the transmitter.

Though the agreement was criticized by the Costa Rican Congress as circumventing the coutry's neutrality, it was initialed in the home of President Luis Alberto Monge[26]. As partial compensation to feelings that Costa Ricans neutrality had been violated, the agreement stated that the VOA may only use the transmitter 60 per cent of the time.

Other U.S. activities in the region also point to an increase in the Central American radio war. The U.S. government has agreed to finance a $1.5 million installation of three television transmitters on the Costa Rican–Nicaragua border. U.S. Army officers in Honduras have been promoting another plan to build an AM/FM transmitter in that country to beam programs to Nicaragua. The station would be located at the airfield in San Lorenzo, which U.S. Army engineers have been expanding to handle increased military manoeuvers. That plan is currently "on hold"[27]. Honduran law prohibits more than one-third foreign ownership of radio stations as well as programming "prejudicial to national sovereignty or democratic institutions"[28].

Part of the Voice of America's expansion in the hemisphere is a $150 million shortwave and medium-wave relay station in Puerto Rico to cover the Caribbean, Central and South America. This project is slated for completion in 1990. Finally, site preparation and engineering studies are reportedly underway for a VOA transmitter in Belize.

DISCUSSION

The U.S. war against Nicaragua is as much an ideological struggle as it is a military one. Armed counterinsurgency and psychological war are part of one common stategy. The CIA's manual on psychological warfare in Nicaragua states:

in guerrilla warfare, every combatant should be as highly motivated to carry out propaganda face-to-face as he is as a combatant. . . . The techniques of psychological operations [maximize] the social-psychological effect of a guerrilla movement, converting the guerrilla into a propagandist[29].

Of course, the *Contras* are not the only side to realize this connection. Everyone in the Nicaraguan war of ideologies is using radio and other electronic and non-electronic means of propaganda to win the hearts and minds of opposing populations. The techniques of bellicose propaganda are as diverse as military tactics. But all sides share one thing in common. As Mattelart has observed regarding Nicaragua:

In psychological war, objectivity does not function. The objective fact does not exist. In psychological war everything is permitted. You can divide reality and deform facts, but you can also invent facts, edit stories and even "white papers".

Mattelart pays special attention to such stations as Radio Impacto:

When you analyze the axis of attack of a station like Radio Impacto, you realize that they mix lies with truth. . . . Psychological war has as its essential method not to "inform" but to put into living color the collective representations of the people. This means to play not solely on reason but also on the emotions. I think that an interesting subject that illustrates this when one hears foreign radio is the emotional exploitation of the Patriotic Military Service theme. The most impressive area for a person who comes from abroad is to see how the whole symbolic level related to the family, women and motherhood is manipulated[30].

Nicaraguan Vice President Sergio Ramírez Mercado addressed the subject of the ideological war against Nicaragua in remarks to students at the School of Journalism of the Central American University in Managua. He outlined the five themes that Nicaragua's enemies are using to discredit and delegitimate the revolution in public opinion:

1. The revolution pursues a totalitarian system; 2. Nicaragua is attempting to be a base for Soviet penetration in Central America to challenge the interests of U.S. national security; 3. Nicaragua is the field of confrontation in the East–West struggle; 4. Nicaragua is attempting a revolution without borders and systematically exports its revolution; 5. Nicaragua's excessive militarism only shows its expansion goals; its Army is ready, in the offensive sense, to invade and occupy other countries of the area; and in conclusion, as long as the

Sandinist Front does not initiate a true national dialogue to include those up in arms, there will be no possibility for peace in the country[31].

Mattelart and Ramírez would certainly agree that very few social or political phenomena have caught the world's attention in the past few years as has the Sandinista revolution. After being an isolated and forgotten country, Nicaragua has become a source of constant news and the subject of debates in the world media, parliaments, universities, mass movements and unions. Without a doubt, this importance is a product of the clear confrontation between U.S. imperialism and a people's revolution in a small, poor country.

Throughout the world, Nicaragua's struggle for security, prosperity, and freedom from U.S. interference has become a propaganda struggle between competing conceptions of how that society should be organized. The methods of this struggle are simultaneously military, political, economic and ideological. Nicaragua is at the center of a worldwide ideological confrontation. It does not have the resources of the giant to the north; the U.S. is investing huge amounts of human, material and technical resources to win this battle. It does have one thing that shines through: the desire of a people's revolution to improve the lives of the majority of the population.

In this sense, *Nicaragua is a threat to the United States*. This threat is not military, for no amount of Soviet or Cuban military aid could ever threaten American predominance. This threat is not economic, for Nicaragua's national product and resources are minor in the hemisphere and, furthermore, Nicaragua has adopted neither a communist nor even a socialist economic model. The Nicaraguan threat to the United States is political and ideological. Nicaragua demonstrates to the other countries of the region — countries who have yet to choose freely a system that improves the majority of people's lives — that a revolution by and for the people can turn an unjust system around, that a majority of the people can benefit from the country's wealth rather than a self-selected elite.

The Nicaraguan revolution demonstrates that there is no contradiction between Christianity and socialism. For Nicaraguan Sandinism is a political manifestation of liberation theology, which has swept throughout the hemisphere since Medellín in 1968. This is the real threat: that other peoples will recognize that they too, using the tools of the Church and of socialism, can topple an unjust oligarchy kept in place by U.S. imperialism, which draws out profit without investing in improving the lives of the people. For this reason, the United States wants to crush the Sandinista revolution.

Foreign radio stations are directing broadcast provocations that threaten regional peace and harmony. The question of the content of communication has been a concern for nations since the founding of the United Nations and before. The first prohibition mentioned in international law is that of war propaganda. Resolution 110 (II) adopted at the 2nd Session

29. Tayacán, *Psychological Operations in Guerrilla Warfare*. With essays by Joanne Omang and Aryeh Neier, New York: Vintage Books, 1985, p. 34 and p. 40.
30. Armand Mattelart and Guillermo Rothschuh Villanueva, *Guerra, Ideología y Comunicación*, Managua: Ediciones Nicaragua al día, 1985, p. 23 and p. 24.
31. *Foreign Broadcast Information Service*, 21 May 1985, p. P11.

of the U.N. General Assembly on 3 November 1947 specifically "condemns all forms of propaganda ... which is either designed or likely to provoke, or encourage any threat to the peace, breach of the peace, or act of aggression." U.N. Resolution 127 (II), adopted on 15 November of the same year calls on governments to study measures that might be advantageous on the national plane to combat, within the limits of constitutional procedures, the diffusion of false or distorted reports likely to injure friendly relations between States. All of these are only recommendations. But the "International Covenant of Civil and Political Rights", adopted on 16 December 1966, explicitly binds States in Article 20, Paragraph 1, to prohibit, by law, any propaganda for war.

In the opinion of this author, stations HRN, the Voice of Honduras, and Radio Impacto from Costa Rica, have violated these proscriptions and should be brought to account before the World Court in The Hague. In addition, the Voice of America's attempt to flood Nicaraguan airspace is a provocation against Nicaragua's sovereignty.

This corroborates what reporters have found out in the region[32]. Martha Honey, reporting for Radio Canada International's program *Sunday Morning* on 4 August 1985, interviewed a terrorist informant in Costa Rica. This young Nicaraguan anti-communist claims that right-wing extremists in the region are provoking incidents while blaming the Sandinista government, thereby providing an excuse for escalating the U.S. war against Nicaragua. These groups have the support of a number of Costa Rican and Honduran businessmen and government officials.

32. Martha Honey, "Sunday Morning", *Radio Canada International*, 4 August 1985.
33. Gary Prevost, "The War and Its Effects on Nicaragua", paper presented at the International Studies Association, Washington, DC, 5–9 March 1985.

For example, Honey claims, the CIA used these groups to bomb Eden Pastora's press conference in May 1984 and blamed the Sandinistas. This informant said that bombing attacks are planned for the U.S. embassies in San José and Tegucigalpa as well as against the offices of the Costa Rican president. In addition, two prominent anti-Sandinistas have been targeted for assassination: Miskito rebel leader Brooklyn Rivera and celebrated Nicaraguan draft resister José Urbina Lara. These groups will then produce evidence blaming these attacks on the Sandinistas. The U.S. government has pledged to strike directly against Nicaragua if terrorist attacks against Americans occur anywhere in Central America. These terror cells can be expected to instigate further dirty tricks in order to bring about U.S. intervention against Nicaragua.

Nicaragua is in a perpetual state of siege. According to Gary Prevost of St. John's University, the number of victims of *Contra* violence has increased from 73 in 1981 to 4,099 in the first six months of 1984[33]. Attacks are increasingly being carried out against civilians. Government workers, particularly field workers of the Ministry of Agrarian Reform and Ministry of Health, have been killed on their trips to the countryside. In 1984 alone, 94 teachers were killed and another 171 kidnapped. Seventy state farms have been attacked or destroyed. Combining physical damage with lost agricultural revenue, the total damage is now in the range of $1.1 to $1.3 billion, approximately three years' normal export earnings.

None of this physical and economic hardship measures the ideological war. The intense penetration by foreign propaganda radio cannot be measured in dollars and lives. But the impact is very real. Only with an end to outside aggressions will Nicaragua be able to move ahead with its programs. In the meantime, its people must suffer physically, economically and mentally.

JOSÉ LUIS CORAGGIO
Social Movements and Revolution

Introduction:
THE THEORIZATION OF SOCIAL
MOVEMENTS AND SOCIAL STRUGGLES

Inspired by new practices in the organization and development of social forces in the European countries and in the United States, the 1970s saw a flowering of new ideas about social struggles. These forces, referred to as "social movements", were organized around specific demands, such as housing or urban services, women's liberation, environmental conservation, and denuclearization. In many cases the state acts as an "interlocutor", but in other cases these movements were aimed at the transformation of relationships in which the state was not a privileged agent.

The multi-class nature of the movements, their capacity for mass mobilization, the protest nature of their demands — to the extent that they could not be resolved without profound changes in the ruling social system — was equally attractive to both political parties and theoreticians.

For the former, the attraction lay in the constant challenge to channel, articulate, and either increase the power of or regulate these forces as part of traditional political struggles. For the latter it was a matter of establishing the consequences of these developments within the context of a political theory which pretended to scientifically orient the practice of social transformation, particularly those of a revolutionary character. In some cases, political urgency caused them to arrive at weak political conclusions which had more ideological than scientific efficacy[1].

This in turn produced a common result. The fashionableness of these social movements led to their "pro

liferation" on a conceptual level. This included the elaboration of systems of classification to characterize the population (gender, age, neighborhood life, consumption habits, ethnic origins, nationality, tax situation, etc.), and speculation about their "oppositional or anti-systemic potential". At the same time, these ideas and their corresponding political practices spread to other continents including, obviously, Latin America. In some cases they corresponded to already existing developments, in others, they were applied *a priori*[2].

This process can be characterized as an *analytical moment*, in which societies are "pulverized" conceptually as well as practically and organizationally, by the simple determinations arising from different social contradictions. But just as the lack of theoretical analysis is a vice of scientific practice when it is not completed by a movement of *synthesis and the reconstruction of the object*, the lack of practical and organizational analysis rapidly exhausts political energy and loses effectiveness, in the absense of a *conjunctural bringing together of social forces* which effectively questions the ruling system.

Thus, from this perspective, on the one hand, the theoretical necessity arises of re-defining the concept of *the people* as a synthesis (articulation) of multiple determinations, and on the other, the political necessity of critically analyzing the role of the *revolutionary party* as articulator (synthesizer) of the different social forces which can potentially oppose the system.

The identification of "the people" with a social class, stamped with a theoretically-predetermined "historic destiny", and the designation of a particular party — representing its "objective consciousness" — with the role of *subject* of the social revolution, be

1. See the pioneering works of Manuel Castells and J. Lojkine on urban social movements and their "explanation" based on concepts of reproduction of the force of labor or the general conditions of production.
2. We have asked ourselves if the Shining Path of Peru is or is not a "social movement".

This text was first published in the author's *Nicaragua: Revolución y democracia*, Managua: Instituto nicaragüense de investigaciones económicas y sociales; Mexico City: Editorial Linea, 1985. It was translated from the Spanish by Janet Jamieson. English translation Copyright © International General 1986. This is its first English publication.

comes problematic from a perspective which brings new elements to the discussion of social revolution. Nevertheless, as long as the "problem of the people" continues to be seen as a question of simple conceptual definition separable from the real problem of the self-perpetuation of the vanguard — whose transitional necessity can nevertheless not be denied without falling prey to wishful thinking — progress would be incomplete.

In our opinion, there is a real rupture when one combines the restructuring of the concept of the people, based on identity and organizational factors, with the determination of a *complex subject* which is constituted as a *hegemonic system* instead of being considered a class, party or movement[3].

The formulation of the concept of the people will no longer be derived from a basically "economistic" theory of inevitable tendencies in capitalist society which, in any case, will be accelerated by the vanguard. On the contrary, the concrete contradictions within the state and civil society, and the differential positions of social *agents* in material, ideological, and organizational terms will form the "objective" base. The analysis of this base from the perspective of power relations will facilitate the elaboration of a strategy for building a popular hegemony. This primacy of the political in relation to revolutionary practice does not exclude — on the contrary it requires — either the need to explain class conflict or the eventual theoretical reconstruction of economic laws and their historic tendencies.

Practice itself demonstrates the impossibility of establishing a "bi-lateral" correspondence between concrete agents and specific identities, such as the determination of gender, class, age, ethnic origins, etc. Given that the diverse contradictions arising from such identities do not necessarily converge in either

individual agents, organizations, or in the people as a totality, it is impossible to reduce "the popular" to a single determination. At the same time an effective hegemonic practice does not presuppose this complex subject as given, but rather, the constitution of the people itself. This, in turn, requires the elaboration of an articulating discourse, a *popular project*, which makes explicit the concrete content of the new society to be achieved. Far from being a utopia, the popular project is a viable proposal for a struggle of solidarity against a system of oppression and privation where effective actions and possible results can be foreseen, where the prospectives and analysis of the conjuncture furthers popular ideologies, respecting autonomies and present identities while articulating and developing them.

Furthermore, to the extent that power relations are not reduced to the relations "between" the state and civil society, but rather that they are understood to be present in the different instances and institutions of society as a whole, the objective of the liberation of the people cannot be reduced to the "taking" of governmental power by a given social conglomerate of opposition. Rather it supposes a permanent *revolution of civil society* and, therefore, a continual *transformation of the subject itself*, the people.

In this study we will attempt to pose the problem of the universal applicability of our thesis, beginning with the experiences of the Sandinista Popular Revolution, some of whose specific characteristics we will point out later. We will return to the theoretical problematic in the final summary.

THE PRACTICE OF SOCIAL TRANSFORMATION IN NICARAGUA: ARMED STRUGGLE, COUNTER-HEGEMONIC PRACTICE AND INSURRECTION

Popular insurrection, the total paralysis of the economy, the enemy kept under permanent siege, the ultimate solidarity of all the population's identities in rebellion against a repressive regime, is an instant in the history of the constitution of a people. But it is precisely a moment of intense contradictions, the effort of social forces towards the same objective: the overthrow of a regime.

In Nicaragua, this goal would not have been achieved in 1979 without the prolonged presence of the FSLN on the political scene. By its very survival as a guerrilla force, with its ups and downs, the FSLN had always kept alive the possibility of challenging the Somoza regime. But its organic link with the masses developed in depth only in the two years prior to victory. Until then, the FSLN had carried out military actions on the one hand, and partial counter-hegemonic actions on the other, participating in the organization of students, women, workers, and neighborhood groups, in what can be called a passive accumulation of forces[4]. "It

3. See Ernesto Laclau, "Socialisme et transformation des logiques hégémoniques", in C. Buci-Glucksmann, ed., *La gauche, le pouvoir, le socialisme*, Paris: PUF, 1983; Chantal Mouffe, "Socialisme, démocratie et nouveaux mouvements sociaux", in the same work; E. Laclau and C. Mouffe, "Socialist Strategy, Where Next?", *Marxism Today* (London), January 1981, and their *Hegemony and Socialist Strategy: Towards a Radical Democratic Politics*, London: Verso, 1985; and Bob Jessup, "The Political Indeterminacy of Democracy" in A. Hunt, *Marxism and Democracy*. [See also the relevant texts on the subject in S. Hänninen and L. Paldàn, eds., *Rethinking Ideology*, New York: International General, 1983, and *Rethinking Marx*, New York: International General, 1984.] In fact, the question of social movements is closely linked to the criticism of "really-existing socialism" and "really-existing democracy", from a point of view which makes the struggle for democracy in Latin America a popular banner, not just a bourgeois one.

4. See Humberto Ortega Saavedra, *Sobre la insurrección*, Havana: Ediciones de Ciencias Sociales, 1981. Concerning the antecedents of the mass organizations promoted by the FSLN before the triumph, see CIERA, *La democracia participativa en Nicaragua*, Managua, May 1984. The FSLN directly led some mass organizations, such as,

cannot be accumulated outside of the conjuncture, because outside it can never accumulate[5]." Insurrectional strategy implies that the organization cease to exist a moment prior to the act, and that there is a simultaneous questioning of all the institutions reproducing the oppressive system, varying in strength, growing in the process, and establishing un-theorized solidarities in the face of a common enemy, so evident at this point that no de-codification is needed. An unquestionable merit of the FSLN as a vanguard lies in their having demonstrated the repressive and exploitive nature of the regime — making the attempts to cover it up or reform it impossible — and at the same time showing its military and political vulnerability. But many times during the insurrectional conjuncture the FSLN would follow and support the people rather than the inverse[6].

Although the FSLN had a more global understanding of the secondary contradictions and their possible articulations, at the moment of insurrection, the different identities of the people faded and the common objective predominated: the destruction of the regime and its political–military agents. Popular organizations served more as a communications network than as a channel for specific struggles. It is important to see that, although organizations arose with obvious specific characteristics from the point of view of the type of struggle or demands which they made against the regime, this was far from a universal pattern and, furthermore, it changed with the conjuncture. For example, the principal struggles of the Association of Women Facing the National Problem (AMPRONAC) were those connected with human rights, missing persons, and with support for the

in the area of unions, the Working Peoples Union Movement (MSPT), the Revolutionary Workers Committees (COR), and the Committees for Worker's Struggles (CLT); in urban areas, the Committees for Rural Workers, organized beginning in 1977 and which included workers, semi-proletarians and small agrarian producers and which in 1978 became the Association of Rural Workers (ATC); in the student area, the Revolutionary Student Front, the Christian Revolutionary Movement, the Sandinista Revolutionary Youth, the Revolutionary Nicaraguan Youth, the Secondary School Student Movement, the Association of Secondary School Students, and the Federation of Youth Movements in Managua; on a neighborhood level, the FSLN brought into being the Civil Defense Committees (CDC) that were to play a crucial role in the insurrection; and in 1977 was born the AMPRONAC (the Association of Women Facing the National Problem) clearly led by the FSLN.
5. Humberto Ortega Saavedra, *op. cit.*
6. *Ibid. Passim.*
7. See Maxine Molyneux, "Women and Socialism: The Revolution Betrayed? The Case of Nicaragua", a paper presented at the seminar "Social Movements and Revolution: The Case of Nicaragua."
8. *Nicaragua: la estrategia de la victoria*, Mexico City: Ed. Nuestro Tiempo, 1980. See also Amalia Chamorro Z., *Algunos rasgos hegemónicos del somozismo y la revolución sandinista*, Managua: Cuadernos de Pensamiento Propio (Serie Ensayos, 5, INIES/CRIES), May 1983.

mothers of the victims of the National Guard, more than with typical feminist demands. In regard to the specific conjuncture, although students and workers organized themselves within their respective specific institutions, as the struggle advanced, the layoffs and the closing of the schools returned them to their neighborhoods. The result was that the Civil Defense Committees (CDC) were able to gather all of this additional organizational capacity and add it to what already arose on a neighborhood level. In reality, the different mass organizations were supported by specific identities not so much as a means of affirming and defending specific interests but rather more as a means of sensitizing and recruiting social forces in the frontline fight against the Somoza regime. Thus, a fundamental role of student organizations was to provide cadres for the rural guerrillas.

The result was a momentary universalization, a *massification* of the people. This is in contradiction to the efforts to organize specific social movements and to recuperate their different demands — an effort which was going to persist after the triumph. In some cases, such as the Luisa Amanda Espinoza Nicaraguan Women's Association (AMNLAE), this effort caused an obvious separation from the usual positions taken by similar organizations in other countries[7]. In addition, the FSLN accompanied the people in their final triumph at the center of a broad anti-Somoza front, which apparently would imply a *fading of class content* from the revolutionary project. Nevertheless, by carrying out the simultaneous total dismantling of the Somoza National Guard and the formation of the Revolutionary Sandinista Popular Army, along with a continuous effort to consolidate popular organizations, the concrete form of victory meant the defeat of the financial bourgeoisie's project to create a hegemony or "dictatorship without Somoza"[8]. At the same time, by keeping a broad social spectrum united against Somozism and its substitutes — supported up until the last moment by the North American government — the FSLN also neutralized all forms of the imperialist project, so that the class content of the revolution could not be questioned on the basis of the characteristics of its social base.

Popular Hegemony As Revolutionary Practice

The experience of the Popular Unity government in Chile is frequently cited to illustrate that without control of the repressive apparatus, with only control of governmental structures, one does not "hold power". According to this view, in Nicaragua the revolutionary forces have really "*taken*" power". Nevertheless, such an understanding comes from a limited definition of power, situating it in one or another state apparatus.

The point of view which clearly separates political society and civil society and which locates power relationships in the sphere of the first (and its link with the second) can be criticized with the concept which attributes political content to the relationships within different social institutions, such as the factory, the school, the family, the church, corporative organizations, etc. According to this criticism, the triumphant Revolution against the Somoza regime, far from having achieved popular power, would only be starting to *build* this power. The slow dismantling of the inherited power relationships should take place simultaneously with the building of a new system of social power. As long as this is not achieved, the old relationships tend to reproduce themselves, likewise reproducing the corresponding ideology of domination in the very heart of the revolutionary process. From this point of view, the building of popular power implies that the *masses* exercise control by means of a process of organization, self-transformation, development of their identities, and the simultaneous appearance of new identities and the disappearance of others. This is because the masses, "massified" by generations of repression and ideological domination also embody identities which must be overcome and transformed, such as racism, machismo, authoritarianism, individualism as these are not the exclusive property of the dominant classes.

And although the FSLN again played a fundamental role in this process, the people themselves, their incipient organizations, their daily struggles, were to have the same dialectic and changing relationship with the vanguard that they had had before the triumph; sometimes led, sometimes leading, and autonomous of the leadership of the FSLN, in general, with no clear definition of the relationship between the revolutionary party and the mass organizations. In this process, the two elements of the relationship, the mass organizations and the revolutionary party, were to be modified in both their form and their content.

As in the insurrectional struggle, the FSLN determined a strategic objective; in this case, the building of a new society starting with the *negation of the global logic of capital*, the subordination of social accumulation to the satisfaction of the basic needs of the population, and the realization of an effective democracy, popular sovereignty and national self-determination. In turn, this determined the immediate task: *the strengthening of revolutionary power*, a necessary condition for confronting internal and external enemies, and keeping open the possibility of trans-

forming society. But within this broad orientation, the masses, continually better organized, had to produce their own answers enriching and concretizing the revolutionary project and giving reality to the slogan of *popular power*. This was to produce changes in the very structure of the revolutionary party.

This task not only called for the necessary material conditions but also for a political–ideological framework. By means of oral or written discourse, but fundamentally through their actions, the FSLN demonstrated the political nature of the revolution. The usual practice of the "dictatorship of the proletariat" — state ownership of the means of production, single party system — was not adopted, but rather one of "popular hegemony"[9], an hegemony under construction together with the historic subject of the Revolution: the Nicaraguan People. Far from homogenizing popular life, differences were admitted and even reflected in the different mass organizations, which expressed the basic liberating demands, such as those of the peasants, the salaried workers in the country and the city, women, youth, and indigenous communities. At the same time, a new identity was consolidated whose beginnings can be found in the revolutionary struggle; the Sandinista Defense Committees, representing the possibility of self-government, of *directly* social relationships in community work without the mediation of mercantile interests[10].

The accumulation of forces cannot be accomplished outside of the conjuncture. In fact, the revolution constantly proposes tasks which are undertaken — not without contradiction — by the masses, which in the process give birth to new identities which effect the liberation and transformation of those who were oppressed. For example, the literacy campaign constituted and gave great social importance to the "19 July Sandinista Youth" organization as a political group directed by the FSLN, through a process which revolutionized the traditional urban/rural relationships, family relationships, and relationships in the school. The resistances produced by the National Literacy Crusade called for an active gathering of these new social forces. At the same time other identities arose, the popular teacher. The more than 19,000 voluntary educators, an essential element in the post-literacy phase, proved that it is possible to break with professionalization and the monopoly of education, and demonstrated the capacity of the people to innovate and become autonomous from the government apparatus if it became necessary[11]. By taking charge of local government, the new Municipal Reconstruction Assemblies provided another example of this process of revealing the ability of the people to govern themselves. One hundred and thirty-six municipalities previously controlled by local bosses or representatives of local economic interests, after the revolution were made up basically of agricultural workers, peasants or urban workers, many of them without a primary

9. José Luis Coraggio, *Revolución y democracia en Nicaragua*, Managua: Cuadernos de Pensamiento Propio (Serie Ensayos 7, INIES/CRIES), May 1984.
10. The Sandinista Defense Committees have organized nocturnal vigilance groups, and the distribution of rationed products. Beginning with the CDC, they currently have some 600,000 members and they are non-partisan and have members from many social classes.
11. Rosa María Torres, *De alfabetizando a maestro popular: La post-alfabetización en Nicaragua*, Managua: Cuadernos de Pensamiento Propio (Serie Ensayos 4, INIES/CRIES), 1983.

Poster, "A man's duty is to be where he is most useful — Jose Marti — National Literacy Crusade".

education[12]. The task of revolutionary defense generated the Sandinista Popular Militia which is possibly the clearest example of this process, but it is not visible to those who see in certain state apparatuses the "localization" of power by definition. The transfer and later consolidation of the masses' combative capacity was not limited to the weekly training courses but rather to effective practical struggle against the counter-revolutionaries continuously infiltrating from Honduras. In fact, in the first phase, the armed struggle against the Somoza forces — which were supported by the U.S. government and the Central American oligarchies — rested fundamentally on the militia and not on the Sandinista Popular Army. First by means of extra-territorial batallions, then in the form of territorial militias, an organized people trained themselves for autonomous self-defense, breaking, here as well, with the professional monopolies that the capitalist state guards so jealously[13].

In other cases, it is evident how a revolutionary context enables a submissive, alienated identity to make a qualitative leap and take on a role in keeping with its importance and social position. The Nicaraguan peasantry had no possibility of organizing themselves under the Somoza regime. Toward the end of 1980, one year after the triumph, their interests tended to be "represented" by agricultural associations controlled by the large producers. In December 1980, the small independent producers from the District of Matagalpa decided at a meeting to break with the Coffee Growers' Central Co-operative and to form the Provisional Committee of Small and Medium Producers which began to call for associations of small producers to be set up in other districts. Based on these associations, in February 1981, the National Union of Farmers and Cattle Breeders (UNAG) was founded. This union immediately made economic demands on the government, but it also demanded to participate on the State Council and in different institutions concerned with agrarian problems. Since then, this mass organization has gone on to win a growing political influence, maintaining a critical attitude in the face of considerable deviations in the agrarian reform policy and influencing its content. If in the first

year of the Revolution the possibility was considered of *opting* for a co-operative course or for a course which would socialize the productive forces through state ownership, the development of a peasant identity called for and encouraged by the revolutionary process, is already clearly affecting the agrarian strategy of year 2000. Both courses of socialization will be developed equally[14]. But, at this juncture, defined by the growing external aggression, it is the combination of production and defense which gives an enormous thrust to this organization and gives it a central place in the revolutionary process. Agrarian reform favorable to the peasants is accelerating far beyond basic technical criteria. In an irreversible process of class consolidation and authentic political and social revolution, the peasants are demanding and getting land and firearms[15].

In July 1984, the UNAG was to go one step further in its position as a fundamental force in the revolutionary process. It announced that its organizations would include agricultural producers *of any size*, with the sole condition that they productively support the process of national liberation[16]. This decision, which in another context would undoubtedly give rise to the domination of the mass of small producers by a limited group of large land owners, who would rely on this mass to strengthen their private interests, in the context of a social revolution implies just the opposite. *Popular hegemony implies the integration of minorities under the direction of the majority.*

In the case of The Luisa Amanda Espinoza Nica-

12. Charles Downs and Fernando Kusnetzoff, "The Changing Role of Local Government in the Nicaraguan Revolution", April 1982, mimeographed.
13. The Obligatory Military Service Law of 1983 further socialized national defense by breaking the bias which had, by various means, previously led the Sandinista Popular Army to be mostly composed of people from the least fortunate classes.
14. See *Estrategia de desarrollo agropecuario y reforma agraria*, Managua: MIDINRA, December 1982.
15. The clearest manifestation of this phenomena is the existence in the border areas of almost 200 Defense and Production co-operatives with nearly 7,000 members.
16. See the declarations of Daniel Nuñez in *Barricada*, the official organ of the FSLN, 7 July 1984, and the notice given at the second meeting of the UNAG in *Barricada*, 9 July 1984.
17. Maxine Molyneux, *op. cit.*

"MPS [Milicia Popular Sandinista] — X-Ray — Is it serious, Doctor?", drawing by Roger Sanchez Flores (Reprinted from his *Muñequitos del Pueblo*, Managua: *Barricada*, ca 1981).

raguan Women's Association (AMNLAE), a different phenomena occurred. Although this organization reappears in force when questions are discussed where women occupy a central position (domestic laws, or recently, a obligatory military service law which would be merely optional for women), its political presence as an organization has not grown as much as the European feminist movements would have hoped. This can be attributed to the greater difficulty, in comparison to the demands of workers or young people, of breaking down the ideological and material structures which subordinate women. Nevertheless, as the directors of the AMNLAE themselves explain it, their priority is to contribute by other means to the defense of the Revolution, a necessary condition for the future battle for women's emancipation[17].

Our hypothesis is, going beyond the schema proposed by a *government* (revolutionary in this case) in a position to regulate, encourage or block this or that demand, *it is the conjuncture which determines the dialectic relation between revolutionary party and mass organizations, and which identities will develop, at what pace and in what direction.* While the progress of the peasants corresponds to their specific demands and at the same time to the material and ideological needs of the Revolution (presenting a real alternative to the capitalist sectors unwilling to be productive, preventing state bureaucracy, developing production, and the consolidation of the defense against external invasions), the specific demands of women would have opened up a complex front of struggle not only against the opposition forces (such as the Church hierarchy) but also within the popular front. This is understood by the party and by the organization itself which has limited its demands, waiting for a more favorable conjuncture in which "the general interests" will not be in contradiction to its specific interests. Thus, there is nothing structural in the revolutionary project which inhibits the full liberation of Nicaraguan women.

A mass organization which is generally not considered as such in theoretical discussions is the Catholic Church. And it also corresponds to a very deep-rooted identity of the Nicaraguan people. Nevertheless, we can illustrate something here which is valid for the other mass organizations as well. Pluralism and democracy are not just problems related to situations in which organizations are linked externally, these problems also occur in the very midst of these organizations. In this case, one is dealing with an institution which obviously preceded the Revolution itself, and which is characterized by being internally guided, in principle, by rules of the strictest hierarchy. It would be difficult to think of an organization more vertical than the Catholic Church. Nevertheless, in actual practice, a certain pluralism exists in its interior, with the coexistence of different tendencies which represent secondary contradictions within Christian thought but which in the social context of a country struggling against imperialism, occupy a central place

in the conjunctural problematic of the Church. In dealing with a Catholic people committed to its liberation, ready to fight against its oppressors to the death, the internal equilibrium within the Catholic hierarchy cannot be dealt with out of context without risking the alienation of its own popular support.

In truth, although the highest authority of the Catholic Church explicitly expresses his disagreement with revolutionary development, Christian and revolutionary identities have acquired a special relationship in Nicaragua, to the point that many clearly Christian principles have been incorporated as revolutionary ideology by the FSLN. Many priests and believers will argue against the counterrevolutionary political positions of their hierarchy, without denying the priesthood or their Christian faith. The counterrevolution has made and will continue to make

"Long Live the AMNLAE" (the Asociación de Mujeres Nicaragüenses Luisa Amanda Espinoza; the mass association of revolutionary Nicaraguan women), photograph by Eva Bendz (Reprinted from *La insurrección de las paredes*, Managua: Editorial Nueva Nicaragua/Ediciones Monimbó, 1984).

enormous efforts to break this unity and make the Church an ideological platform which cannot be offered by the weak organizations of the bourgeois opposition[18]. Paradoxically, the FSLN is firmly determined to maintain the unity between Christianity and Revolution, affirming that there are no contradictions between the two identities.

The clearest evidence that the identities of the masses do not automatically develop in the direction of revolutionary consolidation and success, is the case of the indigenous communities, the Miskitos, Sumos, and Ramas, and the Creoles, on the Atlantic Coast. In August 1981, the FSLN and the government broadcast a declaration of principles in which they promised to support and maintain the indigenous cultural traditions, and guarantee their participation in the country's affairs (the organization Misurasata would have been immediately represented in the State Council). Specifically, this concerned the communities on the Atlantic Coast. The FSLN promised to guarantee and legalize the ownership of their lands, in communal or co-operative form, and to "support their own organizational forms in the different communities, in order to obtain the necessary representation in the social, political and economic management organizations on the Atlantic Coast.[19]" But this was of no value to a community who, exploited and robbed of their resources by transnational firms who exercised real local power, and accustomed to viewing the inhabitants of the rest of the country as "the Spanish", had always a marginal relationship with the State. An additional negative antecedent was the marginal participation of these communities in the Sandinista struggle

against Somoza. But in addition, a revolutionary development in the indigenous identity implied a change not only within the communities themselves and their relationships to those outside their communities, but also within the revolutionary forces, especially difficult as shown by the history of failures in dealing with the ethnic question not only in Latin America but also in other parts of the world. The fact that the *Contras* infiltrated precisely in the Atlantic Zone at the same time that certain community religious leaders were identifying the revolution with the "devil", created situations in which their treatment by the FSLN or the government cannot always be seen as simply a "mistake". Rather, in many cases, it was the inevitable result of the real contradiction between the need to defend territorial integrity from external aggression and the desire to permit self-determination and a gradual re-articulation of the indigenous communities to a society undergoing revolution[20].

This case illustrates how the *process of liberating identities requires a transformation in the relationship (in this case inter-ethnic) on both sides*, and how its development does not depend exclusively on the decisions of a revolutionary party or government, to the point that the enemy itself can determine the conjuncture when to block the desired course.

One case where the FSLN has played a principal role in limiting the "natural" development of a popular identity is that of the salaried workers. The inherited economic restrictions and the additional ones resulting from the deterioration of the exchange rate and the increase in the interest rate, the obvious weaknesses of a State in the process of construction, natural disasters and the financial-economic blockade imposed by the Reagan administration, as well as the political decision to maintain a broad internal front under popular hegemony, called for an end to certain forms of class struggle. These forms would have resulted in the deepening of the unions' old economic demands, mortgaged under the Somoza repression, and also the opening of possible demands for a generalized worker control of the means of production. This limit on the struggle became as extensive as did the limit on the occupation of lands by the peasants[21].

In effect, implanting popular hegemony required maintaining a pluralistic social system. It was necessary to answer the demands of private landowners that their property rights as well as the possibility to make profits would be guaranteed without being stigmatized as an exploiter. The revolutionary government made these guarantees on the condition that private property fulfill its social function under popular hegemony: to produce under acceptable conditions of efficiency[22].

In consequence, class struggle was not frozen but rather took other forms: worker control of the *use* of property[23], the demand for better working conditions, the demand for an indirect salary by the State, and fundamentally, something which the workers' organizations would have once delegated to the government

18. Ana María Ezcurra, *Agresión ideológica contra la revolución Sandinista*, Mexico City: Ediciones Nuevomar, 1983.

19. See: "Declaraciones de principios de la revolución popular sandinista sobre las comunidades indígenas de la Costa Atlantica", included in CIERA, *op. cit.*, p. 156.

20. For an objective report on this question, see *Trabil Nani: History and Current Situation in Nicaragua's Atlantic Coast*, CIDCA, April 1984. [See the extract of this report published in this volume.]

21. On 21 November 1979, the FSLN broadcast a communique ordering "... all entries and confiscations of residences, vehicles and urban and rural property cease immediately...." (see the 21 November 1979 issue of *Barricada*). The FSLN, via the Sandinista Workers Central (CST) and the Association of Rural Workers (ATC) established the principle that maintaining production was necessary for a revolution under attack, but that in the face of predicted escalating external aggression, the Revolutionary Government should have recourse to the 9 September 1981 Economic And Social State of Emergency Law (Decree 812) which punished strikes and take-overs of both land and production centers. See *Leyes de la República de Nicaragua*, Ministerio de Justicia, volume V, July–December 1981.

22. See the Agrarian Reform Law (Decree 782, 10 August 1981), accused of being "protectionist" by ultra-left critics. In *Leyes de la República de Nicaragua, op. cit.*

23. The "De-capitalization Law" (Decree 805, 28 August 1981) would allow the workers to exercise strict vigilance over the management of private capital in this area.

apparatus: the control over the economic surplus by means of an economic policy, and a state monopoly over the financial sector and the commercialization of essential products. This new form of expression of worker identity demanded an understanding of the conjuncture and a clarity with regards to the revolutionary project which not all of the workers had. The situation was aggravated by the general crisis in Central America, which also affected Nicaragua. This crisis made it difficult to increase urban employment. Therefore it is no wonder that given the emergency conditions in the country, the government has had recourse to legal forms of strike suppression, even though union pluralism had resulted in the survival of those unions which made the classic demands, and of some opposition unions which now raise flags which at the time they did not wave against the dictatorship[24].

24. In fact, the unions multiplied after the revolutionary triumph. From 133 unions with 27,000 members, the number increased (as of December 1983) to 1,103 unions with 207,391 members, of which approximately 80 per cent were under the direction of the FSLN. See CIERA, *op. cit.*, p. 45.
25. During the 1983–84 season, approximately 40,000 voluntary workers were mobilized for the coffee and cotton harvests, in what was evidently a new identity for the Nicaraguan people. (See CIERA, *op. cit*, pp. 64–65.)
26. Concerning the subject of worker participation in management, see CIERA, *op. cit.*, pp. 100–123.

At the same time, rural workers, in the absence of external seasonal migratory flows, with historically high figures for coffee production and with a growing cotton production, were able to advance in terms of their traditional demands (better working conditions, social salary, equitable pay for their labor, etc.), and even limit the growing mechanization of cotton harvesting when manual labor was available. The identity of the rural worker as a landowner was sustained without the concrete possibility to return to the land [*recampesinización*]. What did have a definite negative effect on the flow of the salaried work force to the harvest was external aggression, as it caused a greater migration to the cities as well as the displacement of soldiers and militia for defense purposes. Voluntary labor was a recurrent means of covering this deficit[25]. Given the importance of the enterprises of the Peoples' Property Area (APP) in permanent rural employment, a growing demand was making worker participation more effective, which contradicted the tendencies toward bureaucratization among some state officials[26].

The building of popular hegemony assumes not only the development of but also the articulation of the peoples' identities as the subject of the Revolution. And not just this. In addition it implies, contradictorially, the reproduction/transformation/re-articulation of identities which historically have been considered

Poster, "Literacy and Production: Two goals in our Revolutionary Process which will Temper the New Man in a Liberated Homeland — National Literacy Crusade — Minister of Education".

antagonistic to the popular project. In the particular case of the first phase of the Sandinista Popular Revolution, the function of the landlord was hit hard by the revolutionary laws, as much concerning land ownership as urban housing[27]. The popular project had no place for this social identity except in a distorted form and without any economic importance. It happened again in 1984 with the function of commercial speculator which has been hit hard by the new procedures and regulations for warehousing.

On the other hand, revolutionary discussion has, since the beginning, proposed the possibility of a "patriotic bourgeoisie", a basic element in the hegemonic system and in economic, political and ideological pluralism. Independently of the fact that members of the government may issue from the bourgeoisie (and even continue to hold property and to profit from the means of production) the question is whether it will be possible to maintain the identity of the bourgeoisie as a class or if the transformations which it must undergo in order to integrate itself into the popular hegemonic system are in contradiction to its existence. In fact, the Sandinista project implies the buiding of a system of relationships (identities) by means of which private ownership of the means of production can be regulated by earnings in particular instances, but which will be globally subordinated to the satisfaction of the material and spiritual needs of the people and to the support of their sovereignty, thus making accumulation a means and not an end. This is not impossible, above all when based upon the historic conditions of the Nicaraguan bourgeoisie. Thus it would be possible for it to reproduce as an *economic class*, even presenting its corporate demands before the state's economic policy, union

policies, etc. But *in fact*, the project of popular hegemony implies that the organization of the new hegemonic subject, that is to say, of the new system of social and political relationships would block the possibility of the bourgeoisie realizing their class project, that of imposing their specific interests on the majority. As a *political class*, therefore, they would be "alienated"[28]. This does not prevent their participation in different governmental organizations, either as individuals or as representatives of a corporately organized class, or even by means of political parties. The pluralistic project implicit in a popular hegemonic direction even leaves open the legal possibility of the bourgeoisie opting for governmental power. But the development and consolidation of popular power means that such an eventuality will be blocked by a relation of forces that favors the predominant expression of the interests of the majority.

The theories say that in its development capital invaded every sphere of society, commercializing relationships, and making the liberal state and parliamentary democracy the instruments for the ideological and political domination of the masses, fragmented into individuals–citizens. The challenge of the Nicaraguan proposal is to block these global tendencies and at the same time maintain the possibility of the existence of private capital "deformed" by its subordination within a hegemonic system.

An additional question which is raised and which extends to what may be called the non-capitalistic middle sectors, is that of luxury consumption. In some ways the "success" of broad layers of the Nicaraguan bourgeoisie has been more tied to sustaining privileged levels of consumption than to accumulation itself. This aspect of bourgeois identity should perhaps be controlled by considerations of the general interest, but it could nevertheless allow for a certain level of *inequality* (not associated with domination)[29].

The Open Nature of the Hegemonic System

Several decades ago in Latin America we learned that the economic theories which are based on a closed economy are not applicable to our societies which are exaggeratedly open and dependent on the ups and downs of the external marketplace and of transnational forces, as well as on the economic policies of the central states. But dependency and openness also affect the make-up of political systems. To consider hegemonic relationships "as if" the national society were a closed system in which one could compute relations of force on the basis of their social importance, level of organization, and the ideological relationships between social sectors, is to negate the reality of our society.

The case of Nicaragua is obvious. Faced with the popular project expressed and carried out by the FSLN and the mass organizations, the native bourgeoisie had no possibility of opposing hegemony. Limited in their

27. The Government Council for National Reconstruction set the maximum fee for agrarian rentals at levels several times lower than usual for the best land (300 córdobas per manzana [one manzana equals 2.47 acres] for the production of exportable crops and 100 córdobas for those destined for the internal market). See decrees 230 and 263 of January 1980. *Leyes . . . , op cit.* At the same time, as a result of Decree 216, (29 December 1979), the rents for urban housing were reduced some 50 per cent. Although the political–ideological effect has not been lost, the laws of the marketplace have quietly if slowly been revising these levels upwards.

28. Concerning the "bourgeois question" in Nicaragua see J. L. Coraggio, *op. cit.* A recently evolved and growing characteristic of the relationship between the revolutionary government and the bourgeoisie is that an open dialogue is maintained and attention is paid to the demands of specific factions, but the organizations which claim to speak for the class as a whole are not accepted as valid interlocutors.

29. In this aspect, as in others, it is impossible to crystallize a revolution according to a predetermined "model". One of the effects of the Reagan Administration's military and economic aggression, combined with the crisis in the world market, has been to cause the government to introduce a program of macro-economic adjustments which tends to drastically reduce non-essential and luxury consumption which have a relatively slight effect on the mass consumption of goods and salaries.

control of the mass communication media, with no possibility of knocking on the door of the military barracks, with no proposal for economic development and no solution to the crisis other than continued dependency on the United States of North America, they had no possibility of proposing a real alternative to power. Their course was to either leave the country or to become actively incorporated in the "patriotic bourgeois" position, with all of its contradictions, which opened up for them within the system of popular hegemony.

But the Somoza system of domination had not been a "national" system but rather a sub-system in the imperialist relationships of domination, which saw Central America as part of a "back yard", and which had made Somoza the North American gendarme in the area. And overthrowing Somozism is not the same as defeating imperialism. Having lost the battle, the North American administration *immediately* began to besiege the revolutionary government economically and politically, making an attempt to take part in the internal definition of the relations of force. Their economic aid was aimed directly at the bourgeois sectors and their allies, in support of their activities and their organizations. When the revolutionary government put a stop to this direct link, aid was cut off. The undeniable consolidation of the popular forces in Nicaragua rapidly convinced the North American strategists that the only way to stop the Revolution was the re-activation of the outlawed Somoza National Guard, and they began their preparations with the support of the oligarchies in the region. Finally, the aggression once again took on its current form of open North American intervention in the internal affairs of Nicaragua. It is difficult to say what the development of the hegemonic popular project would have been like under other conditions, but the reality is that the actions of the imperialists were a co-determining factor in the development of events and brought out with greater clarity the anti-imperialist identity of the Nicaraguan people[30].

Parties and Movements: The Problem of Articulation

We see that in Nicaragua a social project is being born as a result of the practice of building a popular hegemony in which the mass organizations and their

30. Concerning this identity, formed by the struggles of Sandino, see Sergio Ramírez, *El pensamiento vivo de Sandino*, San José: EDUCA, 1974, and Carlos Fonseca, *Obras*, Managua: Editorial Nueva Nicaragua, 1982.
31. See the recent Political Parties Law and the Electoral Law.
32. This is not so clear in every case. In other countries, social movements organized around the defense of human rights, peace, or natural resources, transcend, without doubt, the level of specific demands and take on the role of criticizing the destruction which is being carried out by humanity itself.

dialectical relationship with the FSLN and with the revolutionary government is a central element. These relationships have been taking the form of laws, of institutions — in many cases provisional — which have made it possible to regulate conflicts, establish mechanisms for participation, and anticipate the consequences of certain behaviors.

Nicaragua is now planning an important step in this institutionalization: the election of a National Assembly, with 90 representatives elected from specifically demarcated territories[31]. A law governing political parties has now been approved. As to the electoral system, the model adopted will be that of a parliament elected by universal suffrage based on a process of electoral competition among *political parties* and in which pluralism is guaranteed through proportional representation. The question which we must ask ourselves is how social movements are going to be represented within these political structures? Or rather, what other structures should be created so that these social forces can participate on the governmental level? At present, the State Council has representatives from political parties and from social movements. In establishing suffrage as the only mechanism for representation, the practical possibility of putting parties and movements on the same level, of having them compete for social representation in the same scenario, appears to remain blocked. This is obvious not only because of the multiple identities of the social agents, but also because of the need to maintain the specificities of movements and parties. The first are more oriented toward the partial demands of popular identities, whereas the second fulfill the task of synthesizers, of integrators of a national project, which must take into consideration many dimensions which do not take on the form of identities and social movements[32].

An alternative is for the political parties to include on their lists representatives of the different mass organizations — which under a system of proportional representation implies a process of negotiating one's position on the lists — and also of including the demands of these movements in their platforms. But if social movements and their leaders become vote mobilizers for the parties, these could tend to reproduce what we already see in an extreme form in North American democracy. It is possible for a party to turn into a detector of contradictions, of specific interests. This party can then collect and transform these contradictions into a mixture of partial promises which as a whole not only do not consistitute a true national project, but when taken together are also usually incongruent and not viable, freezing rather than giving dynamic force to the social situation.

On the other hand, if it is true that the organizational autonomy of social movements as an expression of social forces appears to be a desirable condition in a popular democracy, at the same time the changing character of the identities of the people, which results from the same ongoing process of construction/ transformation itself, makes it difficult to crystallize these identities in clearly defined qualitative and quantitative positions.

An institutional alternative which could be considered is that of creating a second Assembly with a consultation/deliberation character, where the major national problems could be discussed and the principal social forces of the country could express their points of view. In any case, the direct participation of mass organizations in different decision-making instances would not be in contradiction to these new forms of government.

This problematic has other consequences. The dialectical relationship between the revolutionary party and the mass organizations in the context of a pluralistic system can take two forms: either the party can continue as a *leadership party* of selected cadres, which in many cases arise out of the very activities of the mass organizations themselves; or, it can become a *mass party*. This has important consequences with regard to the problem of the articulation with the people. The leadership party makes decisions not only by determining strategic objectives and tactics but also by being physically present in *the administration* of the mass organizations. This is accomplished by incorporating into the party their most outstanding leaders who aspire to become party militants. The mass party is present and almost in a state of symbiosis with the masses, both detecting and nurturing itself on its contradictions and its growth, in which the role of "representative of the people" is joined in a double link with the party and with its specific base of support. It is appropriate to ask ourselves, in the context of a prolonged imperialist siege against Nicaraguan society, if the first model, which would take the form of a "tree", with the FSLN among the top branches of the different mass organizations, would not be more vulnerable than the second, where a horizontal network would exist directly between the different social movements[33].

A final observation is that possibly the Church — Christianity as a current of thought and also as as organization — rather than being seen as a social movement "along side" the others, would be seen as a articulator of social movements, present in their underlying structures as well as in the different levels of their administration. In this sense, the FSLN and Christianity can be either confluent or competitive in this task of consolidating and giving form to the subject of a new Nicaraguan society.

EPILOGUE:
SOME THEORETICAL QUESTIONS ARISING FROM REVOLUTIONARY PRACTICE IN NICARAGUA

In the introduction we attempted to present a summary of a conceptual approximation concerning social movements, based fundamentally on those European developments in the area which have to a large extent been adopted in Latin America. In the center section we attempted to interpret the experience of the Revolution in Nicaragua from that perspective and, after doing so, we continued by pointing out either explicitly or implicitly some of the limitations of the initial conceptual framework. Here we are able to bring up some of the theoretical questions which arise from the Nicaraguan reality in relation to theories of social movements.

In the first place, the *identities* to which the conceptual framework refers cannot be seen as "attributes" which permit the classification (or organization) of individuals in groups (social movements). It is much more productive to think of them as interpersonal or social *relationships*. In addition, they should not be seen as oppressed or alienated "essences" which need to be liberated. Rather they shoud be seen as situations which consciously or in the course of action are transformed through a revolutionary process. Furthermore, they are not yet given in either embryonic or developed form; new identities arise and others disappear only as a consequence of the process.

Just as a theoretically correct movement should be completed through the synthesis and reconstruction of the object, which in this case means giving definition to the concept of the people, this movement is incomplete if it is not combined with the conceptualization of a complex subject, internally contradictory, unified by an internal *hegemonic system*. Insofar as the people are constituted as a *revolutionary subject*, the majority presence of the working classes guarantees the class content of this system by means of a complex interweaving of organizations and institutions. In the domain of political action where the objective is not to invalidate all forms of power but rather to guarantee that social power be exercised by the people, the movement of synthesis mentioned above has its parallel in the process of *articulating* social movements, a process in which the political parties have historically played a central role. In particular, in the process of achieving a correlation of forces which will make it possible to break with the structures that subjugate the people, the role of *revolutionary party* should be re-introduced into this theoretical discussion, not only because it articulates

---

33. In fact, recent developments would seem to indicate that, due as much to the need to strengthen the internal front as to the dynamic of the electoral process, the FSLN will tend to approach more and more the dimensions of a mass party even though the concept of the vanguard may continue to be maintained.

   In a sense, this implies the partial "internalization" of the confrontation of identities and specific interests within the heart of the revolutionary party. The opposition leadership/mass should not be confused with the *party's* role as vanguard. A mass party is perfectly able to fulfill the role of vanguard for those social forces engaged in a process of consciously building a new society.

specific movements within a front of social forces, but also because in many cases it is responsible for the structure of said movements. This does not cease being valid even for situations as diverse as that of Nicaragua or of European societies, where it is likely that the political parties have neither been nor are now foreign to the development and content of social movements.

In this sense, the people are seen as a *historically determined category* which changes not only with the structural development of society but also with the political conjuncture, neither reducible to a predetermined class nor to a collection of universally determined identities. And its internal structure — as hegemonic system — includes the articulation between party(s) and social movements, with no possibility of "choosing" between one or the other form of collective action. The historical and conjunctural character of the movements (and identities) includes the possibility of their disappearance, of their loss of efficacy, of their re-articulation, as a result of the very processes of transformation. This possibility, correctly, makes it difficult to accept the tendency in some authors to predict (or wish for) a substituting of the system of political parties for one of social movements. Nor does it support a more favorable evaluation of the second with respect to, and to the exclusion of, the first, either relative to democracy or their ability to develop the people as subject. It appears more productive to suggest the hypothesis that the presence of social movements on the political scene indicates a real criticism of the parties' efficacy in politically chanelling conflicting social developments, and that their actions necessarily will modify the structure of the political system. Within the context of an authentic social revolution, in a society with a differently constituted civil sphere, these dialectical relationships can take on other forms, also historically determined, which become evident when the possibility arises of going from a leadership party to a mass party, upon moving from a phase of organization and accumulation of forces against the ruling regime to the phase of building popular power in the presence of a revolutionary government.

Finally, having expressed the importance of incorporating political parties in the analysis, the problem of articulation becomes specifically a question of *the form of this articulation* in which two clear alternatives stand out: that of the "verticalist" which puts the mass organizations in a subordinate position with respect to the party, even though they may inform and nurture it, or, the alternative of a mass party which "horizontally" articulates the different identities and corresponding popular organizations.

Far from pretending that these are new contributions to the theory of social movements, we have tried to bring to the forefront certain aspects which appear to have been omitted in some of the more recent forums on this subject. It is in this spirit that we suggest Nicaragua's current experiences can serve as an effective laboratory for testing the universality of some of these propositions — which have perhaps been too quickly extrapolated from other Latin American realities. At the same time we have not eliminated the possibility that this "crusading" comparison may even bring into question for Europe itself the validity of some of the concepts which have continued to issue from the academic world.

FERNANDO CARDENAL and VALERIE MILLER
Nicaragua 1980: The Battle of the ABCs

It is September 1980. Nicaragua is green from winter rains. The countryside that just two weeks ago was bustling with more than 50,000 young volunteer literacy teachers is quieter now. The National Literacy Crusade is over. The peasant-shirt, blue-jean uniforms of the young *brigadistas* ("student-volunteers") can no longer be seen in the far-away hills and valleys. Their footsteps no longer mark the mountain paths between San Rafael and Yalí, but their voices and spirit remain, transformed and replaced by those of their students. Local people from Waslala and Wiwilí now conduct the community study groups begun by the volunteers. From cotton fields to the jungle valleys, reading and writing continues.

In the cities, the buses overflow, crowded again with teenage faces. Endless registration lines of students surround the high schools and universities. The country begins another school year, which on the surface looks like any other. Yet, Nicaragua will never be the same again. The National Literacy Crusade has broken the patterns of the past and has laid the foundations for the future. In five months, more than 400,000 Nicaraguans learned to master basic reading and writing skills, and tens of thousands of young people and their families learned about rural poverty and peasant culture.

Nicaragua recently celebrated an educational victory that a little over a year ago would have seemed impossible. On 23 August 1980, the nation applauded the success of students and teachers of the National Literacy Crusade. We saluted their achievements, and we also saluted thousands of people who could not stand with us, those who had given their lives in battle to free this land. The National Literacy Crusade was a living tribute to their sacrifice, commitment, and hope. Their dedication and faith in the future made the campaign possible. Their memories live on in each one of us. This article is dedicated to them.

Nicaragua's struggle for self-determination had been going on for many years, but finally exploded on a massive scale in 1978. After decades of foreign domination, inequity, and military repression, the mounting rebellion could no longer be contained. As the battle intensified, young people went to the mountains and joined the liberation forces. Directed and organized by the Sandinista National Liberation Front (FSLN), they fought with an unshakable belief in victory and an uncommon courage against extraordinary odds. Civilians, organized into community-defense committees, added to their force. City people dug up the neighborhood streets to form barricades against tanks and troops. When the tear gas became too thick, housewives set out on their porches specially prepared tubs of bicarbonate of soda water for the young fighters to neutralize the burning chemicals. Women's groups organized clandestine hospitals in their homes. First- and second-graders served as couriers carrying important messages across battle lines. Businessmen led strikes and raised funds for arms. Market women hid ammunition at the bottom of baskets brimming with vegetables and carried out their missions walking confidently between rows of armored cars. Families carved out bomb shelters in their patios, using shovels and spoons. They created homemade hand bombs out of firecrackers and collected rocks to throw against Somoza's machine guns.

Despite this extraordinary display of courage and faith, the war was long and costly. Some 40,000 people were killed, 100,000 wounded, and 40,000 children orphaned. Somoza escaped with all the reserves in the Central Bank except $3.5 million, leaving an international debt of $1.6 billion. Yet, less than one year after victory, the nation was transformed from a violent war zone into one enormous school. The spirit and commitment of hundreds of thousands of Nica-

This text was prepared for an International Institute for Educational Planning workshop on "Planning and Administration of National Literacy Programs" held in Arusha, Tanzania on 27 November–2 December 1980, and was published in the *Harvard Educational Review*, Volume 51, 1 February 1981. Copyright by the President and Fellows of Harvard College. Reprinted by permission of the author.

raguans forged in combat became the moving force behind a massive literacy program. Young men and women who had taken up arms and gone to the hills now took up pencils and primers and returned to the mountains.

Where machine guns and bombs had filled the air such a short time ago, the sounds of ABCs and singing could be heard. Along the same paths where young fighters had rushed to battle, young literacy teachers set up blackboards and guided unsteady hands in writing their first words. In cornfields ravaged by war, beside the simple graves of fallen patriots, the literacy volunteers worked the land side-by-side with their adopted peasant families. In bomb-damaged factories, workers taught fellow workers the ABCs. The violence and destruction of yesterday had been replaced by the quiet pride of learning. A new nation was being born. One battle had been won and another begun. In these pages we will describe that second battle by explaining the origins of the campaign and its relationship to development. We will also examine some of the major problems that the Literacy Crusade confronted and the strategies developed to overcome them.

ORIGINS OF THE BATTLE

On 24 March 1980, the entire country became engaged in a nationwide learning campaign. Student volunteers went to the countryside to teach literacy and learn the ways of peasant living, while urban workers and housewives taught and learned from people in the cities. The program was designed to help Nicaraguans acquire the skills, understanding, and empathy necessary for participation in a society undergoing rapid transformation.

The spirit that inspired the campaign had its origins in the early part of the century. The 1980 Literacy Crusade grew out of the liberation struggle begun by General Augusto César Sandino. The tensions that led to the struggle were related primarily to efforts to establish an interoceanic canal in Nicaragua. In 1909 Liberal President José Santos Zelaya refused to grant canal rights to the United States. As a result, the State Department gave its support to the Conservative opposition which, when it took power, agreed to a permanent U.S. military presence and U.S. control of the economy through management of national bank, railway, and customs operations. In the 1920s the tension between the two parties escalated into open fighting. The buildup of the Liberal army in 1927 posed a serious threat to the Conservative regime. Fearing a loss of power and stability, the United States bolstered the marine presence. By a combination of political promise and military threat, the United States ambassador persuaded both parties to halt the fighting. General elections were agreed to and a National Guard was created to maintain the "peace". U.S. Marine commanders were put in charge of its training and organization, and Anastasio Somoza García was among its chosen officers.

However, General Sandino refused to accept the United States-negotiated accords. For seven years, Sandino and his peasant army battled against foreign intervention. Unable to defeat the increasingly popular general, the marines finally were forced to withdraw in 1933. With their departure, Sandino signed a peace treaty with the government, dismantled his army, and retired to organize peasant co-operatives in the north. The United States installed Anastasio Somoza as the head of the National Guard. In 1934 Somoza had Sandino assassinated, his co-operatives destroyed, and their members and families exterminated.

Throughout Sandino's struggle he had always wanted to assure his people's social and economic development. He set up co-operatives for agricultural production and, when possible, urged his troops to learn to read and write. He was especially proud of their educational achievements:

I can assure you that the number of our illiterate officers can now be counted on fewer than the fingers of one hand. Unfortunately, due to a shortage of people who can teach, progress among the soldiers has been almost negligible.
When General Pedro Altamirano first joined us he did not know how to read or write but ... during the fighting and only because I insisted on it, Altamirano learned, stumbling

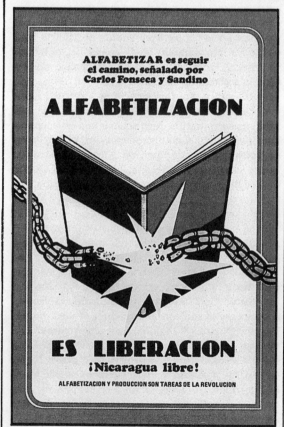

Poster, "To be literate is to follow the way set out by Carlos Fonseca and Sandino — Literacy is Liberation — Free Nicaragua — Literacy and Production are Revolutionary Tasks".

and mumbling as he went along. Despite his age, he has made great strides since then, and now, as amazing as it may seem, he actually knows how to type — even if it is only with one finger[1].

In the early 1960s, the FSLN took up Sandino's challenge. The struggle for both literacy and liberation was once again alive.

DEVELOPMENT AND LITERACY: YESTERDAY

Under Somoza, Nicaragua was run as a family plantation. Development had been narrowly focused on modernizing the economy's agricultural export sector for the benefit of a small privileged minority. The promotion of universal literacy or adult education was irrelevant and potentially threatening. Under this economic system, national development programs were essentially used to enrich Somoza's personal fortune and to buttress the regime's power structure by providing his partners with lucrative business opportunities involving massive graft and corruption. While isolated sectors of the population benefited from the programs, the root causes of economic disparity and political injustice were never addressed. Ultimately, development projects led to the expansion of the government's corrupt patronage system and to the further impoverishment and repression of the majority.

Illiteracy was both a condition and a product of this system. In 1979 a special census revealed that more than 50 per cent of the population was illiterate, a figure which soared above 85 per cent in some rural areas[2]. This problem was never seriously addressed during the dictatorship because the promotion of universal literacy was neither politically advisable for the maintenance of the system nor ecomically necessary for its functioning. The development model of export agriculture depended upon a large pool of unskilled workers, and therefore it neither required nor encouraged an educated labor force. Politically, it was unwise for Somoza to undertake a genuine nationwide literacy program. Basic education would have provided the poor and disenfranchised with the potential tools to analyze and question the unequal power relationships and economic conditions under which they had lived. An illustration from the crusade underlines this point. A peasant is speaking during the dialogue section of the lesson:

Somoza never taught us to read — it really was ungrateful of him, wasn't it. He knew that if he taught the peasants to read we would claim our rights. Ay! But back then, people

1. Quoted in José Román, *Maldito Pais*, Managua: El Pez y La Serpiente, 1979, p. 135.
2. Ministry of Education, *La Educación En El Primer Año De La Revolución Popular Sandinista*, Managua, 1980, p. 162.
3. Auxiliadora Rivas and Asunción Suazo, conversation in literacy class, Masaya, Nicaragua, 4 May 1980.

couldn't even breathe. You see, I believe that a government is like the parent of a family. The parent demands the best of his children and the children demand the best of the parent, but a governor, like a parent, who does not give culture and upbringing to the child, well that means he doesn't love his child, or his people. Don't you agree?[3]

Under Somoza, literacy teaching was used as a cover for counter insurgency operations in the north. The "Plan Waslala", according to the Ministry of Education's own report in 1978, appointed more than 100 literacy teachers to act as spies and identify peasants sympathetic to the FSLN. Many people singled out by this operation later disappeared. Waslala itself was the site of an infamous concentration camp where hundreds of peasants had been savagely tortured and killed.

DEVELOPMENT AND LITERACY: TODAY

With the recent triumph of the Sandinista Revolution, the meaning of development and education changed radically. The ideas of Julius Nyerere, President of Tanzania, seem especially appropriate for understanding the change. In his writings, Nyerere stresses that development means freedom and liberation. Development means people. But, as he emphasizes, people cannot be developed, human beings can only develop themselves. In the new Nicaragua, we also believe that development means freedom, a freedom that is based on liberation and popular participation. Such a process rests on the redistribution of the nation's power and wealth and on the thoughtful, creative involvement of people in community organization. Development in Nicaragua today requires that all aspects of society be examined and recreated to respond to the needs and aspirations of the majority. It involves a profound transformation of the social system and the creation of structures which promote permanent opportunities for learning and enhance equitable forms of economic and political participation.

We believe that in order to create a new nation we must begin with an education that liberates people. Only through knowing their past and their present, only through understanding and analyzing their reality can people choose their future. Education, therefore, must encourage people to take charge of their lives, to learn to become informed and effective decision makers, and to understand their roles as responsible citizens possessing rights and obligations. A liberating education nurtures empathy, a commitment to community, and a sense of self-worth and dignity. It involves people acquiring the knowledge, skills, and attitudes necessary for their new community responsibilities. Education for liberation means people working together to gain an understanding of and control over society's economic, political, and social forces in order to guarantee their full participation in the creation of the new nation. Literacy and permanent programs of adult learning are fundamental to these goals. We believe they are essential to the building of a democratic society in which people can participate consciously and critically in national decision making. The struggle to achieve these aims is long, and we are just beginning.

Soon after the triumph, the Government of National Reconstruction (GNR) and the FSLN proposed their first development plan. Education and literacy were among its top priorities. The program emphasized economic reactivation and national reconstruction and was founded on four major points. First, it established a socioeconomic policy based on a commitment to full employment, improved social services, universal literacy, land reform, self-sufficiency in basic food stuffs, increased production for the common good, and a mixed economy. Second, it encouraged popular participation through a network of citizens' and workers' associations, a representative legislative body, the Council of State, and a variety of public forums for open debate and dialogue between government and citizens. Third, the program called for the birth and affirmation of the "New Nicaraguan", revolutionary men and women, characterized by sacrifice, humility, discipline, creativity, love, generosity, hard work, and a critical consciousness. Finally, to accumulate the necessary capital for domestic investment and to pay the nation's staggering debt, it emphasized austerity. Salary differentials were drastically reduced, wages controlled, and luxury imports curtailed.

In their development plan, conducting a nationwide literacy campaign was one of the first priorities of the young government. In August 1979, just 15 days after victory, Nicaragua's Literacy Crusade was born. The first goal of the campaign was to eliminate illiteracy. Specifically, this meant reducing the illiteracy rate to between 10 to 15 per cent, establishing a nationwide system of adult education, and expanding primary school coverage through the country. Other important goals were to encourage an integration and understanding among Nicaraguans of different classes and backgrounds; to increase political awareness and a critical analysis of underdevelopment; to nurture attitudes and skills related to creativity, production, cooperation, discipline, and analytical thinking; to forge a sense of national consensus and of social responsibility; to strengthen channels of economic and political participation; to acquaint people with national development programs; to record oral histories and recover popular forms of culture; and to conduct research in health and agriculture for future development programming.

Specifically, the Crusade was intended to help people acquire basic skills in reading, writing and to develop an elementary knowledge of the history of the

Revolution, the national development plan, and the emerging political and economic structures. As a whole, the campaign was designed to sensitize the entire country to the problems and rights of the poor and to prepare citizens for their responsibilities in meeting the challenge of national development. The Crusade had one other important function: it gave the young people who had fought and suffered the traumas of the war a channel for their energy and enthusiasm. Their participation as volunteer teachers helped them make the transition between the violence of war and the challenge of transformation.

In its design and implementation, the campaign was eminently political and profoundly spiritual. First, it was aimed at giving the nation's poor and disenfranchised the skills and knowledge they needed to become active participants in the political process. In doing so, it consolidated a powerful new political force and challenged the power of large economic interests. Second, it was spiritual. The act of learning to read and write served to restore and nurture spiritual values which had for so long been suppressed. Dignity and self-worth took on new meaning as people began to gain confidence in themselves and their future. Literacy was considered much more than a basic human right. The FSLN called literacy "an apprenticeship in life because in the process the literate person learns his intrinsic value as a person, as a maker of history, as an actor of an important social role, as an individual with rights to demand and duties to fulfill[4].

The means to carry out such an ambitious educational challenge emerged from both the philosophical principles and the practical experience of the Revolution. The actual strategies of battle provided a model for educational action. One of the fundamental tenets of the GRN and the FSLN was citizen participation: just as in war, victory rested on active community involvement. Triumph over illiteracy meant citizens learning from citizens, neighbors helping neighbors, an entire nation organized to educate itself. The specific strategy depended upon the network of citizens and labor associations that originally had been organized clandestinely for the war. The actual operation of the literacy struggle followed the same general lines as the liberation struggle — from isolated skirmishes and harassment of the enemy in the pilot project stage, to a national insurrection during the main implementation phase, on to the final offensive of accelerated study, and ultimately to the consolidation of the Revolution through the follow-up program.

The metaphors and terminology of the campaign were purposefully military — "The National Literacy Crusade: Heroes and Martyrs for the Liberation of Nicaragua", "the war on ignorance", "the cultural insurrection", and "the second war of liberation". The literacy warriors, or brigadistas, of the Popular Literacy Army were divided into brigades, columns, and squadrons and were located along six battlefronts identical to those of the war[5]. They joined forces with

4. Unpublished Report on the Literacy Crusade by the FSLN, December 1979.
5. Brigades were made up of all those brigadistas in one municipality; columns were made up of four squadrons

Photograph by Ramon Zamora Olivas (Reprinted from C. Alemán Ocampo, *Y también enséñenles a leer*, Managua: Editorial Nueva Nicaragua, 1984).

the Peasant and Workers' Militias and the Urban Literacy Guerrillas. Each battle unit chose the name of a fallen combatant as a means of honoring his or her memory.

In no way was the use of military terminology designed to glorify war or violence. Anyone who lived through the horror perpetuated by Somoza's guard was acutely aware that the pain and trauma of violence and repression were not worthy of glorification. On the contrary, the choice of military metaphors was designed to help young volunteers integrate the memories of the past, transforming terms related to the war into positive associations with teaching and sharing. Military terminology also helped the brigadistas see the Crusade as a vital part of the nation's continuing liberation struggle and to understand that, as such, it demanded the seriousness, dedication and discipline of a military offensive. In essence, we wanted to make clear that peace-time battles demanded the same selfless, disciplined commitment as did the war effort; in fact, they demanded more.

The use of military terms and the naming of fallen heroes had a deeply spiritual significance. The Crusade owed its very existence to the Revolution and to

the sacrifice of thousands of men and women who fought and died for liberation. By calling forth their names and memories, the young volunteers kept alive the courage and example of their fallen compatriots. A spiritual bond joined the living with the dead. It inspired greater levels of commitment and compassion and it spurred people on in moments of difficulty. Over 40,000 Nicaraguans died in the struggle's violence. The Crusade and its symbols were a living testimony to their sacrifice, dedication, and faith in the future.

THE CHALLENGE AND THE PROBLEMS

The challenge confronting the crusade staff would have discouraged most educational planners. At times we were overwhelmed. The lessons of the war, however, provided us with a special source of strength and inspiration. During the insurrection we had learned to take unimaginable risks. We learned about organizing, and about trusting in people's extraordinary capacity for daring, creativity, and perseverance. We were confident that we could translate that spirit into the Literacy Crusade. But, initially, we weren't quite sure how to prepare, organize, and mobilize the large numbers of people necessary for the battle or how to finance it. The problems appeared formidable.

Somaza had left the country destitute. We could not count on public financing. We estimated that we would need to raise approximately $20 million to support the effort. Since the war had affected much of the nation's transportation system, and years of government corruption had impeded the development of a rural infrastructure, new methods had to be devised to maintain communication with the isolated regions of the country, to transport the tens of thousands of brigadistas to the countryside, and to distribute massive amounts of equipment and teaching materials.

The long months of battle had destroyed industry so that supplying even the basic material necessities of the Crusade required herculean efforts. Machinery had to be imported, factories reorganized, cottage industries developed, and materials ordered from foreign markets to provide the necessary uniforms, lanterns, mosquito nets, boots, raincoats, malaria pills, water purification tablets, and study materials. Agricultural production had been interrupted, and scarcity in rural communities was commonplace. Basic foodstuffs first needed to be imported and then distributed to supply the brigadistas.

Because decades of repression had prevented the development of community groups and labor associations, the campaign had to depend on organizations that were still in their infancy for the crucial tasks of mobilizing and supporting the Crusade's volunteer personnel. Long years of neglect had deprived the poor of adequate health care and resulted in high levels of parasitic and skin infections, malaria, and malnutrition. Conditions in rural areas were especially

where possible and each squadron contained 30 brigadistas and one to three education advisors.

severe. Medical supplies and basic health information would have to be provided to the brigadistas. To mount a campaign of such magnitude, a network of offices needed to be established. Since the number of trained and experienced administrators was limited, the Crusade would have to become a learning laboratory for educational managers.

Once launched, the Crusade confronted another series of problems. The rainy season begain in May and continued throughout the duration of the campaign. As a result, many volunteers were isolated, and transportation and communication throughout the country were seriously impaired. Somoza sympathizers and former guardsmen created grave problems and tried to spread fear among the brigadistas and their families in an attempt to paralyze the Crusade. In certain regions, literacy teachers and personnel were threatened and harassed; nine were assassinated.

In the face of such complex difficulties, our inexperience weighed heavily on us. Out of the initial staff of seven, only two had worked in literacy programs, and none had ever been involved in a project of such magnitude. Our strategy for overcoming the team's lack of experience evolved over time. Basically it included study, long hours, hard work, collective problem solving, and hiring experts in adult education.

We spent the first month studying — reading about the experiences of other countries, discussing the small church-sponsored literacy projects that had been attempted in Nicaragua, talking with experts, writing position papers, and outlining a possible primer. We also had to spend time searching for desks and chairs. The Ministry offices had been left empty, and there were times when the team had to take turns using desks and either share chairs or sit on the floor.

To complete our national team, we hired selected experts in education from Argentina, Colombia, Costa Rica, Mexico, Honduras, Puerto Rico, and the United States. During the campaign they were joined by four Cuban specialists who had participated in the 1961 Cuban literacy campaign. As one of their first assignments, they were given a truck to pick up student desks from the university so that they would have a place to sit.

We also requested further technical assitance from a variety of organizations and institutions — UNESCO, the Organization of American States, the World Council of Churches, CELADEC (a Latin American Ecumenical group working in popular peasant education), CREFAL (Regional Center on Adult Education and Functional Literacy for Latin America), and Cuba's Ministry of Education. Cuban teachers who worked in Nicaragua's primary schools participated in the Crusade after classes. Spain, Costa Rica, and the Dominican Republic sent delegations of teachers to partici-

pate in the campaign. During the course of the program, additional international experts joined, including people from Canada, Chile, El Salvador, Peru, Spain, and Uruguay. More advisors also came from Colombia, Mexico, and the United States[6].

At the end of September the core team of seven visited Cuba for a week. We interviewed the former director of the 1961 Cuban Literacy Campaign and spent four valuable days delving into the archives of their Literacy Museum. During October 1979 we organized an intensive one-week planning seminar with a team of experts from Mexico, Colombia, and the United States. After a careful clarification and analysis of the Crusade's proposed plan, we developed some general operational guidelines and began to define program structures and tasks.

As the work intensified, the core team met daily to identify and study specific problems as they emerged, and to seek effective responses. The staff labored 14 to 15 hours a day, seven days week. This combination of commitment, intensive study, group problem solving, and the elaboration of easy-to-follow operational procedures enabled us to overcome many of our initial shortcomings. Before any program could be launched, however, we had to face the legacy of debt, destruction, and corruption left by the dictatorship. Serious problems of financing, health, food, transportation, and communication demanded immediate solutions.

FINANCING THE CRUSADE

The crusade had to be financed from sources outside the government. We called in two specialists from the Ministry of Planning. After providing them with program details such as the Crusade's proposed scope, duration, and personnel and material needs, they developed a tentative budget calling for approximately $20 million (200 million *cordobas*).

We immediately set up a finance office. Requests for assistance were mailed to governments, institutions, and solidarity groups around the world. Official delegations were sent to the United States and to Europe. In Nicaragua, the Crusade established a program of Patriotic Literacy Bonds and encouraged community fund-raising efforts. Employees from all sectors, public and private, tithed one day's salary each month to the campaign. Marketwomen from Managua and peasants from distant mountain villages came to the national office in order to make their contributions personally. For example, three representatives of the Revolutionary Sports Committee of Chontales, two peasants and one young student, contributed 1,000 cordobas collected from community raffles. Enthusiastic high school students filled the city streets carrying tin cans. Following some of the same tactics used in the insurrection, they set up road blocks — to collect "pennies for pencils" — and called on radio stations to read official declarations of war against ignorance and to make appeals for financial help. Dances, song fests,

6. In all, the Crusade's National Office employed the services of the following international experts: 2 Argentinians, 1 Canadian, 1 Chilean, 5 Colombians, 1 Costa Rican, 4 Cubans, 2 Salvadorians, 1 Honduran, 2 Mexicans, 1 Peruvian, 1 Puerto Rican, 4 Spaniards.

concerts, and poetry readings all added to the fund-raising effort.

Including cash and materials, some 120 million cordobas were raised. Since the program had been carefully streamlined by cutting out all excess expenses, these funds covered the costs. Catholic and Protestant organizations were the first to contribute. The countries most generous in their donations were the Federal Republic of Germany, Switzerland, Sweden, Holland, and England, although people contributed from all over the world. In this way, they too formed part of the Crusade and shared in its achievements.

HEALTH PROBLEMS

For decades, life in the countryside had meant poor health and early death. Malnutrition, malaria, measles, gastroenteritis, and mountain leprosy — a widespread skin infection that causes large scabs and scars — were common and sometimes deadly. To protect the brigadistas, inoculations were given, as well as basic health training which included malaria diagnosis and control. Each teaching squadron was provided with a first-aid kit with supplies sufficient for the duration of the Crusade.

Health problems, however, were more extensive and complicated than anticipated. Many older people attending literacy classes suffered from poor eyesight and therefore had difficulty reading. While eyeglasses had been ordered, their delivery was delayed, causing some people to withdraw, at least temporarily, from the campaign. Other program participants suffered from debilitating illnesses, making attendance sporadic. Volunteers suffered similar ailments. In some cases, disease prevented people from enrolling in the Crusade.

The first-aid supplies which had been carefully calculated to last five months usually ran out within two weeks. When confronted with the extent of illness and disease in the countryside, the brigadistas placed their first-aid kits at the service of the community. Medicine was immediately shared with their adopted peasant families. As a result, new supplies had to be ordered and special medical brigades formed. After a brief intensive training program, some 700 university medical students were placed throughout the country to serve as mobile health teams. Besides providing basic medical attention to volunteers, they also prepared them to give community classes in elementary health eduction. In addition, the brigades gathered vital information on national disease patterns and health conditions to be used in future health programming.

Food was also a problem. Without the timely organization of an emergency distribution system, food shortages would also have affected the brigdistas' health. Through the Institute of Basic Grain Distribution (ENABAS) volunteers were provided with double rations of basic foodstuffs both to feed themselves and to assist their host families. Weekend visits by parents and care packages from home helped improve the community diet.

TRANSPORTATION AND COMMUNICATION

Nicaragua's poor transportation system hampered many aspects of the Crusade. Mobilization operations, supply distribution, and communication were all affected. For the March mobilization, brigadistas were dispersed gradually, their departures staggered over a four-day period. To accomplish the massive operation, the Crusade worked in co-ordination with the Ministry of Transportation and the Farmworkers' Association. They located, employed, and co-ordinated every available means of transportation — buses, boats, ferries, trains, dump trucks, jeeps, ox carts, horses, mules, donkeys, canoes, rafts, and, finally, feet. Some volunteers had to walk for two or three days to reach their assigned communities. During the campaign, helicopters were used for emergency medical rescues. Vehicles from every ministry and government institution were pressed into service for the distribution of supplies. Food, boots, uniforms, notebooks, pencils, pens, primers, medicine, lanterns, hammocks, and mosquito nets had to be delivered to all 144 municipalities. As winter approached, an emergency plan was instituted to accelerate the distribution process in order to provide sufficient supplies to those areas which would be isolated by the rains.

At the conclusion of the Crusade, the poor network of roads and almost total lack of bridges exacerbated the problems of demobilization. By August, the winter rains had made many roads and rivers impassable. The lovely streams that the brigadistas had crossed on foot in the dry season had become swollen torrents, and the dirt roads had turned into muddy swamps. What had been a two- or three-day walk in March became a five- or six-day journey.

A carefully orchestrated eight-day demobilization program was put into action. At each point along the way, community organizations provided accommodations and hospitality for the footsore brigadistas. From the farthest sites, the young volunteers walked to area transportation points. From municipal centers, they were transported to department capitals, and then finally to Managua for the August 23rd celebration. Although there were many blistered feet, everyone arrived home safely.

Communication, while always a problem, was greatly improved through a network of 48 shortwave radios. Department offices and selected remote municipalities were given radio equipment and their personnel provided with training. A rotating team of volunteers staffed the central office 24 hours a day from March 10 to August 22. Besides maintaining communication in technical and administrative matters, the network served as a lifeline in case of medical emergencies.

THE ESTABLISHMENT OF RECORDS

Since government statistics were outdated and notoriously inaccurate, one of the first campaign tasks was conducting a census to establish actual levels of literacy and to ascertain the availability of volunteer teachers. With expert assistance, the census was planned and executed. Teams of volunteer census takers were trained and sent out into the field, and the results tabulated by citizens and labor organizations. Since this was our first experience in mass mobilization, the effort was not without its problems. Because the volunteer response in Managua was much greater than anticipated, not enough public vehicles had been secured for the operation. It was Sunday and all offices were closed. Not wanting to dismiss needed recruits, the Crusade's administrative co-ordinator borrowed money from his mother to rent private transport. No one was turned away. In all, the volunteers surveyed 1,434,738 people. Since the census tabulation would have absorbed all the nation's computer capacity for two weeks, a group of 2,500 volunteers received special training, and the tabulations were completed in ten days. The results indicated that 722,431 Nicaraguans were illiterate.

In addition, the census gave us a more complete picture of the country's illiteracy levels and their geographic distribution. As the Crusade progressed, however, it became clear that people's notions of illiteracy varied. Some who classified themselves as totally illiterate could recognize the alphabet and read simple words, but could not write. Exact skills were not known until brigadistas give program applicants a qualifying test. This brief exam was the first in a series of three given during the campaign. The initial test was designed to determine the actual skill level of each participant, beginning with a simple exercise — drawing a straight line. This step was included so that those unable to continue beyond the first question would have some sense of accomplishment and understand that they too possessed the potential to master the alphabet. The next level of skill tested was the ability to write one's name, followed by reading and writing exercises — single words first, then short sentences. The test concluded with a comprehension exercise. People who completed all sections successfully were considered literate, and those who could read and write a few words were classified as semiliterates. Illiterates included people who could not read or write more than their own name.

An intermediate test was given to assess learner progress and diagnose individual study needs. The ability to read and write different syllabic families was determined so that specialized review could be oriented toward practicing those that had not yet been fully mastered. The final exam was administered by the literacy volunteer under the guidance of a technical advisor. It consisted of five parts which tested reading, writing, and comprehension skills. To be considered literate, participants had to write their name, read

Photograph by Ramon Zamora Olivas (Reprinted from C. Alemán Ocampo, *Y también enséñenles a leer*, Managua: Editorial Nueva Nicaragua, 1984).

aloud a short text, answer three questions based on the reading, write a sentence dictated to them, and write a short composition. They were expected to be able to read with comprehension, pronouncing words as a whole and not as a series of isolated syllables. They were to write legibly, leaving appropriate spaces between words, and to spell phonetically. With such skills, participants were prepared within their vocabulary range to read newspapers, application forms, technical information pamphlets, and books.

Records kept on each student included such general information as name, age, sex, date of enrollment, residence, occupation, and past school attendance. A monthly progress chart indicated the lessons and exercises completed in both the primer and math workbook, as well as the total number of sessions attended. Test results for each of the three exams were recorded, as were observations about individual learning difficulties, health problems, and areas of personal interest for future study.

These reports reveal the history and progress of the Crusade. They also indicate the poor conditions under which the majority of Nicaraguans have lived and the tragic human costs of underdevelopment. According to the 1979 census, Nicaragua had an overall illiteracy rate of 50 per cent, 30 per cent in urban areas and 75 per cent in the countryside. Children between 10 and

14 years of age accounted for 21 per cent of the illiterate population. In the course of the campaign we discovered other dimensions of the illiteracy problem. As much as we did not want to accept the fact, some people simply did not have the capacity to master reading and writing skills in the campaign. Reports from volunteers and technical advisers indicated widespread learning difficulties and cases of disability. Poor health was the principal cause. Extensive malnutrition handicaps many Nicaraguans, impairing sight and hearing, limiting memory, and often causing early senility. Health statistics indicate that 25 per cent of all newborns fall into the high-risk category. Many do not reach five years of age, and those who do suffer serious mental and physical disorders. About 9 per cent of the population had severe learning disabilities that prevented them from studying.

Despite debilitating health problems and extreme hardships, 406,056 Nicaraguans leaned basic reading and writing skills — an achievement that testifies to the creative power and determination of students and teachers alike. But initial statistics revealed that Nicaragua still had an illiteracy rate of 13 per cent to overcome (6 per cent urban and 21 per cent rural). We believe, however, that by 1981 the rate will decrease as a result of the Crusade's follow-up program and the campaigns in English, Miskito, and Sumo.

STRUCTURAL ORGANIZATION: FROM MOUNTAINTOPS TO MANAGUA

The success of the Crusade's administrative and support structure depended primarily on the participation of the citizen and labor associations. Though we did not know the kind of structure that would facilitate their involvement or exactly how to organize it, we learned much from the process. Since the campaign was an intensive, short-run nationwide project, it required setting up a massive organizational network that could effectively reach from isolated mountaintops down to the neighborhoods of Managua.

7. The Technical/Pedagogical Division had four sections — Curriculum, Research, Training, and Library/ Museum — and was designed to provide the educational expertise for the program. The Technical/Organizational Division essentially served as a support–control structure for the literacy promoters and as a liaison to the different sponsoring organizations. It had four sections: Statistics and Census; the Popular Literacy Army (EPA) and the Urban Literacy Guerrillas (GUAS); the Mass Citizen and Labor Organizations; and the Internal Technical Secretariat. The Administrative Division was separated into two departments: Logistical Support, which was made up of Supplies, Health, Food Distribution, Transportation, Communication and Maintenance, and Plant Maintainance; and the Department of Administration, which contained Control, Accounting, Personnel, and Budget. The departments and municipalities were each structured along lines similar to the national — Technical/Pedagogical, Statistics and Census, Logistical Support, and Publicity.

With that in mind, we tried to develop a system that would be flexible and responsive at the local level and yet maintain a clear central direction and control. A single national co-ordinating structure took on the general management functions. Operational responsibilities were decentralized through a regional institutional network. In the field, the teachers' organization, ANDEN, and the Sandinista Young People's Association carried out organizational and implementation functions. Citizen groups, labor federations, and public institutions participated and supported the work at all levels. Two national congresses were held which brought together participants and staff to discuss program needs, problems, and solutions. Conferences began at the community level, proceeded to the municipal, on to the departmental, and finally to the national. In all, over 100,000 people participated.

To co-ordinate the campaign structures, the Crusade functioned in consultation with a National Literacy Commission. Presided over by the Minister of Education, Carlos Tunnerman, the National Literacy Commission, composed of delegates from 25 public and private institutions, workers' associations, and citizens' groups, assisted with resource mobilization and co-ordination. Parallel commissions were established on both the departmental and municipal levels with representatives from the same institutions and organizations as the national structure. Subcommissions were formed at the comarca and neighborhood levels.

The Literacy Crusade was organized as part of the Ministry of Education and therefore could draw upon any of the Ministry's technical or administrative support services. The campaign itself, however, was co-ordinated and managed by a single executive structure, the National Co-ordinating Board, headed by a National Co-ordinator and consisting of six divisions: Technical/Pedagogical; Production and Design; Technical/Organizational; Public Relations; Financial Promotion; and Administrative. A special subdivision was also established to design and implement the bilingual program[7].

This administrative and organizational network was complemented by the actual operational structure in the field. The field network was directed by a variety of organizations and co-ordinated by the Crusade. For the rural work, the Sandinista Young People's Association was responsible for the organization, enthusiasm, and discipline of the teaching brigades. Made up of high school and college students, this group, known as the Popular Literacy Army (EPA), formed the bulk of the rural education corps. The Farmworkers Association (ATC) organized a small but effective teaching unit called the Peasants Literacy Militia (MAC) which worked alongside the EPA.

The Nicaraguan Educators Association (ANDEN) was in charge of the teachers who served as the technical support staff for the brigades and militia. Each squadron of about 30 volunteers was assisted by three professional teachers. ANDEN was also responsible for two of the Crusade's auxiliary activities, the Retaguardia, a summer daycare program for primary school children, and the Quincho Barrilete project, a literacy and basic education program for child street vendors. Cultural brigades for some 450 students were organized by the University and the Ministry of Culture to collect oral histories, promote popular culture, and conduct different types of research studies. In the cities, the volunteers were organized into two main forces: the Urban Literacy Guerrillas, coordinated directly by the Crusade and made up of housewives, working students, professionals, and private citizens; and the Workers' Literacy Militia (MOA), co-ordinated by the Sandinista Worker Federation and composed of factory workers, office personnel, market vendors, and government employees.

PEDAGOGY IN PRACTICE: REVOLUTION AND EDUCATION

In designing the materials and methodologies for the Crusade, the liberation struggle served as inspiration and teacher. Its lessons were many, some pedagogical and some philosophical. Educational experiences carried out over the long years of fighting and community organizing had demonstrated the validity of a variety of teaching approaches and learning principles. Small study groups had met throughout the struggle to analyze, plan, and carry out war-related tasks; clandestine literacy efforts had been conducted as well. Learning in this context had been based on action and reflection. Lessons had a direct, urgent, and immediate application to reality. These experiences had combined such methods and techniques as experiential learning, dialogue, group discussions, and collective problem solving. They also revealed the tremendous creativity and capacity for learning that existed within people regardless of their educational background.

These experiences were enriched by the ideas and practice of Paulo Freire and others. At the beginning of the campaign, Freire had challenged us to create the best learning program we could. He stressed the importance of providing opportunities for learners to practice their creativity and added that within a liberating revolutionary process people would learn to read and write even with mediocre materials. The revolutionary context and methodology were more important than any isolated study program or particular teaching techniques. Literacy, he said, could only "have a genuine meaning in a country which is going through a revolutionary process"[8]. With his challenge in mind, we faced two technical questions: how to design literacy materials for use by volunteer teachers and how to translate young people's enthusiasm and

commitment into a minimum set of pedagogical skills.

The Crusade's education team attempted to address these questions first by studying Nicaragua's experience in clandestine literacy teaching and then by analyzing other countries' programs in light of local needs. Cuba's literacy campaign was examined closely, as was that of Peru and those of the African nations of São Tomé and Guinea-Bissau, both of which had been greatly inspired by Freire. His thinking along with many other lines of Latin American thought and experience influenced the campaign, but the most important elements of the program emerged from the reality and needs of Nicaragua and the creativity of the Crusade's national education team. In all, five intense months were spent in developing and pilot-testing materials and methods. The resultant education program was a product of their collective effort. It was founded on dialogue and on a standardized national literacy primer.

We believed, as did Freire, that dialogue is critical to a liberating education and that, combined with a phonetics approach to teaching literacy, it surpasses any other method. Since we were engaged in carrying out a national literacy campaign in the context of profound social transformation, we focused on themes that were concerns of the society at large rather than on narrow issues of interest only to individual communities. Because it offered participants the power of the word and of history, the dialogue was highly political. By expressing their own opinions about their lives, their culture, their past and future, people would begin to develop and strengthen their creativity and analytical abilities as well as to see themselves as makers of culture and history. As Carlos Carrión, the FSLN representative to the Crusade, expressed it:

The literacy methodology is intrinsically political. How? It's not just that we speak of Sandino or of Carlos Fonseca, or of the Frente Sandinista. The most political, the most revolutionary aspect of this literacy approach is the fact that we are providing scientific knowledge and analytical skills to our brothers and sisters in the fields and factories who do not know how to read or write — the skills to reason, think, compare, discern and the ability to form their own human and political criteria, their own critical framework[9].

To help volunteers promote the process of dialogue we provided them with concrete, step-by-step guidelines. The five-step process contained a series of suggested questions designed to help participants develop both analytical skills and a profound sense of social responsibility. The questions proceeded from simple to difficult and encouraged the students to describe the contents of a photograph; analyze the situation portrayed; relate the particular situation to the life of the learner, to the community, and to the problems facing them; solve problems around issues identified by the group; and engage participants in transforming reality, committing themselves to solving the problem, and becoming active in the national programs of social change. During the course of the

8. Paulo Freire in conversation with Fernando Cardenal, Nicaragua, October–November 1979.
9. Carlos Carrión, speech before First Congress of the National Literacy Crusade, 17 June 1980.

Crusade, however, we came to realize the obvious — that dialogue occured both during the literacy teaching process itself as well as in the daily living experience, and that the latter was perhaps the richer and more profound exchange. We discovered that photographs needed to be chosen with great care to stimulate a critical discussion. The team had been limited not only by a certain inexperience but also by a lack of photographs from which to choose. After experimenting with line drawings, they discoverd that photographs, despite the limited selection, were far more effective in stimulating dynamic discussion.

After 20 minutes or so of dialogue, the direct study of reading and writing skills began — first with a sentence, then a word, and finally a syllabic family. We expanded Freire's single-word approach by using a short phrase or sentence based on the photograph's theme as the starting point for literacy practice. The team felt that a sentence provided a smoother transition from complex discussion to the concrete study of syllables. Because sentences encompassed a whole thought, they were considered more appropriate for adult learning as well as more flexible in generating the study of syllabic families. After reading the sentence, a key word from each phrase was chosen and divided into syllables, from which one family of syllables was selected and studied. For example, in the second lesson the name Fonseca was divided, Fon-*se*-ca, initiating a study of the syllabic family, sa, se, si, so, and su. Writing exercises were introduced and recognition exercises were used to help the participants identify the syllables as phonetic units. As learners mastered the individual syllables, they went on to use them to build new words, thus practising their creativity and skills in manipulating the written language.

The specific teaching materials we used consisted of the elementary literacy primer, *Dawn of the People*, a teacher's manual, the *Teachers' Guide for Literacy Volunteers*, and an arithmetic workbook, *Math and Economic Reconstruction: One Single Operation*. During the Crusade, teaching games stressing learner creativity, such as a type of syllabic Scrabble, were developed and distributed. In addition, during the entire year of 1980, the national match factory produced all matches in special boxes decorated with the alphabet to be used as letter building blocks.

The primer was divided into 23 lessons, each accompanied by photographs and practice exercises, and was organized into three major areas: the history and development of the Revolution; the socio-economic programs of the Government of National Reconstruction; and civil defense and community participation. Some of the specific lesson themes were "Sandino, guiding force of the Revolution"; "Work is the right and duty of every citizen"; "Spend little, save resources, and produce a lot — that is Revolution";

"The FSLN led the people to Liberation"; "With organization, work, and discipline we will be able to build the nation of Sandino".

The teacher's manual provided step-by-step instructions on the use of the literacy methodology and also contained detailed back-up reading for each of the 23 themes. It gave the brigadistas the necessary social, political, and economic information to generate a knowledgeable discussion and dialogue. Since the Crusade was considered a reciprocal learning process, the handbook also outlined a systematic set of study activities for the volunteers. The basis of their learning was their own living and teaching experience. As such, they were responsible for conducting a careful research study of their communities and keeping a field diary of their activities.

A PEDAGOGY OF
SHARED RESPONSIBILITY

To prepare the immense teacher corps to use the program's materials and methods, a national training program of short, intensive workshops was conducted. The first training materials explained to the brigadistas their revolutionary educational role as literacy promoters:

You will be a catalyst of the teaching–learning process. Your literacy students will be people who think, create, and express their ideas. Together, you will form a team of mutual learning and human development. . . . The literacy process is an act of creation in which people offer each other their thoughts, words, and deeds. It is a cultural action of transformation and growth[10].

Training, therefore, required that all participants take on new educational roles in what we called a pedagogy of shared responsibility. The traditional model of the active, all-wise professor and passive, ignorant pupil was specifically rejected and replaced by one in which the traditional teacher became a type of learning co-ordinator. The role of the workshop director was one of facilitator, a role that involved motivating, inspiring, challenging, and working with the participants who were encouraged to become active problem solvers. Participants were the foundation and wellspring of the process. Their responsibilities were to explore, research, and create. Small-group study, team teaching, and problem solving affirmed this new relationship. Under the co-ordination of two facilitators, workshop members were given a variety of educational tasks to accomplish. During the training, they reflected upon the group process and their progress, integrating both theory and practice.

Our primary purpose in training was to have people master the materials and methods while developing skills necessary to solve social problems creatively and sensitively. Methods were chosen to enhance the initiative and imagination with which people acquire and apply knowledge. The specific techniques used were simulations, role playing, group discussions,

10. Cruzada Nacional de Alfabetización, *Cuaderno de Orientaciones*, Managua: Ministry of Education, 1979, p. 1.

debates, murals, poetry, drawing, songs, and some artistic forms of expression from Nicaraguan folklore. Each workshop began with an introductory presentation exercise to acquaint participants with each other and to establish a congenial, dynamic learning environment. The participants were initially divided into working teams of about six people each, which formed the principal base of learning for the entire workshop. The small group chose the name of a fallen combatant for their symbol and wrote up his or her biography, hanging it on the wall for others to read. In their teams, participants then discussed the meaning of the Crusade and why they had decided to become volunteers, listing their responses on large sheets of paper and tacking them on the wall for presentation to the group. To conclude the first exercise, they were asked to create some two-line, rhyme-slogans which summarized their discussion. This technique had its roots in Nicaraguan traditional culture, where couplets are a popular literary expression, and in the war. During the long years of struggle, short chants which synthesized and captured the spirit of popular demands and aspirations had been used to animate demonstrations and harass the National Guard.

During the workshop, the rhymes took on a life of their own. Groups used their spare time trying to create new and more imaginative ones. They would practice them together in a corner and in a moment of relative silence between activities shout out their creation with great pride and enthusiasm. They then prepared a carefully written copy of their work so others could join them in shouting their couplet. The effort generated a spirit of lively rivalry and boosted energies when long hours of work became heavy and fatiguing. It also served as a positive means to gauge involvement and comprehension levels. If for example a group didn't understand an exercise or a reading, invariably a humorous couplet indicating their confusion and frustration would surface. At the end of the workshop the walls told the story of training. They were covered by summaries of group discussion and popular poetry.

To implement the training program, a decentralized four-stage model was designed. The program's success depended on its multiplier effect: beginning with seven national trainers, it was expected that in less than four months almost 100,000 people would be prepared. From December to March, workshops were held across the country. The driving force behind the training was the "group of eighty". Forty university students and 40 teachers were specially selected for an intensive two-week preparation program and a one-month field experience. From their ranks, 40 were chosen to train approximately 600 students and teachers in the next phase. During late February these 600 people prepared more than 12,000 people, most of whom were teachers. They, in turn, conducted the eight-day intensive workshops for thousands of literacy volunteers. Once the Crusade began, permanent training workshops were given for those people who still wished to enter the program. A radio show broadcast twice daily, together with special Saturday seminars conducted by squadron technical advisors, provided a continuing in-service training for the volunteers.

THE CONTINUING CHALLENGE

We are presently involved in designing and establishing a permanent system of adult education. In October 1980 three new Crusades began — in English, Miskito, and Sumo — for Nicaraguans who do not speak Spanish as their native language; and in 1981 we are hoping to launch a Health Crusade along the same lines as the literacy campaign. So much needs to be done. The hundreds of thousands of Nicaraguans who mastered basic reading and writing skills have just begun their studies. Their skills are still fragile.

The Literacy Crusade is only a first step in a long process of education and social creation. For the moment, we are in a transition that began in the final month of the Crusade — a time for people to practice and strengthen their literacy and math skills. The transition program arose from a natural phenomenon occurring in the literacy groups. As the most advanced students finished the primer, they began to concentrate on helping fellow students in mastering skills. When the campaign terminated, outstanding literacy graduates or educated members of the community were chosen to continue the work of the learning group. After being given some basic training by the Crusade's teaching supervisors, the new educational co-ordinators were provided with a carefully designed teacher's guide and a set of follow-up reading materials that stressed collective study and action as the fundamental basis for community learning. These community learning groups are supported by the network of mass citizen and labor organizations. The work of the co-ordinators is bolstered by specially selected traveling 'promotors' who serve as liaisons to the regional adult education offices and provide the community groups with encouragement, orientation, and extra learning materials when available. Rounding out the transition program is a radio show for the study groups, broadcast twice daily on all national channels.

The challenge for the future is awesome. Expectations are great, problems complex, and resources scarce. In the face of new tasks, the example and lessons of the campaign provide the inspiration and hope for tomorrow. As one young literacy volunteer expressed in August, "The Crusade is like the source of a river of popular knowledge which will flow onward forever."

LIFE AS A BRIGADISTA

Before we conclude, there is one more aspect of the

Crusade that needs to be presented — the experience of bring a brigadista. Life as a volunteer in the countryside was hard work. Tasks filled the day. Mornings were spent laboring alongside peasant *compañeros*; late afternoons and evenings were dedicated to leading study sessions in homes, patios, or front yards. The experience can best be described by those who were there. We have gathered some quotes which convey how the brigadistas lived and worked and how the campaign touched their lives. No one can explain it better.

"Dear All,

I arrived here on this mountain top yesterday on the back of a mule. . . . We left Saturday from Manuaga at 3 a.m. in a caravan of 70 buses and dump trucks, about 1,500 university students in all, complete with a gasoline truck and an army escort to protect us during the 20 hour journey. We spent most of the time singing, shouting cheers, and waving. It was incredible, really! Even though it was nightime in every village and town along the way, people left their homes to wave at us. Of course, they knew we were members of EPA. Women would offer us oranges and bananas and shout up at us, 'Take care! See you when you return. We love you!' They would throw us kisses too. One old man, he must have been at least 70, ran beside the bus smiling up at us shouting EPA, EPA, EPA. I didn't know whether I was crying from the dust, the cold, or the wind, or the emotion I felt at seeing what a revolution can really mean. . . ."

Many Hugs, Gabriella

"I am really impressed how some of these kids came prepared and equipped. One of the boys looks like he is ready to fight the crocodile that always shows up in the jungle movies wanting to eat Tarzan. Another one has all the trappings of a walking Boy Scout Store. It's a sure sign of how ignorant most of us are about how people live in the countryside.

The hardest part for the volunteers is the loneliness and isolation, finding themselves suddenly living among strangers with whom, at least up till now, they have little in common. The feeling is one of anguish and insecurity. Thank God because of their political spirit and Christian faith, none of my brigadistas have deserted. Everyday they seem to adjust and find themselves enjoying life here more.

I can understand the horror of some of the parents from the capital when they come to visit their children and find them living in peasant "homes". What I don't understand is why they are so horrified that their kids will have to spend 5 months in these conditions and not that 70 per cent of the Nicaraguan people have to suffer this misery their entire lives."

Educational Advisor
Los Santos

"To my literacy teacher and companero: Guillermo Briones Cisnero

My friends, Nicaragua is free.
The oppression of Somoza is defeated
For with the rumbling of bullets,
    Anastasio and son ran far away.
And now with the shouting of ABCs,
    Ignorance flees and joins them in Paraguay.
These verses I do recite
    in honor of Guillermo, my friend and companero
because I respect him like no other
    and love him like an older brother."

Anselmo Hurtado Lopez

"Dear Mom and Dad,

I am fine. I arrived safe and sound but please send me 20 cans of grape juice. The well is filled with mud and the river is far away. . . ."

Love, your son

"Dear Folks,

I'm learning a lot. I now know how to milk a cow and plant vegetables. The other day I was with Don Demesio roping a steer but I'm so stupid that I frightened the thing and we had to work twice as hard to catch it again. . . . The rains are constant. The soles of my boots came unglued and I had to sew them with a needle they use to make sacks with."

Love, David

"It's difficult sometimes. Tomasita is smart and wants to study but her baby cries a lot and she can't put him down. I visit her three times a day just on the chance she'll be free but . . . she's only on lesson 4. . . . Camilo doesn't seem to assimilate his sounds very well. Of course he does need glasses. He's 67. . . . Socorro and Joaquina are way ahead on lesson 14 but Julio left to pick coffee and Catalina's in bed with malaria. . . . Vicente has improved incredibly since he fell off his mule. He was really a lazy bum before. But now, with his broken arm, he's quite serious and dedicated, even though he's had to learn to write all over again with his left hand."

Guadalupe from the Brigade Enoc Ortez
in a report to her teaching supervisor

"Eight ex-national guardsmen crossed the border from Honduras yesterday and murdered the literacy teacher Georgino Andrade."

Newsbroadcast, Managua
19 May 1980

"The struggle is long and sometimes cruel. What's needed above all, my dear friend, is love and commitment. Remember, 'the freedom of a people is not won with flowers'. We are young and we are called upon to build the new, to create what our heroes and martyrs would have wanted. Put yourself in the place of Georgino Andrade. You wouldn't like it, if out of fear, the cause you gave your life for wasn't continued."

Letter to boyfriend Brigadista
from girlfriend Brigadista

"The Literacy Crusade taught us two things. One, what our own children are capable of doing and of becoming. Two, what our country is like and how gentle and how poor our people are in the countryside."

Mother of three literacy volunteers

"We take our malaria medicine twice a week and we're supposed to use our water purifying tablets. . . . The sicknesses among the children are many. Eight children in the next valley died last month of measles, three from the same family. It's unbelievable the inhuman conditions these people live under. I feel indignation and rage at not being a doctor."

Brigadista
Atlantic Coast

"The Crusade has been carried out by the kids of Nicaragua, the wonderful kids who under the leadership of the *Frente* fought the tyrant — intelligent kids, sacrificing, determined — idealists and realists all at the same time. For me the principal lesson of the campaign is that now Nicaragua knows that it can count on this treasure for its future. Not all the best children died in the war. With the living, we can carry out the other necessary wars to be fought, the war against social injustice, the war against poor health, the war against disease.

The Crusade is over. The People of Nicaragua and the commitment of the *Frente* made it possible. Thanks to their efforts Nicaragua will be totally different in the future. It will be a better nation, a nation that all Nicaraguans deserve. If that's not a triumph, excuse me, but then what the hell do you call a triumph?"

Priest,
Squadron Teaching Supervisor

REFLECTIONS

Thinking back over the last year, the most important lesson we learned will probably be the most difficult for educational planners to apply. In the final analysis, the success of the campaign depended not on scientifically tested educational theories, or complex planning systems, or even sophisticated curriculum design. The ultimate success of the Literacy Crusade depended on a commitment of the spirit — a commitment of a people and a government born of a liberation struggle. Only that kind of creative force could generate and maintain the levels of sacrifice and dedication required to accomplish such a task.

For when all is said and done, the crusade is not a story of complicated techniques or complex cost-benefit analysis. It is a story of people and the extraordinary potential for liberation and creation that exists within nations. It is about thousands of problems, big and small. But most of all it is a story about the creative intelligence of people and the courageous sacrifice of thousands of Nicaraguans who gave their lives so that intelligence and creativity could flourish. It is a beginning.

Its promise can probably best be described by the words of a peasant speaking to the mother of his young literacy teacher: "Do you know I am not ignorant any more. I know how to read now. Not perfectly, you understand, but I know how. And do you know, your son isn't ignorant any more either. Now he knows how we live, what we eat, how we work and he knows the life of the mountains. Your son, ma'am, has learned to read from our book."

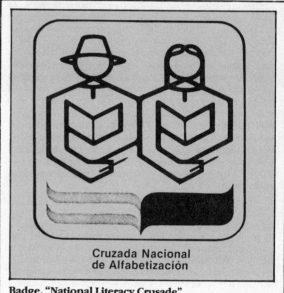

Cruzada Nacional
de Alfabetización

Badge, "National Literacy Crusade".

TOMÁS BORGE MARTINEZ
Participatory Communication

One thing we must do at this meeting is to break down a bit those inevitable barriers of solemnity which are produced by a space as small as this and tend to inhibit us all. I have noticed that some people are even embarrased to cough. This does not happen in large public spaces nor in places where we normally get together to dialogue with the people. Therefore, we will begin by trying to establish an authentic communication with you, and at the risk of stating the obvious, by pointing out that never before has such a small and dangerously select group — nothing less than the communication leaders of the country — has been brought together. I think I should add that I am not a specialist; I am not a communication theoretician. As a political leader I consider myself obligated to be a transmitter, as you would call it, and at the same time a receiver.

This has been an important seminar. Although I have been told that seminars have been held in other Latin American countries, I understand that this is the first to be held in Nicaragua. However, more important than this seminar has been the creation of the Centro de Estudios y Capacitación de Comunicación [CECCOM, the Communication Study and Training Center] which organized this seminar.

It should not surprise us, *compañeros*, that the study of communication has been so delayed in Nicaragua or even that it has taken us so many years to be able to think seriously about the problem of adequately adjusting our conceptual apparatus to our day-to-day communication practice. Both the changes in the Journalism School's curriculum and the efforts of the Nicaraguan Journalist's Union to better prepare their members have been equally important.

As someone here already said, in spite of the fact that we are virtually without the necessary means, i.e., that we are under-developed from a technical point of view, we have produced a creative journalism which has not broken it's wing and which has not become, at least generally, submissive, mechanical and boring.

We have established a certain type of communication using only the scarce communication media which we have in this country.

As *compañero* Castillo said the challenges in Nicaragua are threefold: one, to transform the mass distribution apparatuses into means of communication; two, the need to introduce new practices and to be as audacious here as we have been in other areas; and three, to irreversibly incorporate the people into the communication process.

There has been a great deal spoken here about the relationship between the transmitter and the receiver; this is not unrelated to the interests of the social class to which both belong. All humans are part of a specific social class; and this position determines each person's concrete interests. When the transmitted message persuades a receiver even though the nature of the message does not coincide with the social interests of that receiver, a phenomena is produced which we could call, to give it a name, an apocryphal or false consciousness.

If the principal transmission belt of the Nicaraguan bourgeois, the COSEP, repeatedly sends the message that it "represents the interests of all of society" and calls upon the working class to fight for "union freedom" and this convinces the working class listener and even recruits them into the political struggle, a contradiction is produced which is at the origin of false consciousness.

If a "revolutionary" sends the message that class reconciliation and the redemption of the oppressed are possible at the same time, they are lying. If some bourgeois believes the message, it does not matter; the problem arises if the workers also believe it.

In contrast, when the political message coincides

This text was first presented as the closing speech at the First Seminar on Participatory Radio held on 24 November 1984 at the Centro de Estudios y Capacitación en Comunicación, Universidad Centroamericana in Managua. Published by permission of the author. It was translated from the Spanish transcript by Janet Jamieson. English translation Copyright © International General 1986. This is its first publication.

with the interests of the receiver there is harmony and the contradiction disappears.

In political terms, in an advanced society the contradiction between ideology and everyday existence will basically disappear. But in a society in the process of transition such as ours, riddled by poverty and the rifles of the enemy, the analysis of the role of communication is limited and thus often we are forced to generalize. As far as I know, the analyses which have been done from the theoretical point of view have been very global and there has not yet been a serious sectorial analysis of our media.

I also understand that there is no theoretical synthesis of the history of communication media. Evolving from the most primitive communication forms to the most refined advances in electronics, the development of the means of production and of the productive forces called for the concurrent development of the communication media. We would even go so far as to say that human beings have developed to the extent that the means of communication have developed and vice-versa.

It has been fruitless for theoreticians to try to agree on which communication instrument has priority. However, what still seems to predominate — and, I repeat, I am not a theoretician — is the thesis that the school is the fundamental means of communication. Antonio Gramsci said this and during the same period it was repeated by José Carlos Mariátegui[1]. Later it was given impetus by Louis Althusser who gave the school priority followed by social organizations, religion, the print media, audiovisual media, and, almost at the end, radio.

This ranking, in my opinion — and it is almost a sacrilege to contradict Gramsci — has ceased to be valid in global terms. The audiovisual media in countries as developed as the United States have left all other forms of influence over human beings and their consciousness far behind, including the school. In the United States it is not in the school where this strange mixture is concocted, this rare quintessential ideology that has the North American people stupefied. Rather, it is through the audiovisual media.

However, in countries such as Nicaragua where the technical means are underdeveloped it is the school that is in first place. This applies not just to our country where a revolutionary situation exists but also to societies dominated by mediocre bourgeoisies, to the most backward countries of Latin America, and of course, to the most politically advanced societies or those in a transitional process towards a new society in the Third World. For this reason, in my opinion, the few means of communication which we have at our disposal in direct competition with the enemy's communication media, should be converted into an important complement to the school inasmuch as the

school is a disseminator of ideas that do not contradict but rather re-affirm the project of a more advanced society.

The last drop of sweat must be extracted from the media; they must be converted into a school; a complement to the school which transcends the school. This is why on other occasions we have emphasized the revolutionary need to further horizontal communication. The concrete experiences which have taken place in Nicaragua such as the radio and TV programs "The Face of the People", "Direct Line", "Context 6.20" and others must become the rule rather than the exception.

We are in a position to go beyond the level of artisan communication. These seminars and the School of Journalism have contributed a great deal. We have already acquired the right of possession and even property rights over the basic means of communication in this country. To avoid misunderstandings, I should point out that we should firmly challenge any manifestation of verticality and what you called unidirectionality, of authoritarianism and alienation, that is to say, a submission implied by an absence of constant valiant criticism. This means that we must take an unavoidable subversive position in the face of any manifestation of lying, corruption, deliquency, lack of critical analysis, bureaucracy and the ferocious ideologies which so frequently enter as wolves in lambs' clothing.

This ideological ferocity is powerful. Just as the armed counterrevolution has its nocturnal viewfinders and automatic grenade launchers, the more dangerous ideological counterrevolution — which is infinitely more dangerous than the armed counterrevolution — has its radar, computers, satellites, news agencies, radio transmitters installed on our borders, newspapers, television series, movies, and even a refined counter-insurgency manual. This manual teaches how to kill both the soul and the body which, without wishing to enter into poetic or religious considerations, is not exactly the same. A person ceases to have a soul when they give up critical thinking and will remain soulless as long as they are trapped by egotism and lies.

We must confront this enormous, overpowering communications apparatus, confront it with our own poor technical means; and we must win the battle. Of course, when an analysis of the relations of force is made, we must be honest; there is no comparison between the fire power from the North American army and the fire power from our forces in the military field. We are not going to defeat the armed forces of the United States; we are going to defeat interventionism, even though we have less fire power.

In the field of ideological struggle we have a greater advantage, historically speaking. When in the United States it is said that we constitute a threat "to the internal security" of this powerful country one can only assume that they are making a bad joke. Or when they say — and they have been emphasizing this

---

1. José Carlos Mariátegui, one of the first and most important Latin American Marxist theoreticians, died in 1930. He is the author of *Siete ensayos de interpretación de la realidad peruana*, Lima, 1928.

recently — that we constitute a threat to the neighboring countries and then speak of a mutual assistance pact between the United States and Honduras. This is a dangerous pact because it can be the first step in establishing a legal basis for intervention after a supposed aggression on our part against Honduras. As we have said many times to the North Americans, it is impossible for us to invade Honduras. We cannot; and besides, we do not want to. For reasons of principle, we are not going to resolve the social contradictions in Honduras by means of an invasion. The subjective and objective contradictions there are going to be resolved by means of the specific transformations that will take place in Honduras.

Independent of the fact that we respect the integrity and the sovereignty of other countries, we are not going to resolve the problems of Honduras artificially, nor are we going to make Honduras disappear as an instrument of imperialism through a military decision. From a practical point of view, we cannot invade Honduras because if we invaded Honduras, the next day the United States would intervene. We cannot give ourselves the luxury, even if we want to, of invading Honduras or Costa Rica.

They say that we are a danger. Using the most elementary analysis, common sense indicates that we are not a military danger. Therefore, why are they so afraid of us? Because in the field of ideological struggle, we are dangerous. The representatives of the North American Government and its ideological concepts say that democracy — in reference to the North American concept of democracy — is desired by all the people of Latin America and the world. They say that their concept of justice corresponds to the great expectations for equality in Latin America and the world, and that people reject what they call totalitarianism and exotic ideas.

If it is true that all the peoples of Latin America are hungry for democracy as conceived by the United States, where is the problem? What are they worried about? In reality, what worries them is ideological competition; and this is the field in which we are going to win. The little steps which are being taken, such as this seminar, constitute the laboratory where powerful arms are being invented, the simple, modest and effective arms with which we are going to beat the imperialist enemy in the ideological field.

Every process of communication is integrated in a concrete social formation. Is ours a central social formation or is it a peripheral social formation? We are accused of being a military, political and ideological appendage. We must declare bravely that we are no one's appendage. But does this mean that we are on the periphery of history and of the ideological concepts which derive from it? This is not the case either. Dependency is a socio-economic reality joined to an ideological concept which is very elegant in the hands of the empire and very comfortable in the hands of submissive bourgeoisies. A revolutionary ideological concept implies independence and national sovereignty. We are independent because we are revolutionaries and we are revolutionaries, among other things, because we are independent.

Each social class has identical class interests independent of the fact of whether this class is or is not in power. Therefore, its messages are consistent with its structure, especially with regards to content and often with regards to form. The propaganda of all bourgeois societies is the same; it is mercantilist, refined and relentless. The homogeneity of its messages is explained by their social origin.

In bourgeois societies there is political pluralism and ideological totalitarianism. Its political pluralism is the rainbow of a single ideological ensemble. Generally, revolutionary political and ideological expressions are marginal and insufficient, and the bourgeoisie tolerates them as long as they do not constitute a danger to their ability to dominate, a danger to their power structures. In a revolutionary society such as ours a similar but inverse phenomenon occurs. The revolution tolerates ideological pluralism insofar as it does not endanger political power.

Tolerance, in the case of Nicaragua, will not be resolved by means of police coercion but rather by means of ideological struggle and persuasion. That is to say, bourgeois ideological manifestations and their media will disappear in this country through starvation, by natural death. We are not going to decree their extinction. Rather, we are going to persuade and win this ideological struggle. We aspire to an all-inclusive revolutionary concept and not a totalitarian political concept. Pluralism and a mixed economy is a concession, an act of generosity and a political necessity at the same time.

Reality itself is not the same as an understanding of reality. Understanding reality is a process. As long as reality is not understood it will not be possible to transform it. Revolutionary ideological concepts are the only known lever which can raise society from a backward to a more advanced state. This means that the role of the transmitter in our society is to share the revolutionary ideological message by sending it to receivers who by virtue of their social condition are disposed to receive it. A message will be received when it is well elaborated and is not a decree, an imposition or an authoritarian act.

One must go the the masses to learn from the masses and to teach the masses. Only the humble learn, only the humble can teach, and only the humble can understand that one must be at the same time transmitter and receiver.

We must help our message transcend our borders by giving it credibility which is a problem specific to the means of communication as they have enormous power to distort the image of reality and convince an important sector of the population. For example, convince the people of the United States that Reagan represents their hopes for peace or that the invasion of Grenada was an act of heroism by the North American army. It is very difficult to locally fool a community.

Somoza could not fool anyone in spite of the fact that he controlled many communication media. But far from a community, it is easy to create a distorted image of it, different from reality.

At times we also are influenced by outside information about realities of which we lack knowdedge. I do not know what idea you have of Mengistu, the President of Ethiopia; perhaps none, very little or a distorted one. But I can assure you that the image that the world has of Kaddafi, for example, is very poor because our point of observation is so uninformed about the concrete reality. Through images such as those we see in films, the media can easily sell us an image of gray, opaque, sad societies. In contrast, when we go there in person we are often surprised to find a happy, shining city. This has often happened to us when we visit these countries. This means that we have to make an extraordinary effort not just within Nicaragua but outside as well. The role of the communicator transcends our national borders.

I understood that radio was to be the only subject discussed here, but it seems that other media have been discussed as well. I believe it is important to transfer your evaluations and the conclusions to all the other communication media, including the cinema. I think that CECCOM should plan some seminars about the appropriate role which the dissemination apparatus in a society in transition should play. In the course of practical experience, CECCOM should also formulate a temporary synthesis which can serve until we accumulate, by means of permanent practice, a superior synthesis and thus have the real conditions to express a communication theory based on concrete experience.

As is mentioned in the conclusions reached by this seminar, this revolution and its specificities require an analysis of the apparatuses which are opposed to the revolutionary project. There should be liberty; yet everyone knows that concepts of liberty depend on ideological concepts. We will never convince the directors of the newspaper *La Prensa* that they are the main enemies of freedom of the press in this country.

The major challenge to CECCOM is how to use the means of communication in general, and the radio in particular, toward educational, organizational and socially participative ends. We cannot lose sight of the revolution's rhythms and cadences. We cannot lose sight of the experiences of other countries, even those experiences which we have the possibility to transform into higher experiences. We cannot lose sight of our own experience of these last five years and especially the last one.

I want to repeat the necessity of promoting the horizontal model of communication by the radio, cinema, television and the print media. All these media must open themselves more to the popular project, creatively and without falling into either populism or empiricism. At the same time, we should deepen our own marginal experiences and sensitize all of society which is not conscious of the importance of communication, the transcendent importance of the dissemination apparatuses in the building of the new society. In Nicaragua we are fully aware of the military defense apparatus, as we should be, but we are not aware of the role of the communication media.

The consensus needed by the Sandinista Revolution to carry out its historical project can be either furthered or obstructed by the communication media. This depends upon us. We must be capable of selecting messages taking into account their content and even their form, independent of any bureaucratic concept or any political dispute. We cannot compete with the enemy in technical or in military capabilities. We are going to defeat the enemy by completely winning the conscience of our people by converting the ideological concepts of the revolution into arms to raise the consciousness of all Nicaraguans.

Hopefully this effort which you make will continue. We should fight the tendency to begin something, take a few steps and then sit down to watch the sunset. We must begin walking, sweating and harvesting as part of the effort made by the Consejo Nacional de Educación Superior [The National Council of Higher Education], the CECCOM, the School of Journalism and the Union de Periodistas de Nicaragua [the Union of Nicaraguan Journalists]. You, *compañeros*, are part of the defense of the homeland; you are part of the ideological regiments of the revolution. I hope that you will be good soldiers.

DEE DEE HALLECK
Nicaraguan Video: "Live from the Revolution"

Any public event in Nicaragua that attracts more than 30 persons will also draw a video crew. Not the U.S. network crews who limit their coverage to interviews with irate *La Prensa* editors and impatient consumers in food lines. Not the European crews who work the solidarity brigades from both East and West Germany. Not the independent U.S. and Canadian crews who line up *en masse* for a Mary Hartman (the nun, not the soap opera dip) tour of La Granja, the model prison farm, or wait for a visit with Ernesto Cardenal at the former Somoza estate, headquarters of the Ministry of Culture. No. The *public* events — the concerts, the neighborhood meetings, the elections rallies, the funerals of martyrs, the marches of mothers, the openings of hospitals, the bombing of hospitals, the openings of schools and likewise their attacks by *Contras*, the school graduations, the theatre festivals, the ceremonies for land title distribution to *campesinos*, the Cara Al Pueblo meetings (Face the People) — all these are documented by the video crews of the new Nicaragua. Their work constitutes what is the only authentic video revolution, that much-touted new phenomenon in the world today. Video is part and parcel of the reconstruction of Nicaragua.

Portable video has been an essential tool in recent social struggles in the U.S., but because the movements it has been a part of are so marginal, it has remained marginally seen — at organizing meetings here and there, on public access cable and late nights on public television. In Nicaragua it is a part of a social dynamic that is transforming a country. Video is not just documenting that process. It is very much a part of that process.

The following are notes from two visits to Nicaragua — in November 1983 and in August 1984. It is also based on information supplied by my son, Ezra, who lives and works in Managua as a video liaison person for X-Change TV, an organization devoted to cultural exchanges between Central America and the U.S.

The first thing one realizes about Nicaraguan media, and the revolution of which it is a part, is that there is no single party line imposed. This is a diverse society, a nation brought together under a broad coalition of groups, with a wide variety of beliefs and styles. This variety is reflected in the various groups producing and distributing video. There is a different feeling in their work spaces and in the tapes they make.

There are five main centers of production in Nicaragua. The largest and best-equipped is the Sistema Sandinista — the national television system. The second is the video workshop that is part of the Agrarian Reform Ministry — Communicaciones Midinra. The third is Taller Popular De Video (People's Video Workshop), which is a part of the Sandinista Workers Union. The fourth is INCINE, under the Ministry of Culture, whose main product is film, but whose work includes video production. The last is Pro-TV which documents the Cara Al Pueblo meetings and produces programs for the Ministry of Education.

SISTEMA SANDINISTA

The Sistema programs two channels every day — one from noon onwards, and the other from 4 p.m. The programming, like much of Nicaragua, is an amazing assortment of contradictions — from the saccharine *novelas* from Mexico and Colombia, to the dubbed adventures of Barnaby Jones. It has ads for MacDonalds (yes, there is one in Managua). Coca-Cola and Soviet tractors. In November 1983 the station logo was a group of tiny animated peace doves who flapped their way around a globe to form the letters SSTV as a voice-over, while an accompanying vertical crawl proclaimed "Todas Las Armas al Pueblo!" (All Arms to the People!). Despite its revolutionary station breaks, the Sistema's productions are often reworking of U.S. network formats. Television everywhere has been so completely dominated by the U.S. model that

This text was first published in *Radical Science* (London), 16, 1985. Reprinted by permission of the author.

"professionalism" has come to be defined as how closely Nicaraguan TV resembles NBC.

The Soviet film that developed in the 1920s was forging new paths and was able to leap over what few conventions existed in film at the time. Nicaraguan TV comes 40 years into a TV world in which 180 national TV systems look as though they were all housed on the 40th floor of Rockefeller Center.

The most unusual item on an evening's schedule is apt to be the news, partly because what is happening in Nicaragua is unusual and interesting, but also because the form in which it is broadcast is apt to be more open-ended and spontaneous than most of the Sistema offerings. Activities are shot hand-held. This doesn't mean they are wiggly. Most of the cameramen (in Nicaragua the Sistema camera people that I saw *were* men) are rock-steady and have no real need for tripods. Their stories are often visual essays — not many interviews and no "on-the-scene-reporters". Information is supplied by the newscasters in voice-over, but often long pieces of visual material run without comment — in a style that is leisurely and flowing — more like U.S. public access, where time is free and information isn't sandwiched between commercials. I have the feeling that this is more from lack of enough tightly edited material than from any theoretical concerns of management. On one news show I saw 15 minutes of inchoate drunken revelling at the Santo Domingo Festival. Church festivals are always covered. This is a country where the institutional church is in direct opposition to the policies of the government, but where three priests hold cabinet-level positions. All church activities are news: from the Purissima Festival to the bitter pronouncements of anti-Sandinista Archbishop Obando Bravo. Participants in the ongoing church debate are endlessly interviewed in the TV studios. On most nights the church is at least a third of the news.

The segments on the news that are produced in the studio are often awkward and replete with transitional errors and shaky chroma-key edges. The occasional goofs and missed cues have made the administration of the Sistema reluctant to distribute their news programmes abroad. X-Change TV has repeatedly tried to get samples of the news for distribution, but Sistema executives would rather lend out their "professional" work — slick entertainment specials — in the "Live-from-Lincoln-Center" genre. These canned and controlled artsy shows are a long way from the "live-from-the-revolution" programmes that X-Change has in mind. But the Sistema is probably ashamed of the news. The open informality may charm Northern visitors, the transitional goofs may denote self-referential process consciousness to a *Screen* sub-

Weekly Sandinista Television System programming during March 1984 (From *Barricada* (Managua)).

scriber, but they only give ulcers to the Sistema's producers.

The attraction of X-Change to the more primitive news is an example of the kind of solidarity activity that has been one element of an ongoing debate within the Ministry of Culture and the artistic community in Managua. One of the results of the revolution has been an explosion of creativity among the campesinos; native writing and primitive painting have proliferated. This type of art is always popular with solidarity groups. A German art gallery sponsored huge editions of primitive painting posters — reproduced on expensive paper with an elaborate graphic technique. Likewise, editions of campesino poetry, produced by internationalists, have been printed and bound and distributed widely. The national folklorico dance movement is doing great, receiving donations from all over the world. But professional artists have asked: where, in this scheme, is the support for serious artists who may be developing a more complex and probing aesthetic? The attraction of revolutionary tourists for primitive posters leaves out Nicaraguan artists who have spent long careers in the arts. In a country where every piece of paper and every pencil is a precious resource, the Ministry of Culture cannot afford to put out editions of *their* works. Economic concerns are not the only issue, as there are many who believe that the arts should be mass-based and that supporting an elite group of university-trained artists only perpetuates the class differences that still exist from pre-revolutionary times.

While the debate continues, an important role of the Sistema has been to make national performance of both the folklorico and the professional theatre and dance groups available to a wide audience. *Sandino-Santo Y Seña* (Saint and Symbol), their most elaborate presentation to date, is a dance and music spectacular that was recorded at a live performance in a ruined hotel that has recently become the opera house of Managua. The building is a crumbling shell with an eerie presence that forms a poignant reminder that this is NOT a typical theater in a typical Latin American country, but constitutes an art built on the destruction of resistant traditions. I saw a performance there in August, where the vigour and enthusiasm of the production burst through the decay of the surroundings. The technical virtuosity of the lighting, the dancing and the hundred-piece string(!) orchestra was in stark contrast to the extreme poverty of most of the audience and with the decrepit state of the theater. Imagine that an earthquake has destroyed the Plaza Hotel and you are sitting in its ruins watching Ballet Hispanico with an audience of 3,000 unemployed workers from the South Bronx. Needless to say, there are a few differences. For one thing, because of the revolution, the theatre is THEIR theater. You feel it when you are there with them. That sense of empowerment is a part of the event; it is also a part of the TV presentations that record it. The audience cutaways are therefore different. They serve the function

of reminding the TV audience of just whose show it is anyway. (Come to think of it, maybe the Lincoln Center cutaways serve the same purpose. . . .)

MIDINRA

Comunicaciones Midinra is part of the Agrarian Ministry. The offices are a little outside of Managua on the road to Masaya, in what was a rather well-to-do hacienda-type house with a large interior patio surrounded by grandiose archways. When I was last there the patio was being used to store empty VCR boxes. Below the arches, the desks and files are an amazing collection of types — from Danish Modern to Ramada Inn Inquisition style. Their walnut and teak finishes are stencilled in prominent places like subway graffiti tags with huge numbers in bright red and white paint. The numbers designate which farm the furniture was confiscated from. Many of the large farms in Nicaragua were abandoned after the revolution and the confiscated property from these *ranchos* gives Midinra a material edge among the video groups. Desks and files they may have, but the office desperately needs more telephones. Over 70 persons work there, and their single telephone is the kind of frustrating bottleneck through which any work in present-day Nicaragua must eventually pass.

Video isn't the only thing that Midinra does. They have several printing presses and do the work of documenting and explaining the agrarian reform process. Their primary aim is making the agrarian reform work understood by and available to the peasants and farm workers in the countryside, and secondarily informing a wider public — city dwellers in Managua, Leon and Granada, but also other countries and international organizations. Several of their publications are in English. Arturo Zamora is director of Comunicaciones Midinra. It is indicative of his self-effacing style that he has no desk or office, but hangs out from work space to work space jumping up apologetically to give this or that worker back his or her seat. Arturo directs the printing, audio-visual and video. The audio-visual is a large department with a still-photo darkroom for both color and black and white. They have produced over a dozen slide shows with synchronized tracks. Subjects include "The Benefits of Soy Beans" and "Nutrition for Pregnant Women". Midinra is planning an audio studio and hopes to do a regular radio series in the near future.

The video department consists of four rooms — an editing room, a tape library, an equipment room and an office. Needless to say, the office is the furthest from the air-conditioner. In Nicaragua, equipment and tapes are treated with the utmost respect. This is not mystified Third World awe, but a concrete understanding of the hassles involved in part-replacement and tape purchase. Augusto Tablada is director of the video department. He likes to tell how he was caught in monsoon-type rains in an open field with their new

Sony N-3 camera and a 4800 VCR deck. He took off his rain gear and put it as additional protection over the already plastic-encased equipment, and spent seven hours in pouring rain trying to hold the equipment out of the mud. "The camera costs dollars," he grins. "I'm only worth cordobas." Exchange dollars are practically impossible to get, and cordobas won't buy equipment. All of the video groups in Nicaragua rely heavily on donated equipment.

Midinra films are available in both 3/4 and Beta. Most production is shot and edited on 3/4, then transferred to Beta for distribution to the countryside. Each regional headquarters has a Beta player and has regular showings of Midinra tapes. They also show work by U.S. independents and even a few Hollywood films. *Julia* was going to the mountains in the week I was there.

Miriam Carrero comes to work at Midinra with a shopping bag full of powdered milk. The boxes have a smiling blond and blue-eyed toddler on the front. The lettering on the box is Cyrillic: the milk is Russian. Powdered milk from the U.S. is difficult to get here. All U.S. products are harder and harder to get. Miriam has two children — a four-month-old baby and a three-year-old girl. Her mother assists in the childcare, as in many Nicaraguan extended families, but even so, working as a video editor is difficult with two young ones. Miriam gets up at 5 a.m. to go to the market to be sure she can get the week's supply of powdered milk for the baby. Miriam started out in film work at INCINE. She recently changed initially because the pay was better. INCINE pays only 3,700 cordobas a month ($130) while Midinra gives 6,000. Now Miriam is very enthusiastic about video and wants to learn all aspects of production. She now runs the editing machines but is very much involved in content decisions. From what I could gather of the post-production process, tapes at Midinra evolve organically (to use an agricultural term) from the material collected. The camera person works with the editor. Input can come from many persons at Midinra and the atmosphere is that of a collective, not a heirarchy. Technical advice is supplied on occasion by agricultural advisors; for example, a cattle geneticist was working closely on a recent tape on cattle production.

Midinra's work is primarily focused on agrarian topics, but, like Jaime Wheelock, director of the Agrarian ministry, their interests extend to theoretical and historical issues as well. Midinra recently completed an historical tape to commemorate the 50-year anniversary of Sandino's death. This tape is a mixture of archive footage, recent war footage and agrarian images. Of all the tapes I have seen from Nicaragua, it takes the most risks. It is a passionate experimental tape, using Eisenstein-type montage juxtapositions to rev up emotions. (After a shot of a U.S. helicopter being shot down, there is a close-up of a bull being castrated.) This anniversary was the focus of a series on the Sistema. Each of the *comandantes* had hour-long interviews in which they answered questions posed to them by the Sistema. Midinra took Jaime Wheelock to the countryside, where he discussed the issues with the *campesinos*. They then edited this into an hour program and wanted the Sistema to run that instead of the stuffy studio format interview. The television system refused to air it, saying it did not fit their series. (This type of evasion is a familiar story to independents who try to deal with U.S. public TV.) Actually the relationship of Midinra to the Sistema is one of the more baffling issues for an outsider to comprehend. Midinra has to BUY time on the Sistema: 60,000 cordobas for each hour of program. They do a monthly program, but all the time is paid for, and their programs are subject (as in the interview case) to rejection by the management.

Midinra has been a haven for foreign independents. Its open atmosphere and friendly workers have made it a place where U.S. independent filmmakers could align their cameras, splice light cables or just hang out and screen tapes. In a sense, Midinra's video grew out of the independent movement in the U.S. Prior to 1979, Augusto spent time in the U.S. and worked with Eddie Becker, an independent producer in Washington. After the revolution, Eddie came to Midinra to help train agricultural workers in video skills. The students from his class are still the mainstays of video people at Midinra. Eddie found that they picked up camera techniques quite easily. What he ended up spending most of his time teaching was how to make a good solder. He brought with him three connector kit bags from Radio Shack and several hundred yards of cable. The cables they produced are still in use. A trouble-shooting manual that he designed for them is the basic handbook of their equipment room.

Most internationalist media people sooner or later find their way out of the Carretera Masaya to Midinra's workshop. Before they leave, they are given a list of missing parts and needed equipment to send back. Video people from Germany have been active in their support of Midinra and have raised money from trade unions for essential equipment. A major effort is underway at the present time to do a TV series with West Germany; Miriam is co-producing it with a woman producer from Munich. This show will be a docu-drama series on farm life. It is a children's series: the first program shows a young boy visiting his grandfather on a coffee farm. The grandfather explains in detail just how things have changed since the revolution.

Midinra would like to develop their co-production possibilities. They have been aghast at the enormous sums of money that U.S. (and Canadian and European) producers spend on equipping a production in Nicaragua. Arturo suggests, "Why not use our equipment and work in co-production with us? That way we can all benefit." Arturo recently assisted Bianca Jagger on a documentary about ecology in Nicaragua for distribution in the U.S. Just as with their printed materials, Midinra sees their audience as including not only Nicaraguans. "We want to do our part to counter the disinformation that the world hears about Nicaragua", Arturo explains. He has embarked on a series called *Alternative Views* (not to be confused with the Austin cable show of the same name) to begin to counter Western press bias. This type of production could also be done as co-productions, he feels.

Future plans at Midinra include a feature film on the history of Sandino. Wilfredo Ortega Mercado, who is currently the tape librarian, has a plan for a program on cultural seduction — how young campesinos lose their minds to American consumer goods. Miriam hopes to produce a program on women agricultural workers. And the ongoing work continues — the documentation of land reform, the construction of co-operative dairies, the research into ecological methods of pest control and health care in rural areas. Midinra also serves as a liaison from the producer to the consumer. Of their tapes that have been most popular here in the U.S. as part of the X-Change TV series, two are on very parochial specific topics: *Qué Pasa Con el Papel Higiénico*, and *Qué Pasa Con Las Papas*. The first, "What's Up with the Toilet Paper?", is a sort of point–counterpoint about why there isn't enough toilet paper in the country. Why the shortage? Humorous and catchy interviews with people on the street convey the range of feeling about toilet paper. There IS a real shortage in Nicaragua, and this lack has become one of the major complaints by the sectors of the population that are most against the revolution. By repeating these complaints and disseminating them, Midinra itself has been criticized. The criticism against the tape only increased its popularity, and the tape became an important element in the ongoing discussions about shortages, hoarding and rationing. The second tape is about potatoes. Potatoes grow well in Nicaragua, but poor farming methods have slowed production. This is a tape in praise of the potato that includes instructions for successful harvests.

TALLER POPULAR

Taller Popular de Video Timoteo Velasquez is a workshop named for a fallen comrade. It is part of the Central Sandinista de Trabajadores (CST), the largest union in Nicaragua. Like Midinra, they also have a regular series on the Sistema, and also distribute via Betamax to union locals throughout the country. It is housed and shares resources with Tercer Cine, a private production company composed of Jackie Reiter, Wolf Tirado and Jan Kees de Rooy. The Taller began as a Super 8 workshop taught by Julia LeSage. She went to Nicaragua in 1981 on a special project sponsored by the United Nations. "We worked mostly on editing techniques and alternatives to synch sound interviews, such as the use of music, other taped verbal material and background sound. At the suggestion of Amina Luna, one of the CST filmmakers, we began filming a project on working women's participation in the revolution, which the group has since completed in video."

Super 8 processing soon became too difficult, as Kodak withdrew all trade with Nicaragua. The workshop now works almost entirely in video. Amina is still one of the producers, along with Francisco Sanchez, Oscar Ortiz and Ileana Estreber. Their productions center on people — close shots of faces alternating with their homes, their land, their work. *Así Avanzamos* is a tape about a cattle collective, faced with all the problems of building up production, together with the stresses and material losses of the *Contra*-inflicted war damage. The determination of the people to keep on working ("Así Avanzamos" — so we advance) is evident on their hopeful faces. There is a dreamy, romantic quality to many of the Taller productions. This is not, however, the romantic view of "primitive" life that we sometimes find in the work of Gringo anthropologist/filmmakers. The faces of the people emanate a hope that is reinforced by the real accomplishments they have gained in the face of incredible odds. The ease with which the peasants *participate* with the video production gives the discourse an intimacy that transcends the interview format. This *sharing* with the videomakers is what characterizes the work of U.S. independent Skip Blumberg. There is a one-to-one relationship with the camera that is as close as video can get to an authentic human relationship. This intimacy can, on occasion, make the Taller tapes deeply tragic. *Las Mujeres* is about two women who work in the reconstruction in one of the northern areas. They describe some of the hardships they have encountered in their work, but go on to list the accomplishments of the literacy campaign and the agrarian reform work in the face of the fear and intimidation that the *Contras* impose. The bravery of these two women included their willingness to talk with the video crew. Shortly after the tape appeared on television, they were both killed — brutally murdered. One was tortured and raped along with her six children. This type of *Contra* terror is not unusual; their targets are those who work with the revolution. The *Contras* rarely attack the army. Instead they go after the schoolteachers, the doctors, the nurses and agrarian reform workers — and, on occasion, those peasants who share their hope and dedication with a video crew.

INCINE

INCINE is the film production unit of the Ministry of Culture. It was born under fire in the mountains before the revolution. I talked with Noel Rivera, who was one of the "muchachos" who formed the mainstay of the army of insurrection. He was only 15 years old when he left home to fight against Somoza's National Guard. In his battalion was a film crew, which needed someone to run the Nagra, the basic audio recorder used for film documentaries. He became the sound man after a few days training and has worked with

INCINE ever since. INCINE has made one feature — *Alcino and the Condor* and many documentaries. Their newsreels are often shown before the feature films in the theaters around the country. Half of the theaters in Managua are privately owned and INCINE has to pay for the time for newsreel projection. The theater owners refuse to play shorts that are longer than ten minutes. Noel recounts the story of a newsreel he helped make that was 12 minutes long. When he saw it at the theater, it was strangely truncated. The theater owner had just lopped off the last two minutes of the documentary in mid-sentence.

Movie theaters in Managua show the same junk films that we get on Times Square. Kung Fu movies are the most popular and audiences line up at 7.30 a.m. to see a 9.30 show on Saturday morning. The Cinemateca is a state-owned theater that shows a few Eastern European films (Czech, Hungarian) and occasionally an independent feature from the U.S. Cuban films draw large crowds.

INCINE has a video department directed by Rosanne Lacayo. The Lacayos are the main force behind INCINE and some have accused the organization of being a family affair. Their most recent tape is a homage to Julio Cortazar, poet and friend to the Nicaraguan revolution. Within the cultural debate mentioned earlier, INCINE stands squarely with the "serious art" contingent. Their main interest lies in producing film versions of Latin American novels.

INCINE has been on the receiving end of lavish gifts of production equipment and production assistance. The immediate successes of ICAIC, the Cuban film production institute, led many to hope that Nicaragua's film production would accomplish similar feats. Several factors mitigate against this. The most important is the strain and pressures of the war situa-

HOY EN EL CINE

Miércoles 6 de Abril de 1983.

MARGOT – 3:30, 5:45 8:00 p.m. "FUGA A LA VICTORIA" – Todo público.

CABRERA – 3:30, 5:45, 8:00 P.M. "TRISTAN E ISOLDA" – Todo público.

CINEMA 1 – 4, 6, y 8 p.m. "UN ARDIENTE VERANO" – Todo público.

CINEMA 2 – 4, 6, y 8 p.m. "EL DIABOLICO DOCTOR FU MAN CHU" – Todo público.

JARDIN – 3:30, 5:45, 8:00 p.m. "FUGA A LA VICTORIA" – Todo público.

AMERICA – 3:30, 5:45, 8:00 p.m. "LA HUIDA" – 12 años.

DARIO – 3:30, 5:45 y 8:00 p.m. "EL CARTERO LLAMA DOS VECES" – 18 años.

DORADO – 4, 6, y 8 p.m. "EN BUSCA DE JESUS" – 12 años.

MARIA – 4, 6 y 8 p.m. "JESÚS DE NAZARETH" – Todo público.

AGUERRI – 3, 5 y 7 p.m. "EL MARTIR DEL CALVARIO" – Todo público.

REX – 4, 6 y 8 p.m. "SAUL Y DAVID" – Todo público.

BLANCO – 5:30, 7:30 p.m. "LA PROXIMA VICTIMA" – 18 años.

VERACRUZ – 5 y 7 p.m. "EL REY ESTA VIVO" – Todo público.

SALINAS – 6 y 8 p.m. "CRIMEN EN EL CAMPO DE CEBOLLAS" – 12 años.

MEXICO – 11 a.m. 2, 4, 6 p.m. "EL PROCESO DE CRISTO" – Todo público.

CHAPLIN – 11 a.m. 2, 4, 6 p.m. "PASAJE PELIGROSO" – 12 años.

MARIBEL – 6 y 8 p.m. "TRIANGULO DE URANIO" – 18 años.

TREBOL – 4, 6 y 8 p.m. "SCUM-BASURA HUMANA" – 18 años.

MIERCOLES 6 DE ABRIL DE 1983

4:30 — Barras de Ajuste
5:00 — Dibujos Animados (Color)
5:30 — TV Funnie (Color)
6:00 — Taller Manual (Color)
6:30 — Zoología (Color)
7:00 — Super Estelar (Color)
7:30 — Revista Internacional (Color)
8:00 — Noticiero Sandinista (Color)
8:45 — Telenovela EL ASESINO VIVE EN EL 21 (Color).
9:15 — Cine del Miércoles.

MIERCOLES 6 DE ABRIL DE 1983

3:00 — Barras de Ajuste
3:30 — Dibujos Animados (Color)
4:00 — Carlos Dickens (Color)
4:30 — El Rey Arturo (Color)
5:00 — Momentos Familiares (Color)
6:00 — Telenovela SEÑORITA ANDREA (Color)
6:30 — Desde la A a la Z (Color)
7:00 — Telenovela LA COSECHA (Color)
7:30 — Telenovela ROJO Y NEGRO (Color)
8:00 — Noticiero Sandinista (Color)
8:45 — Palco del Misterio (Color)
9:45 — La Naturaleza (Color).

SISTEMA SANDINISTA DE TELEVISION
ESTA PROGRAMACION PODRIA VARIAR SIN PREVIO AVISO
DESARROLLANDO LA NUEVA TELEVISION EN NICARAGUA

Daily film schedule for Managua cinemas, and the Sandinista Television System programs for all of Nicaragua on Wednesday, 6 April 1983 (From *Barricada* (Managua), 6 April 1983).

tion in Nicaragua. Except for the Bay of Pigs fiasco and the imposed economic constraints, Cuba has not had to withstand the brutal forces of reaction that attack Nicaragua daily. Second, and certainly a part of the first, is the worsening economic situation, with the price of film and processing in Mexican laboratories rising daily. Third is more internal to INCINE. Their organization seems the most chaotic of the media groups that I visited. INCINE is built on grandiose schemes that get hung up in the simplest of details. While I was there, a group of technicians from Los Angeles were sponsoring technical workshops. The group came with a large donation of lights and equipment. They were surprised at the lack of the most *basic* tools, however, and were unable to use most of their lights. There was only one circuit capable of running ONE of their lights in the workshop building. These workshps were funded by the Common Sense Foundation. Perhaps they could have had more common sense and have been more utilitarian in scope. But quien sabe? Maybe some nascent cinematographer was tapped by the classes and will emerge as a leader of the budding Nicaraguan film industry. In the meantime, the video production unit is becoming more and more important as a center of activity at INCINE.

CARA AL PUEBLO

The other video production unit is the audio-visual department of the Department of the Interior. A unit from this department produces weekly Cara Al Pueblo meetings and also does production for the Ministry of Education — both documentation and tapes for instructional purposes. The Cara Al Pueblo are weekly meetings of the *comandantes* with the people — in the barrios around Managua and in the countryside. These are perhaps the most characteristic public events of the revolution; they are to Nicaragua what Fidel's speeches are to Cuba. It is a significant difference that these are two-way — not the voice of a single leader, but the questions of the people directed to a group of their leaders. These may include local leaders, the directors of the local block associations. The questions range from specifics on the new sewer lines for the neighborhood to more philosophical questions on the relationship between church and state. When the meetings are held in Managua, they are broadcast live from a mobile van. These programs are very popular and would have high ratings if the Sistema botherd to measure that. There have been accusations that these meetings are orchestrated by the local CDSs (neighborhood committees for defense of the revolution), and that only acceptable questions are allowed, but the shows I saw were spontaneous and often highly critical of the government. The Cara Al Pueblo meetings will become increasingly important as economic conditions worsen. Their value is not as a safety valve, but as an effective way for people to have input into national decision. The degree to which these meetings express the authentic fears, angers and hopes of the people will be an important measure of public accountability. This process is very much the national dialogue, and the participation of video is crucial. The Cara Al Pueblo has a well-equipped van which is the envy of the other video producers of Managua. One of the ironies of the situation there is that, despite the collaborative attitude at the highest level of government, there exists among departments a great deal of competition and possessiveness. There is very little communication among the various organizations. INCINE has no idea of what Midinra is doing. Midinra has no way to gauge their schedule on the Sistema, because they are not privy to the Sistema's long-range planning and do not know month-to-month where their slot will be positioned. The Taller has no contact with INCINE. They have only one 4800 portable recording deck. If that is in the repair shop, they have to cancel all their shoots — even though there are at least six other decks that could be loaned from other workshops. There is only one engineer who works at the Sistema who has put his job on the line by sometimes sneaking a workshop deck into his shop to repair. There are healthy aspects to the independence of the various groups — there is no monolithic look to Nicaraguan video — but all the groups would benefit more from more sharing of resources.

It is sobering to contemplate the future of Nicaraguan video. Even if the vicious *Contra* War stops (which would happen almost immediately if the U.S. stopped funding it), the economic situation is so difficult that conditions will probably worsen in the short run. As the dollar pinch gets harder, there will be increased struggles within the trade unions. Rampant inflation has hit most workers, even though the prices of staples are fixed. Midinra, INCINE, the Sistema and the Cara al Pueblo are all part of the government. They are the "voice of the people" only in so far as the government remains true to the ideals and aspirations of the revolution. As a voice of the workers, Taller Popular de Video may play an increasingly important role in articulating their needs and dissatisfactions. The real work of the revolution is in the future and video can play a constructive role in so far as expression retains authenticity and pluralism.

The U.S. independent community has been an important source for Nicaraguan video — a source for technical assistance, for equipment donations and for programming exchange. But perhaps most important has been the inspiration of video use. The kind of personal human community video that has characterized our marginalized independent video work here in the U.S. has become the standard for a video community in Nicaragua whose cameras are the eyes of their nation, and whose nation stands at the heart of current human history.

CENTER FOR ATLANTIC COAST RESEARCH AND DOCUMENTATION (CIDCA)
Trabil Nani: Historical Background

Until the overthrow of the Somoza regime by the FSLN caught the world by surprise on 19 July 1979, Nicaragua was seldom in international media headlines; few even knew where this small country of three million people was. And even after Nicaragua became an important point on the Latin American political map, the tropical expanse known as the Atlantic Coast remained virtually ignored.

Coverage of Ronald Reagan's inauguration had barely faded from the news, however, before reports began to surface of tensions between the new Nicaraguan government and the various ethnic groups on the coast, particularly the Miskito Indians. The situation continued to deteriorate until January 1982, when the revolutionary government precipitately evacuated all the Miskito communities along the border with Honduras — about 8,000 agreed to the evacuation while another 10,000 crossed over to Honduras. It was then that the issue hit the mass media with full force, and an unusually high degree of misinformation.

Steadman Fagoth, self-exiled Misurasata leader, charged that about 400 Miskitos had been murdered by the Sandinistas, another 3,500 were missing and the rest had been forced to march to "concentration camps" without consideration for women, children, the sick or elderly. U.S. Ambassador to the United Nations Jeane Kirkpatrick declared in a TV interview that 250,000 (four times the *total* Miskito population) had been herded into concentration camps. General Alexander Haig, then Secretary of State, brandished a photo published in the French magazine *Le Figaro* which purportedly showed the Sandinistas burning Miskito bodies. (The photo's author quickly clarified that it was in fact a photo of the Red Cross in the Pacific burning the bodies of those killed by Somoza's National Guard in 1978.) President Reagan proclaimed the Nicaraguan government the worst violator of human rights in Central America.

In the wake of such a campaign, trust in the Nicaraguan government's version of events was a prime casualty. Who was prepared to believe that *no* one had died on the trek to the resettlement area; or that pregnant women, children and the elderly were airlifted out; or that the destination was not a concentration camp? By the time independent delegations discovered the extent of the untruths, the damage was done. Suspicion about Sandinista motives abounded, complex historical issues were reduced to unhelpful stereotypes, and viewpoints on all sides became increasingly entrenched.

Since that time, little had happened within Nicaragua to create an environment in which the underlying issues could be identified, examined and resolved by those most directly affected. Rather, the last two years have seen an escalating military intervention which has seriously hindered this effort. Like its counterpart in the Pacific, this war is financed and directed by the U.S. government through Somocista leadership, and counts on the active assistance of the Honduran military. While the numbers of Indians — mainly Miskitos — in the ranks of the counterrevolution are testimony to the fact that there is something seriously wrong on the coast, they are not *prima facie* evidence, as its champions claim, nor is what is being fought a genuine or popularly supported indigenous liberation struggle.

In the exterior, the war for hearts and minds has escalated proportionately. One of the latest contributions is the testimony by Dr. Bernard Nietschmann to the Organization of American States' Inter-American Commission on Human Rights. According to his testimony, Dr. Nietschmann spent two and a half months during the summer of 1983 visiting Misikito acquaintances from Nicaragua who are now in Costa Rica and Honduras. He states that while there he was invited by

This text was first published as part of the author's mimeographed report entitled *Trabil Nani: History and Current Situation in Nicaragua's Atlantic Coast*, Managua, April 1984. Reprinted by permission of the author. This is its first publication.

"Trabil Nani" means "many troubles" in Miskito.

what he calls the Miskito, Sumu and Rama Nations to visit the Atlantic Coast of Nicaragua. According to his testimony, he did this, apparently illegally, spending several weeks traveling through undisclosed villages in the region.

Dr. Nietschmann, a geography professor at the University of California, Berkeley, charges with graphic detail that there have been "widespread, systematic and arbitrary human rights violations in Miskito Indian communities." Previously, such dramatic accusations had been made only by leaders of Misura in Honduras and Misurasata in Costa Rica, splits which emerged from Misurasata, the former Indian organization in Nicaragua, founded in 1979. In response to their charges, independent organizations such as Americas Watch conducted their own investigation *in situ*. Although these investigations were necessarily of short duration, they demonstrated that accusations of deliberate, massive brutality were false, exaggerated or could not be conclusively substantiated[1].

And still the disinformation continues. The *piece de resistance* is an article in the *National Catholic Register* (8 January 1984), based on an interview with ex-Green Beret medic Jim Stieglitz, who claims to have visited the Bluefields area of the Atlantic Coast. He describes mythical concentration camps, forced labor, rampant smallpox, tiger cages and checkpoints *en route* where Russian is the *lingua franca*. The article is such an audacious fabrication that even his geography is incorrect. Teotecacinte, named as the site of one supposed Miskito concentration camp, is in reality the northernmost border community in Jalapa, in the Pacific. (Nicaraguan immigration files show that Stieglitz was in the country for two days, not enough to make a round trip to Bluefields by land.)

Although knowledgeable observers in the exterior discount such excesses, a purpose is served. They shift the field of inquiry. The very real conditions of war in the Atlantic Coast are ignored in the effort to find out the "true" story about human rights violations. Regarding the Atlantic Coast, for example, the Nicaraguan government has been the object of continuous criticisms for its violations of indigenous rights as a result of the evacuation of 39 Miskito communities from the conflictive border with Honduras. But these criticisms have been virtually without reference to the military situation in the region. If it is mentioned at all, the aggression is generally underestimated or, as in the case of the Nietschmann testimony, completely misrepresented.

While the fact that the region is under attack cannot excuse human rights violations of innocent citizens, or explain away failures or errors on the part of the Sandinista revolution in grappling with more fundamental problems, neither can this fact be dismissed as

an irrelevant factor or willfully distorted by those who claim to be disinterested, apolitical observers of the process.

In an effort to help concerned organizations and individuals to better understand the complex situation on the Atlantic Coast, as well as because of recent documents such as the Nietschmann testimony, CIDCA — an autonomous research center recently attached to the National Council on Higher Education (CNES) — has conducted its own investigation. Our study has included interviews with 170 individuals from 30 Miskito and Sumu communities in Special Zones I and II (recent political–geographic designations roughly corresponding to the northern and southern parts of the former department of Zelaya respectively). We have conducted lengthy interviews with local pastors, as well as with bishops and other regional representatives of the major churches in the Atlantic Coast (Moravian, Catholic and Anglican). In addition, we have interviewed officers and personnel of the military and security forces and examined the activities of ministries charged with providing services to the region (health, education, store provisions, etc.). This has given us a far more ample panorama than that offered by Dr. Nietschmann who, by his own admission, only interviewed Miskito community members or those in exile, presumably including leaders of the military aggression against Nicaragua.

As our research progressed, we found ourselves compelled to understand the military situation in the region — the strategy and tactics of the aggressors, their geographic reach and the extent and nature of their social base. The following section of this report re-examines the antecedents to this struggle, necessarily tracing their roots back to the colonial period, in order to better evaluate the contradictions that have specifically arisen between the indigenous communities and the new government. This background section extends to the middle of 1981, when Steadman Fagoth left for Honduras with the avowed purpose of waging war against the Nicaraguan government, followed shortly afterwards by Misurasata general coordinator Brooklyn Rivera, who announced the same goal.

THE HUMAN GEOGRAPHY

The area commonly known as the Atlantic Coast bears little resemblance to its Pacific counterpart. Instead of the fertile land that produces Nicaragua's mainstay export crops of cotton, rice, sugar cane and vegetables, or the coffee-rich highlands of central Nicaragua, much of the coastal area of the Department of Zelaya is swamp, thick tropical forest or pine savannah. Hundreds of tiny streams flow down from the mountainous mining region in the northern interior, converging into a dozen rivers that twist through the lowlands and finally empty into ample

1. *Americas Watch on Human Rights in Nicaragua*, May 1982, pp. 62–63; Amnesty International, "Nicaragua Background Briefing," *AI Index* 3/10/82 (London), p. 8.

lagoons along the coast proper, many of which in turn open on to the Caribbean. During the extensive rainy season, huge pockets along these waterways are flooded, creating insect and mosquito-ridden swamps. Except in the extensive pine plains in the northeast triangle, streams and rivers, rather than roads, provide the main transportation routes.

Ethnically homogenous communities varying between 100 to 2,000 people are clustered around the lagoons and river mouths along the coast, growing more dispersed further inland along the rivers or the few dirt roads. With luck their crop clearings of rice, beans or cassava are close outside the village, but in many cases they are a day's travel or more by canoe, beyond the ubiquitous swamps. Those who live close to the coast or along the large rivers depend for their protein primarily on fishing, others on hunting, though a few cows, pigs and chickens can be seen in every village. Communities in reach of the few commercial centers such as the mining towns of Siuna, Rosita and Bonanza, or the port towns of Bluefields and Puerto Cabezas, sell fish and agricultural surpluses

to meet their cash needs. Other, more isolated communities mainly do without, or their men migrate to the sawmills, fishing operations or other wage labor operations scattered though the region.

Wage labor figures for 1980 in Zelaya include 1,500 workers in mining and 2,700 in the 100 other manufacturing and agro-processing activites[2]. In all, with just under 10% of the national population, the Atlantic Coast produced 4.7% of the country's gross domestic product in 1980[3].

The predominant ethnic minority is Miskito (estimated at 67,000 in 1981), concentrated primarily in the northeastern area and down along the coast as far as Pearl Lagoon[4]. Along the southern coast as well are several communities of Rama (700), Gariphone, or black Caribs (1,500), Sumu, and Afro-European descended Creoles. The majority of the 5,000 Sumus, however, traditionally live in the interior highlands near the mines, and the greatest portion of the 26,000 Creoles are found in the urban centres of Puerto Cabezas and Bluefields or on Corn Island. The demographically dominant population is the mestizo (Indian–European) peasantry (180,000), which pushed into the department of Zelaya beginning in the 1950s, as an expanding cotton and cattle economy and Somoza's army expelled them from their tiny plots on the Pacific. Many made their way to the mines and port towns, but the majority settled in the rural interior. (Since the new political divisions were created in Special Zones I and II, an undetermined number of

2. Ministerio de Planificación, *Diagnostico del Departamento de Zelaya*, Managua, 1983, pp. 72–94.
3. *Ibid*, p. 29.
4. CIDCA, *Demografia Costena: Notas sobre la historia demografica y población actual de los grupos etnicos de la Costa Atlantica nicaragüense*, Managua: Centro de Investigaciones y Documentación de la Costa Atlantica, July 1982, p. 49. Note: An estimated 20,000 Miskitos have gone to Honduras since this study was prepared.

Los Pueblos de la Costa Atlántica

MISKITOS
SUMOS
RAMAS

Mestizos	182.000
Miskitos	70.000
Criollos	26.000
Sumus	5.000
Ramas	700
Caribes	1.500

La autonomía significa reconocer derechos iguales a todas las etnias, independientemente del número de habitantes.

"The peoples of the Atlantic Coast — Autonomy means to recognize equal rights for all ethnic groups, regardless of their number" (Published in *El Tayacán* (Managua), 1985).

these Spanish-speaking mestizos are now part of the Matagalpa and Chontales regions.)

EXOGENOUS INFLUENCES

There have been three major outside influences on the coast. First were the British who, beginning in the 1560s, established trade relations with receptive Indians, particularly those around Cape Gracias a Dios. In exchange for turtles, lumber, fish and their own cheap labor, these Indians received metal tools, firearms and rum from the British bucaneers. Soon this initial contact began to produce important changes in their culture. The variant of English they mastered to engage in commercial relations influenced their own language as well. There was also a phenotypal change, as the coastal Indians mixed with both Europeans and their African slaves. While debates remain about their origins, by the end of the 17th century this grouping had become universally known as Miskitos. Today they are a self-identified cultural grouping which has tenaciously preserved language, land adscription and kinship structures at the same time that it has demonstrated great agility in adapting to or adopting exogenous cultural impositions. While the more traditional Sumu and Rama have decreased demographically, the Miskito population has constantly expanded.

The British allied with the Miskito to fight Spanish efforts to colonize the Mosquitia region (during this period extending from northern Honduras down into Costa Rica). The British saw in the alliance the means to protect their commercial domination of the Caribbean region; the Miskito's goal was to avoid the fate of their race throughout Hispanic America — extermination. Miskitos made frequent armed forays against Spanish positions in the interior and in the process used their military advantage to sack weaker Indian communities such as the Sumu, enslaving their occupants or selling them to the British[5].

The British assured their furure in this alliance by promoting the notion of an indigenous monarchy within the loose Miskito social structure. For more than 200 years a family line of kings, educated in England or Jamaica, presided over the coast, loyal always to the British Crown.

By the middle of the 19th century, the two other outside actors had entered the stage. The first was the Moravian church which, with British encouragement, sent its first permanent German missionaries to the region in 1849. They lived the simple life of the Indians and provided badly needed social services to the communities. Learning their language and re-

counting their own period of persecution by the Catholic Church, they soon converted the majority of the Miskito population to their version of Protestantism. In the process they reinforced existing hostilities toward the catholicized Pacific.

The Moravians translated their hymns and later the Bible into Miskito and the church and its teachings became the unifying element for the dispersed population. To this day, the church is at the very center of community life.

In 1916, responsibility for the mission was transferred from Germany to the United States, under the auspices of the church's Society for Propagating the Gospel Among the Heathen. Since that time, U.S. funding and staff have been responsible for the majority of the educational and health facilities in the region. (Most of the rest has been provided by the Catholic and Seventh Day Adventist churches, leaving the coast populations with virtually no concept of state-provided services.)

Although Miskito lay pastors have now replaced the U.S. missionaries, these pastors have assimilated many of their mentors' cultural and political values. It is important to note that not until 1974 was the administrative body of the church exclusively native, and even then it was predominantly Creole. Leaders readily admit that the majority of the village pastors are narrowly educated and ill-equipped to deal with the complexities now confronting them, despite the fact that they are often the most educated and respected members of their communities.

The other new force was the U.S. government itself, which had its expansionist eye on Nicaragua as the likely site for an interoceanic canal. By 1843, 22 years after Nicaraguan independence, Great Britain had manoeuvered itself into a position as the legal "protector" of the Mosquitia. But its declining power could not stand up to U.S. advances in the region. Arriving at the brink of full-scale war with the United States, Britain capitulated. In 1860, it signaled the end of its territorial aspirations by signing the Treaty of Managua with the Nicaraguan government. This treaty created a Miskito Reserve under Nicaraguan sovereignty, with powers of local self-government granted to the Miskito monarchy. Tellingly, this treaty was negotiated without the participation of any representative of the Miskito Crown.

By 1880 the Miskito king was granting concessions to U.S. lumber and banana operations throughout the region. Within a decade, U.S. investments in these activities and in the steamship lines which serviced them totaled $10 million[6]. It is estimated that 90% of the commerce of the region was under U.S. control. Bluefields grew quickly as a new commercial center. Starting in 1884, Chinese and Chinese–American immigrants began to arrive and move into the retail trade, to the consternation of their coastal competitors; within 11 years the latter had pushed through a law forbidding further Chinese immigration to the coast[7]. Miskitos, who had already lost their early posi-

5. Mary Helms, *Asang: Adaptions to Culture Contact in a Misquito Community*, Gainesville University of Florida Press.

6. Eduardo Perez-Valle, *Expediente de Campos Azules, Historia de Bluefields en sus documentos*, Managua, 1978. (See document "Intereses Norteamericanos en la Reserva 1882–1892," pp. 137–144.)

7. *Ibid.*, p. 241.

tion as commercial middlemen for the British traders, were drawn into wage labor on the 20 or so banana plantations in the area. An influx of English-speaking black Jamaicans were given low-level administration jobs.

There is no evidence that the coastal government itself did much to improve the life of its subjects. A law requiring obligatory education, for example, was never made effective; the Moravian school, the only educational institution on the coast at the time, noted that it had fewer students in 1893 than it had had in 1868[8]. By that period control was in the hands of the Jamaicans, and the growing commercial sector was the main beneficary of government policy[9].

REINCORPORATION TO REVOLUTION: ISOLATED ENCLAVE ECONOMY

In 1894, the Managua government of J. Santos Zelaya took advantage of the relative power vacuum in the coast resulting from U.S.–British contradictions to militarily occupy Bluefields and wrest full control away from the local government. The move was promoted by the U.S. government, which wanted the British out once and for all.

The Reincorporation Decree, otherwise known as the Mosquito Convention, was signed by the Managua government and delegates from each of the local communities[10]. The key concessions to them were tax and military service exemption for the Indians, and the local reinvestment of all locally-generated revenues — under the administration of the central government. A new agreement, called the Harrison–Altamirano Treaty of 1905, again negotiated exclusively between Nicaragua and Great Britain, included Creoles in the tax and military exemptions, but limited the period to 50 years. Addressing the question of land rights, the treaty promised to acknowledge the legal titles held by Miskitos and Creoles for all properties acquired before 1894 or, if since adjudicated to other owners, their nearest equivalent. Those who held no title would receive eight manzanas of land for each family of four, plus two more for each additional family member. Finally, public grazing lands would be recognized for each community. In the main, these land agreements were adhered to only in part, and the reinvestment agreement hardly at all[11]. Historic distrust and hatred of "the Spanish", as the coastal peoples still called the population and government of

8. *Ibid.*, p. 141.
9. *Ibid.*, p. 143; Larry Laird, "Origenes dela reincorporación nicaragüense de la Costa Miskita," *Revista Conservadora* (Managua) No. 141.
10 For texts of this and other treaties and decrees mentioned in this section, see *Expediente de Campos Azules*, listed chronologically by year.
11. *Ibid.* (See "Exposición de los costenos," pp. 335–342.)
12. Bernard Nietschmann, *Between Land and Water: The Subsistence Ecology of the Miskito Indians, Eastern Nicaragua*, New York: Seminar Press, 1973.

the Pacific, continued unabated.

Under the Liberal government of Zelaya, U.S. companies were soon receiving even more concessions on the coast than before — reaching at its peak 10% of the territory, and included mining rights. Typical of the enclave activity, profits were shipped abroad, and nothing was reinvested locally that did not benefit the operations themselves. When in the 1930s a banana plague hit the plantations, and General Sandino's army attacked as well, the companies ripped up their railroad lines or left them to rust, and departed. By the 1950s, the lumber companies had ravaged much of the hardwood and pine forests, and they too began to abandon the region. Meanwhile, conditions in the gold and silver mines deteriorated as old machinery was not replaced; workers with tuberculosis or silicosis were let go without pension. The Somoza government, in power since the 1930s, looked the other way.

The last wave of investment to hit the coast was fishing — turtle, shrimp and lobster for export. Freezing plants were built in the 1960s according to no rational conservation plan, Miskito fishermen increased their catch to meet the demand, and soon unregulated competition depleted the waters[12].

With each new investment wave, indigenous workers migrated out of their villages to join the labor force. Three centuries of exposure to British mercantilism had facilitated Miskito receptivity to U.S. exploitation. Traditional subsistence agriculture, turtling, fishing or hunting gave way to a preference for canned goods bought at the company commissaries. With each retreat, workers returned to their old ways with less willingness, satisfying cash requirements by selling surplus rice, cassava, fish or turtle to the communities that still had a wage labor force, or to the port and mining towns. No successive investment wave was ever as big as the banana boom, and after the 1930s, the coast was in a constant state of semi-depression.

Charity shipments of food and used clothing supplemented meager earnings and further whetted the appetite for American goods. One Catholic priest recalls that community members would fight over the clothing provided by Caritas. More than one community lost the incentive to continue sowing their own subsistence crops given the option of wage goods and such handouts. This was only exaggerated when Alliance for Progress shipments began to arrive in the early 1960s.

The people in the area were not paternalized only by the churches and the U.S. government, however. Somoza employed a strong dose of paternalism on the coast as well, and for this reason views about him were mixed. He gave large donations to the Protestant churches, which never spoke against him. In fact, some Moravians saw him as a bastion against "communist penetration". It is also said that his image was aided by his close ties to the United States, the fact that he spoke English and is reported to have given speeches in Miskito. Even Alpromisu (Alliance for Progress of Miskitos and Sumus), an indigenous rights organization founded in 1973, only suffered a brief period of repression. Somoza soon discovered he could better neutralize it by funding its projects and offering jobs to some of its members.

The National Guard, too, was less repressive than in the Pacific, limiting itself for the most part to collecting a cut of foreign corporate profits and participating in the active contraband trade in the port towns. The fighting that left 50,000 dead during the final years before the overthrow of Somoza barely touched the Atlantic Coast, although a few Miskitos studying on the Pacific during the late 1970s worked with the Revolutionary Student Front or indirectly with the FSLN.

Attitudes on the coast about Sandino himself were also mixed. Some Miskitos along the Rio Coco had fought in his army in the late 1920s, and Deputy Adolfo Cockburn had even risen to the rank of Brigadier General[13]. Others participated in the incipient agricultural co-operatives he spawned. Sandino's struggle thus represents the first alliance between the exploited of the Pacific and the Atlantic. But since so many Miskitos identified with their foreign bosses, they shared the view of the United Fruit Co. and the

13. Anastasio Somoza, *El verdadero Sandino o el Calvario de Las Segovias*. 2da. Edicion, Managua: Edit y Lito, "San Jose," 1976.

Moravian church that Sandino's guerrillas were bandits and murderers. For them, Sandino's qualities as an anti-imperialist patriot has not had the same historical and emotional relevance as on the Pacific.

Nonetheless, most people on the coast met the fall of Somoza with general enthusiasm and optimism for the future, though this meant different things to different sectors, as it did on the Pacific.

INDIGENOUS ORGANIZING IN A REVOLUTIONARY CONTEXT

In November 1979, four months after the fall of Somoza, Junta member Comandante Daniel Ortega was invited to attend the fifth annual assembly of Alpromisu in Puerto Cabezas. In attendence were some 700 delegates, ranging from older Moravian pastors and traditional village headmen, to young professionals and students recently returned from the Pacific. All wanted to know what the implications for the coast would be of this new revolutionary situation.

While the FSLN had done virtually no work there, its political program, published in 1969, had included a section called the "Reincorporation of the Atlantic Coast", which stated:

The Sandinista Popular Revolution will put into practice a special plan favoring the Atlantic Coast, submerged in the

Poster, "Integration will be realized with literacy — Atlantic Coast of Nicaragua — 1980 Year of Literacy — National Literacy Crusade — Minister of Education".

worst abandonment, in order to bring it into the life of the nation.

A. It will end the vicious exploitation that the Atlantic Coast has suffered throughout its history by the foreign monopolies, particularly by Yankee imperialism.

B. It will prepare lands of the zone deemed apt for the development of agriculture and cattle.

C. It will take advantage of favorable conditions for the development of fishing and forestry.

D. It will stimulate the flowering of local cultural values of the region, growing out of the original aspects of its historical tradition.

E. It will do away with the hateful discrimination to which the Miskitos, Sumus, Sambos and Negroes of this region have been subject[14].

On 15 November 1979, at the time of the Alpromisu meeting, tensions already existed. On the basis of reports from mestizos living on the coast that Alpromisu was a separatist organization, the FSLN had arrested several of its older leaders. Another Miskito, Lesther Arthur, accused of being a Somocista, was killed by persons who were popularly referred to as Sandinistas and "Lesther Arthur" became a rallying point for agitation.

However, at the end of the meeting, it was agreed to create an indigenous mass organization that would represent all three groups and work together with the revolutionary government and the FSLN for the improvement of their conditions. Out of that November meeting was born Misurasata (Miskitos, Sumus, Ramas, Sandinistas Working Together). The young, charismatic Steadman Fagoth Mueller was elected general co-ordinater.

A potential for tensions exists between any organization that views the world through an ethnic prism and one which understands it primarily in class terms. In class terms, it is necessary to first change material conditions and the social relations of production, leaving until later the transformation of aspects of the superstructure which concern ethnocultural discrimination. In this sense, there is a tendency to underestimate the experience of cultural oppression, as well as the historic ethnocentric legacy. But since most members of any ethnic minority suffer both class and ethnic oppression, the two struggles should be seen as inextricably linked. In principle, then, the two groups have common strategic and tactical interests.

In the case of Misurasata/FSLN efforts at an alliance, additional elements exacerbated the tendency toward mutual distancing: (1) the Miskitos had experienced a long period of relative political autonomy, and even after 1894 had virtually no history of participation within the context of the nation-state; (2) their experience with the dominant political and cultural power (the "Spanish") had been bitter and historically combative, and they identified the FSLN as an extension of that power rather than a break with it; (3) the FSLN envisioned a strong role for the state in con-

solidating the revolution — history has shown the need to be prepared to face frequent aggressions from the government of the United States; this approach came into direct conflict with the ambivalent positions of Misurasata; and (4) the FSLN promoted a world view that clashed strongly with that of the Miskito and other groups on the coast, i.e., they expected the Miskitos to share their view of the U.S. government as a threat to the revolution when the Miskitos tended to view it and its representatives as benefactors. While this view is changing somewhat, the initial reaction to the revolutionary positions was to reject them.

For the Sandinistas to encourage the growth of such an organization in the context of a new and still very vulnerable revolutionary state implied a major risk. Misurasata had the potential of uniting its followers behind an antagonistic project in an unprotected section of the country which could easily be used to its own advantage by the U.S. government. It is little wonder that rumors of a separatist undercurrent within the indigenous movement provoked doubt and suspicion within the FSLN.

In the publication of its political line at the beginning of 1980, however, Misurasata defined itself as an organization that would "defend and consolidate the Sandinista revolution in our own social sphere," aligning itself ideologically within the framework of the revolution:

The Sandinista Revolution is founded on the basic principles of Nationalism, Anti-Imperialism, Internationalism, Classism and popular democracy. We the national indigenous peoples declare that these are the most significant and applicable principles for our national reality in general and our indigenous reality in particular[15].

THE FIRST YEAR:
IS THE GLASS HALF EMPTY
OR HALF FULL?

On that basis, and given that the indigenous groups did not have a broad class spread that would be likely to lead to a defense of policies in contradiction to the popular base of the revolution, the Sandinista government gave Misurasata its full support as an indigenous mass organization. Where Alpromisu had been virtually moribund a year before the triumph, with the space opened by the revolution Misurasata grew by leaps.

Misurasata leaders had two particularly strong public criticisms by the end of 1980. The first was that they had to constantly fight for their cultural rights within the revolutionary programs for the coast. To this, the Sandinistas acknowledged that they knew nothing about the Indian cultures and had erred in assuming that the structures and attitudes growing out of the Pacific experience could be easily adopted by them. But, they argued, that is what a mass organization is for — to give collective form and substance to the needs and demands of its sector and to struggle for

14. *El Programa histórico del FSLN*, Departamento de Propaganda y Educación Politica del FSLN, 1981, 3ra. Edición Registrada.

15. Misurasata, *Lineamientos Generales*, 1980.

those rights within the national framework and the limitations of an incipient revolutionary process.

The second criticism was that Misurasata was marginalized and had no voice in making important decisions about the coast. Brooklyn Rivera says that its members were systematically denied local leadership positions and that they were not consulted about any of the development plans or other policies for the region.

Defined as a mass organization, it is hard to fault the space that Misurasata was given in that first year. It was certainly recognized at the time by Cultural Survival, a U.S.-based organization working on behalf of indigenous rights, which wrote in its publication in 1980:

An expensive bilingual component was added to the impoverished nation's literacy campaign. A national Indian organization has a seat on the Council of State. The government has accepted the Indians' right to their traditional land and is presently negotiating the limits of that territory. These are rights which most indigenous people in Latin America do not enjoy[16].

To this must be added that Misurasata was encouraged to organize, was given the same opportunity to petition for government funding of projects as the mass organizations on the Pacific, and made ample use of government resources on the coast. Not only did it argue for and win the right to a literacy crusade in written coastal languages (Miskito, Sumu and English), but was also given the responsibility for co-directing the campaign in the Miskito and Sumu areas and providing all the literacy workers.

Not surprisingly, Misurasata cadres used the vehicle of the literacy crusade very successfully in their own organizing drive. Also not too surprisingly, given late revelations about Steadman Fagoth's personal ambition and political antipathies toward the Sandinistas, he and his closest followers used the opportunity to organize against the revolution's projects on the coast. What happened in Tasbapounie, according to one Miskito resident of that community, is probably not atypical.

Tasbapounie is a predominantly Mikito community of about 2,000 people, including a number of Creoles. It lies on the ocean side of a narrow stretch of land bordered on the west by Pearl Lagoon. It has received extensive assistance from the new government, perhaps because of its size, relatively high level of education and ease of access for commercial trade. Among other projects in the first two years were electrification, a local state store, improvements and increased staff in the health clinic, a 500,000-Cordoba loan for a fishing co-operative and funding for an agricultural co-operative by INRA, the agrarian reform institute. INRA's goal was to make the lagoon area self-sufficient in rice production and provide it to the population at government-subsidized prices.

The traditional Miskito organization of agricultural labor is called "Pana-Pana" (hand-to-hand work) — a sharing of labor on each other's private crops, in which the land itself is the property of the community. While that system ia beginning to break down in some areas, it is still the method in Tasbapounie. People were initally wary of the INRA offer, fearful that they would end up in debt to INRA or that their private plots would be abandoned. They were also not quick to embrace the idea of sharing profits from their work. After numerous discussions, INRA representatives assured them it would be theirs and that INRA would guarantee purchase of the crops at a fair price by ENABAS, the state distribution agency. Sixty people were convinced to give it a try, and formed three co-operatives of 20 people each. With the tools and seed provided by INRA they cleared new land way out in the bush and planted their first crops.

Soon afterward, at the height of the local literacy crusade in November 1980, Brooklyn Rivera came to Tasbapounie, a strong Misurasata community. (Rivera by then had become general co-ordinator after Fagoth was elected Misurasata representative to the Council of State.) With government and FSLN representatives standing beside him, Rivera reportedly told the assembled crowd in Miskito that this was the way "communists" always worked — they give you something at first, then start taking it all over later, depriving people of the fruits of their labor. He also intentionally mistranslated the FSLN and government representatives — a common phenomenon, according to other interviews. The co-operative members apparently never returned to their plots again, and the crop was lost — as was the opportunity to test Rivera's charge in practice.

Despite such growing hostilites, Sandinistas themselves still refer to this year as one in which there was an essentially fruitful working relationship with Misurasata. They also point with justifiable pride to the accomplishments on the coast, which include major advances in the provision of health care. The first cross-country television and telephone relays were constructed and work was begun on an all-weather road that linked the two coasts (completed in 1982). The abandoned pine resin plant, Atchemco, was reactivated with a 72 million-Cordoba investment and the Nicaraguan Development Bank provided 36 million Cordobas in loans to small and medium producers, three times the amount provided in Somoza's last year[17]. One hundred million Cordobas were invested to improve the standards of the 77% of housing on the coast that either lacked running water, had dirt floors or roofs made only of straw. Dance and musical groups were funded, a radio program in Miskito was initiated and by August literacy teachers were in the countryside with their primers in Miskito, Sumu and English.

Studies were being developed in all the ministries to assure culturally and economically appropriate development projects. A ministerial level body called

16. *Cultural Survival*, September 1980.
17. CNPPDH, *Nicaragua y los derechos humanos*, Comisión Nicaragüense para la Protección y Promoción de los Derechos Humanos, 1983, p. 81.

INNICA (Nicaraguan Institute for the Atlantic Coast) was created especially to deal with the particularities of the region. Comandante William Ramirez was made minister of INNICA, Comandante Lumberto Campbell, a Creole from Bluefields, the vice-minister, and Brooklyn Rivera was offered a high-level position which he rejected. Armstrong Wiggins, another Misurasata member, had an administrative position for the coast within the Casa de Gobierno, and was advising the government informally on indigenous policy.

The Sandinista leaders were aware that the eyes of the world were upon them. As they were doing in so many other areas, they would find new, creative solutions to the problems on the coast, despite the fact that there were few progressive models to learn from. Many ministry officials we interviewed recall the pervasive revolutionary enthusiasm for seeing "the giant awaken", as billboards across Nicaragua proclaimed. But even the slogan backfired. What had been intended as a show of respect for the coast and its future was sneered at. "We've been awake all along, and you Spanish just never noticed," was Misurasata's retort.

At the same time, official openmindedness was not necessarily reflected among FSLN cadres sent to work on the coast. To anyone in Nicaragua in 1980, one of the chief reasons for this was all too obvious. Given the low level of education throughout Nicaragua, and the difficulties of political organizing under Somoza, the demand for politically and professionally skilled cadres vastly exceeded the supply. To this must be added the language barrier, cultural and ideological differences, the different attitudes and role of grass roots religious personnel in the two regions and the prior lack of contact between the two coasts. The sum is a tremendous potential for cultural insensitivities, misunderstandings and disrespect. When to this is added a strong component of mutual prejudice, the potential for problems becomes a near certainty. In such an environment, every perceived sign of disrespect, much less overt racist abuses, accrues not to the responsible individual, but to the "Spanish" in general, and the Sandinista revolution in particular.

STEADMAN FAGOTH: PLANS OF HIS OWN

A relevant, though now hypothetical question is what might have happened had all of Misurasata'a leaders had the interests of the indigenous and Nicaraguan people at heart. Working together with FSLN leadership and other Moravian pastors (who are only now beginning to take a fair and honest look at the revolution), could they have staved off the escalation of cultural and ideological antagonisms, and developed an atmosphere of greater trust in which to negotiate mutually acceptable solutions?

Unfortunately, Fagoth and his group had different plans. He used the historic animosity of the indigenous

groups toward the Spanish, together with every error the FSLN committed, as a powerful mobilizing force, converting it to a banner of separatist aspirations. Given the limited interest of the majority of the Miskito population in state policy questions, he and his followers never had to elaborate what kind of political or state structure they had in mind. But the demagogic potential was tremendous. One example of this was a Misurasata community assembly at the beginning of 1981 in which Fagoth reportedly regaled his audience with visions of a time when the Spanish would have to show passports to come to the coast. Such imagery takes on added power when the Sandinistas are portrayed as atheist communists by some religious leaders, and the period of greatest U.S. economic penetration and exploitation is recalled as "the golden days."

The power of Misurasata grew rapidly. By the end of 1980 its leaders were defining Misurasata proudly as the vanguard organization of the indigenous people on the coast. At least a few Miskitos we spoke with now feel that Misurasata's leaders abused that power to the detriment of real Indian interests. Over the course of 1980 Fagoth and his followers had redefined Misurasata's role from that of a mass organization mediating indigenous interests to one which directly challenged the principles of the revolution.

Some of the leaders were undoubtedly influenced by the historic decision on the right to self-determination taken in the 1977 United Nations conference on discrimination against indigenous peoples of the Americas. They saw it as a green light to push for immediate political autonomy. In their immaturity and exhilaration they did not seem to contemplate the possible strategic consequences this could have on their fragile alliance with the Sandinistas. By November 1980 Ronald Reagan had just been elected on a platform which included open hostility to the Nicaraguan revolution, and the Managua government was braced for an escalation of tensions.

Under the influence of Steadman Fagoth, other leaders were motivated by his opportunistic personal ambition. Like he, they not only used every Sandinista error to their own advantage, but turned every beneficial Sandinista program into a Misurasata achievement. To this day, for example, many Miskitos believe that the literacy crusade in maternal languages was won by Misurasata only after pitched battle with the government. When they couldn't do this, they twisted the meaning of the programs to make them appear diabolical plots of the "Sandinista-communists". The clearest example of this can be found in a half-page interview with Fagoth in the 11 July 1981 issue of the Spanish-language Miami daily, *Diario las Americas*.

In a *Miami Herald* interview published on 3 August 1981, Fagoth stated that "on January 16 we took the decision to declare open war against Sandinismo." And indeed, the beginning of the end occurred in February 1981. A major point of negotiation between

Misurasata and the government had become ratification of historic land titles. The antecedents to this struggle date back to the 1860 treaty creating a Miskito reserve, and the issue by 1980 was riddled with competing claims, legal complexities and major political implications. The government had mandated Misurasata to survey the situation and present evidence and a recommendation for discussion. The survey was funded by Cultural Survival, and Misurasata members proceeded to gather up all existing community land titles for the presentation of their map.

The government's understanding was that under discussion were traditional private and communal village properties, but in February 1981 it learned that Misurasata planned to present a demand for 33% of all Nicaraguan territory, including the mines. Apart from the touchy question of strategic resources, the Sandinistas linked such a claim for contiguous territory to U.S. interests in splitting the country and thus weakening the revolution.

It should also be kept in mind that Misurasata was demanding three-fourths of Zelaya, even though the indigenous groups make up no more than a third of the regional population. Misurasata had already antagonized some Creole communities which shared croplands with neighboring Miskito villages by suggesting that they would have to "go find an island somewhere" once Misurasata controlled the region.

Some suggest that such a demand was only a recognized negotiating tactic and that a satisfactory agreement could have resulted from good-faith discussions.

But this was not the plan. Fagoth and Rivera intended to unveil the land claim before thousands of receptive Miskitos in Puerto Cabezas at the closing ceremony of the literacy crusade and invite the Junta of Government for National Reconstruction in order to force its full capitulation. The Sandinistas also claim that Misurasata had orchestrated a series of armed confrontations to coincide with this bid for increased power. The government's response was the pre-emptive detention of 22 top and second-level leaders. The arrests were an effort to avoid an unnecessarily ugly and dangerous situation.

However, the results were not all that had been hoped for. The Sandinistas had not prepared the political ground-work for such a drastic move, and it resulted in turning many Misurasata members against the revolution. The situation was further aggravated by the events in Prinzapolka on 20 February 1981, when members of the EPS tried to arrest Elmer Prado and other Misurasata literacy workers. At the time, Prado was leading a celebration at the end of the crusade in a Moravian church. Not content to wait until the end, several soldiers entered and announced that Prado was under arrest. The enraged crowd confronted the soldiers and in the ensuing melee eight persons — including soldiers and civilians — were killed.

The most unforgivable thing from the Miskito point of view was that while the other leaders were quickly released, Fagoth was not. Documentation from the Office of National Security, Somoza's intelligence

Poster for the National Literacy Crusade.

apparatus, released to the newspapers, showed that Fagoth had been an informer during his years as a student in Managua in the 1970s[18]. But the systems of communication on the coast are not reliant on radios and newspapers, and many Miskitos who gathered for massive demonstrations in Puerto Cabezas and Waspan did not know why he was being held. Others did not find the reason particularly damnable, and still others cynically questioned why the Sandinistas had chosen that moment to reveal the information.

In later comments, the Sandinistas admitted that they had had suspicions about him even before Misurasata's formation, but that in accord with their revolutionary principles had wanted to give him a second chance.

FAGOTH JOINS CONTRAS IN HONDURAS

The clamor for Fagoth's liberty did not abate, and in May he was released on the provision that he go to the coast to calm the people, then accept a scholarship to study abroad. He did go to the coast, but promptly crossed the border into Honduras. Soon he was broadcasting wild accusations against the Sandinistas back into the Atlantic Coast in Miskito over the clandestine radio transmitter of the September 15th Legion, a band of ex-National Guardsmen operating from Honduras.

Fagoth's broadcasts combined historic and religious symbols with fabrications about Sandinista atrocities against Miskitos, and he exhorted others to join him in Honduras. Due both to his strongman popularity and to Sandinista military excesses, he was able to entice several thousand followers to join him. From the ranks of the refugees he put together his initial fighting force. (As early as August 1981, Mazta, an indigenous organization in Honduras, denounced Fagoth's training camps and expressed fears about his plans to invade Nicaragua[19].) Brooklyn Rivera visited the refugee camps in Honduras in June and returned claiming that the Miskito refugees had been tricked into going by

Fagoth and were now denied permission to leave[20]. Rivera urged government-to-government efforts to permit their return. Misurasata published a denunciation of Fagoth and urged international groups to ignore him[21].

Government representatives and remaining Misurasata leadership attempted to maintain dialogue for several months after Fagoth's departure. On 19 July, during his second anniversary speech, Daniel Ortega announced that the Ministry of Agricultural Development and Agrarian Reform would be in charge of studying the land problem in the Atlantic Coast[22]. But when Rivera presented the same territorial claim in July, relations, already extremely tense and suspicious, broke down entirely.

In August, the FSLN and the government issued their joint 8-point "Declaration of Principles Regarding the Indigenous Communities on the Atlantic Coast[23]." The document has been criticized both on the coast and internationally for several points, among them its abrupt focus on Spanish as the official language, without mentioning the existence of other national languages. This criticism does not acknowledge the fact that the Council of State had already passed a law requiring classes to be taught in maternal languages through the fourth grade[24]. But the main purpose of the declaration was to clarify the government's bottom-line position on the territorial issue, unequivocally stated in point 1:

Nicaragua is a single nation, territorially and politically, and cannot be dismembered, divided or damaged in its sovereignty and independence.

Point 5 reaffirmed that:

The Popular Sandinista Revolution will guarantee, and legalize through property titles, the land on which the communities on the Atlantic Coast have historically lived, be it in communal or collective form.

At this point Rivera recognized that Misurasata's claim had been defeated. Accusing the government of "parcelling" land which he considered to be Indian territory and claiming that his life was in danger, Rivera fled the country. Comandante William Ramirez, then Minister of INNICA, responded by announcing the withdrawal of recognition from Misurasata, giving as reasons that its leaders were in Honduras and its function as an intermediary with the government had thus terminated[25]. He acknowledged several FSLN errors, including having relied on such intermediaries, and said that communications would henceforth be directly with the communites. He also admitted that the government had launched enterprises on the coast without understanding the region sufficiently, and as a result had abused people's sensibilities.

The government set up a commission to discuss the question of land titles directly with the communities affected, that is, those who had never had clear title, or had migrated after receiving royal title in the previous century. Rivera still refers to INRA's power to decide land issues on the coast, but when the Agrarian Reform

18. *Barricada*, 25 February 1981; *El Nuevo Diario*, 25 February 1981. The *Barricada* article includes photostat of hand-written letter by Saul Torres, signed by Steadman Fagoth in parentheses.
19. *Tiempo* (San Pedro Sula, Honduras), 27 August 1981.
20. *Barricada*, 30 June 1981.
21. *Barricada*, 29 July 1981.
22. Second anniversary speech by Comandante Daniel Ortega, printed in *Segundo aniversario del triunfo de la Revolución Popular Sandinista y veinte aniversario de la fundación del FSLN 19 de julio de 1981*, Dirección de Divulgación y Prensa de la JGRN, Julio 1982.
23. Declaration of Principles Regarding the Indigenous Communities on the Atlantic Coast, 21 August 1981, reprinted in *Cultural Survival Quarterly* (Cambridge, MA.), Vol. 6, No. 1, Winter 1982, p. 23.
24. Decree No. 571, Ley sobre Educación en Lenguas en la Costa Atlantica, published in *La Gaceta*, No. 279, 3 December 1980.
25. Ley de Reforma Agraria, Decree No. 782, 23 July 1981, published in *La Gaceta*, 21 August 1981.

MARGARET D. WILDE
Issues For Dialogue:
The Position of the Moravian Church*
(Extract)

Four Steps Toward Peace

The "boxes-within-boxes conflict" in Nicaragua has confused and divided the church as well as the people directly affected by the war. Yet while we pray for clarity and grieve over the division, the church should also give thanks for the opportunity of Christian presence on all sides. Moravians are present in Nicaraguan villages and resettlement towns, in Honduran and Costa Rican refugee camps, in the capital cities of all three Central American countries, and in the capital city and several key legislative districts of the United States, which is also a party to the conflict.

That Christian presence enables the church to carry out a ministry that is at once pastoral, prophetic and reconciling: serving and consoling those who suffer, admonishing those whose actions cause suffering, and building bridges. Its objectives must be peace and security for the people it serves: not the peace of resignation or the security of dependency, but a peace built on equity, self-direction and full participation in the life of the community and the nation.

These were the objectives laid out by the Rev. Ted Wilde, executive director of the North American Moravian Board of World Mission, after he participated in the visit to Central America with Bishop Maynard, the Rev. Joe Gray and Rev. Howard Housmann[1].

The following steps must be taken on the road to achieve peace, the safe return of people to home villages, and the self-direction of their personal and communal existence:
— In co-operation with other organizations, our church can enlarge its ministry to people in their needs for physical assistance and pastoral care.
— The Moravian Church must continue as part of an ever-broadened communication and dialogue throughout the region.
— The Moravian Church must continue to raise the concerns of the people with governments and agencies. We confirm the efforts of Nicaraguan Moravian leaders to dialogue with their government to attain reconciliation and redress of grievances suffered by the East Coast people.
— North American Moravians should continue to urge the U.S. government to stop armed intervention from outside Nicaragua and to give full attention to the negotiations fostered by neighboring Latin American countries.

Physical Assistance and Pastoral Care

The sudden displacement of thousands of east coast people brought enormous needs for financial assistance, food, clothing, basic tools and equipment, and medical supplies and services. World Relief, the agency delegated by the United Nations High Commission on Refugees, quickly and effectively took up the challenge in Honduras; local churches have worked closely with that program and with other groups in Nicaragua and Costa Rica, to channel assistance from Moravian and ecumenical sources inside and outside the region. The Managua church became home to scores of people fleeing the fighting on the east coast, or visiting relatives imprisoned in the capital area. Local Moravian churches also helped organize legal services for the prisoners in Nicaragua, and for refugees in Costa Rica whose legal status needs clarification.

Many pastors are among the Nicaraguan Indian villagers who were relocated by the government or who fled to other communities, inside and outside Nicaragua, as a result of the fighting. Under extreme hardship, church life has continued and even undergone new growth. In Nicaragua in the midst of military confrontations and controversy over church–state relations, 78 voting delegates and several international visitors attended the church's triennial synod in February 1983. At the end of the year the newly elected superintendent, the Rev. Andy Shogreen, reported:

Very important to mention is that despite the fact that some congregations happen to be without the leading and caring of trained pastors, due mainly to fear of some pastors in going to remote communities, these congregations have been able to develop new leadership and have carried on the good work of the church.... The celebration of pastoral retreats served as a good means of curing some of the above mentioned problems in our church, bringing as a result more communication, reconciliation and new inspiration and strength for the mission of the church to which we have been called[2].

After visiting refugee communities in Honduras, Ted Wilde reported that the refugees in that country

... by their own effort have organized and built whole communities, including homes and churches, in less than a year.... Village people are making and implementing decisions about how they should build and run their communities and their churches. With few trained pastors, congregational organization and the life of worship and discipline have sprung up again from the practices firmly set in the hearts of the people[3].

Says a report from Costa Rica:

The challenge of the Costa Rica church is to both serve the Nicaraguans in the country, both English-speaking and Miskito-speaking, and also to reach out to the Spanish-speaking Costa Ricans.... Special committees of the Moravian Church in the capital city of San Jose and in Puerto Limon, strive to meet the great needs of the refugees in their midst. Those in Puerto Limon are still confined in a refugee camp[4].

Christian Communication and Dialogue

The second step toward peace, safety and self-direction for the Nicaraguan coastal peoples commits the Moravian Church to facilitate communication and engage in dialogue throughout the region. Says Wilde:

Other Moravians must be expediters of the broadened communication which may some day contribute to peaceful negotiations. We need more fraternal visits and continuing dialogue with Moravians of different viewpoints and political affiliation throughout the region. We need to listen to the Nicaraguan refugees in our own country.

We can directly explore how the Moravian provinces or international organizations can help Nicaraguans exchange letters and messages with families and friends in

*This text is an extract from a mimeographed report entitled "The East Coast: Issues for Dialogue", prepared by the author for the Board of the World Mission Moravian Church in America in June 1984.

The Moravian Church, introduced in Nicaragua in 1849, is the eastern region's principal grass-roots institution (as the Catholic Church is in western Nicaragua); the Catholic, Anglican and several evangelical churches also work on the east coast. The Nicaraguan Moravian Church, with locally trained Indian and Creole leadership, became an autonomous province within the world-wide Unitas Fratrum in 1974.

Honduras and Costa Rica. Their interest in such communication is great. Brother Gray, for example, received more than 500 letters from people in Nicaragua for him to carry to the refugee communities in Honduras[5].

The North American Moravian magazine regularly serves as a vehicle for communication. Its publication of widely varying viewpoints on the Nicaraguan conflict has drawn an equally wide range of criticism, and a recent suggestion that "any article about a complex or fluctuating situation be preceded by an editorial statement that puts it in perspective"[6]. Editor Bernard E. Michel replies that such a statement might suggest an editorial bias, and not sufficiently respect the reader's intelligence; the magazine will continue publishing divergent interpretations and challenging readers to seek both sides of every controversial issue.

The Board of World Mission's new program, "Mission to North America", sponsors about five visits each year from leaders of sister provinces and mission churches; this year it is focusing particularly on Nicaragua[7]. Central American Moravians have also visited the United States under similar programs sponsored by the Presbyterian Church and ecumenical bodies. Another important communications link is provided by North American church members who have visited Central America, individually or in church-sponsored programs, and returned home to share their experience and interpretations.

Meanwhile, the Board of World Mission continues to engage in public and private conversation with pastors and lay leaders on all sides of the conflict — missionaries, government officials, scholars, activists, supporters, opponents and victims of official policies — and encourages other Moravians to do the same. "Within the framework of the above broadened discussion, [the church should] remain fully supportive of the approach and dialogue with government of the Nicaraguan Moravian leaders", says a recent internal policy guideline of the Board of World Mission[8]. That does not exclude criticism of the positions with which we or other Moravians are in dialogue; it does mean speaking the truth in love, listening with respect, building bridges and inviting others to cross with us.

Raise the Concerns of the People

The third step confirms the Nicaraguan Moravian leaders' dialogue with their government in search of reconciliation and the redress of the east coast people's grievances[9].

Such dialogue would normally be taken for granted, as a Roman Catholic sister pointed out in 1982: "In more peaceful times, problems would be solved through ordinary communication between the church and the government. In a state of emergency, these problems become major crises[10]." To further complicate the process, under pressure any break in the dialogue may lead to new violence — and any violent incident may cause a breakdown in the dialogue. This is no place for long-distance advice and criticism; only the people directly engaged in the discussions, and those whose cause they are pleading, are in a position to judge its day-to-day progress. However, those who watch the dialogue from a distance can contribute significantly to its success or failure. It is within our power to create the atmosphere for dialogue, or to fill the air with static and self-perpetuating resentment.

The agenda is wide and varied. MISURASATA and the Indian warriors speak of de-militarization, political autonomy and Indian responsibility for the security of the Atlantic Coast. Americas Watch seeks a public accounting for the Leimus incident and the disappeared, compensation for the destroyed villages, freedom of movement and communication among the divided families. Pastor Bent and other church leaders add to the list the release of the remaining prisoners, the establishment of a truly representative Indian organization, and improved local security (including discipline in the use of authority by the Sandinista forces).

Three basic themes underline the various expressions of the agenda: redress for past injuries, security on their land, and participation in community and national decision-making. The memory of disappeared family members remains an ache that even grief cannot heal, until their fate is known. Their tie to the land is at the very heart of Indian cultures, and is important also to the Creole and Spanish-speaking peasant families that have lived for generations on the east coast. Every community has a right to participate in the decisions affecting it. Most of the relocated people will not adjust to their new homes — will not plant the trees that symbolize permanence, or invest their energy in the success of the settlements — until they are offered a real choice and a real participation in the direction of their new lives.

Where Spanish-speaking, western Nicaraguans are concerned, the current Nicaraguan government has respected land rights and participation more consistently than its predecessors. In the case of the coastal peoples, the government has so far refused to account publicly for disappearances and alleged executions, has made paternalistic substitution rather than compensation for alienated and destroyed property, and has resisted attempts by the Indians to develop a new, self-generated organization. Ethnic prejudice is almost certainly a factor in the denial of these rights on the Atlantic Coast, but another factor is the international manipulation of east coast claims for political propaganda and subversion. Most of the coastal people are not a party to this manipulation — many are not even aware of it — but while it continues, the dialogue continues to falter and all are denied justice.

Stop Armed Intervention

That brings us to the fourth step toward peace, which is uniquely within the power of North American (primarily U.S.) Christians: to call a halt to armed intervention and support the efforts of friendly governments to achieve a negotiated political solution to the U.S.–Nicaraguan box of the conflict.

Nicaraguan Moravian leaders have repeatedly asked U.S. Moravians to work energetically for such a solution. They know that a withdrawal of U.S. pressure on their government would not guarantee success for the dialogue on east coast issues, but it would clarify those issues — and their position, and that of their government. Far from encouraging a liberalization of Sandinista policy, as the supporters of covert action sometimes claim[11], the use and threat of armed force against Nicaragua gives the government an easy pretext on which to reject all accommodation. By polarizing the country's internal political process it also strengthens the doctrinaire, divides and weakens the pluralistic forces in that process; many people who would normally support the east coast claims either fall silent, flee, or reluctantly join the armed opposition.

The most promising alternative to military confrontation is the one proposed by the governments of Mexico, Panama, Venezuela and Colombia: the four nations nearest and most vulnerable to the Central American countries, popularly known as the Contadora group of nations. They have proposed mechanisms not only to resolve the immediate conflict but to correct the underlying internal conditions that produced it.

The 21-point Contadora peace plan begins by advocating compliance with international law; observance of human, political, civil, economic, social, religious and cultural rights; establishment of pluralistic, participatory political systems; and guarantees of international security and national sovereignty. Seven points are aimed at removing the temptation to use armed force in order to impose, destabilize or overthrow a government. One supports humanitarian aid to refugees and measures for their eventual repatriation. Others propose law was published in August, there was only one reference to the coast. Article 30, titled "Special Disposition," speaking of the possibility of transferring additional lands to the communities, stated:

The State will have the power to make available the necessary amount of land so that Miskito, Sumu and Rama communities can work them individually or collectively and so that they may benefit from their natural resources, with the goal that their members be able to improve their level of existence and contribute to the social and economic development of the Nicaraguan nation[26].

In September, Rivera, who had joined Fagoth in Honduras, issued a vituperative document in the name of Misurasata effectively exonerating Fagoth and claiming that the Sandinistas left no room for peaceful resolution of indigenous issues. Relations between the Sandinista government and the population of the Atlantic Coast were tense.

26. *Barricada*, 30 August 1981.

THE MILITARY SITUATION ECLIPSES THE SEARCH FOR SOLUTIONS

Since that time, debates about appropriate economic programs, the form and degree of indigenous political participation, control over land use and titles, etc., have been forced into the background by the military escalation in the region. With the regionalization of government and ministerial structures that were initiated in September 1982, however, direct access to decision-making bodies has been facilitated.

It is essential to point out that these debates reflect the far-reaching concerns of a small sector of the Miskito and coastal peoples. The majority of those living in the isolated indigenous communities, on the other hand, are simply feeling confused and uncertain about the control they have over their precarious lives and livelihood in the face of decisions being made by the government based mainly on military contingencies. Furthermore, their preconceptions are being turned upside down as once-revered leaders kidnap

---

"national actions toward reconciliation in cases of deep social divisions", and multilateral social, economic and trade policy measures to remove such divisions in the interest of lasting peace.

The Contadora governments, and the Latin American and European governments that have firmly supported their initiatives, are respected by the parties to the conflict and by the international community as a whole. Their role in economic assistance makes them logical mediators and guarantors of a negotiated settlement. In addition, their own political and economic experiments are among the models and pointers used by Central American revolutionary movements in the search for alternative administrative and developmental structures[12].

A negotiated political solution would not require the United States to withdraw entirely from the region. The United States and every friendly nation can offer encouragement, support and even guidance in the development of alternative political and economic models. Most Central Americans, including most advocates of revolutionary alternatives, are still urging the United States to exercise that role. But we cannot do so as adversaries, and we cannot do so unilaterally; we can only do so in partnership with other friendly governments, and with the Central American people themselves. What is missing in the current policy equation is the element of partnership, and that can only be added if we halt the threat and use of armed intervention.

The Board of World Mission seeks, and urges other concerned North American Moravians, to engage in dialogue with members of Congress and U.S. administrative officials in support of the Contadora proposals and other initiatives toward a reduction of hostilities with Nicaragua[13]. This dialogue should ideally be undertaken together with other concerned Christians — many U.S. church bodies have already committed themselves to the same process[14] — but does not depend on ecumenical action in every instance. People are looking to Moravians for expertise and leadership on the issue of the Nicaraguan east coast.

When Moravians discuss this situation, it should be on the basis of a sober and frank appraisal. We should speak without idealizing or condemning any country, with an awareness of how difficult it is to achieve peace in a sinful world. But we should speak with hope: as Christians we have a great hope for peace, great dedication, and great resources for effectiveness. With God's grace and guidance, we are the answer to our own prayer for peace.

Footnotes

1. The Rev. Ted Wilde, "Mission Team Visits Remote Areas" *The North American Moravian*, March 1984.
2. Rev. Andy Shogreen, "A Troublesome but Significant Year", *The North American Moravian*, May 1984.
3. Ted Wilde, "Mission Team Visits Remote Areas". *The North American Moravian*, March 1984.
4. "A New Moravian Work", *The North American Moravian*, May 1984.
5. "Mission Team Visits Remote Areas", *The North American Moravian*, March 1984.
6. Letter from Ruth and Gerhard Miller, *The North American Moravian*, June–July, 1984.
7. Kevin Frack, "The Gospel Comes Home", *The North American Moravian*, May 1984.
8. From a policy statement affirmed in February 1984 by the Board of World Mission, Moravian Church in America.
9. See also Margaret D. Wilde, "Moravian–Sandinista Dialogue", *Christian Century*, 11 May 1983.
10. Sr. Margaret Cafferty, Congregational Superior of the Sisters of the Presentation, quoted in the editorial column of *The North American Moravian*, January 1983.
11. The Kissinger Commission preceded its divided opinion in favor of aid to the insurgents with the claim that "after the U.S. actions in Grenada, Managua has hinted at some accommodations in its external and internal policies." *Report of the National Bipartisan Commission on Central America*, January 1984, p. 116.
12. For further analysis of the Contadora proposals, see PACCA (Policy Alternatives for the Caribbean and Central America), *Changing Course: Blueprint for Peace in Central America and the Caribbean*, Washington, Institute for Policy Studies, 1984; and Penny Lernoux, *Fear and Hope: Toward Political Democracy in Central America*, New York, The Field Foundation, 1984.
13. Canadian Moravians can press for their government's support to the Contadora process at the international level.
14. See *Adventure and Hope: Christians and the Crisis in Central America*, Report to the 195th General Assembly of the Presbyterian Church (U.S.A.), New York, 1983.

whole villages, destroy their jobsites and offer little in return but more suffering. The Sandinistas, on the other hand, are beginning to demonstrate at close proximity that they are not the devil incarnate, as they had been painted by Misurasata leaders. Some adapt to the new realities with relative ease; others retrench into a silent fatalism, trusting in their religious beliefs to see them through; still others actively integrate into whatever organizational option they think will best benefit them; others join relatives in Honduran re-settlements. It is not a moment when honest observers can identify Fagoth's and Rivera's position as a "Miskito position."

In final contrast, many of the foot soldiers of the counterrevolutionary war on the coast — those whom Nietschmann romanticizes as "Indian warriors" — are the poorest and least educated of the isolated village populations; the illiteracy rate of rural Zelaya before the crusade was 80% and is still more than 50%. And they are steeped in anti-political, religious beliefs. No one knows better than Steadman Fagoth and Brooklyn Rivera how to appeal to their fears which are deeply rooted in 400 years of exploitation.

Nietschmann and others accuse the Sandinistas of racist condescension for insisting that these Miskito recruits have been "tricked" by such leaders. It is a morally powerful attack, and not utterly devoid of basis. But the Miskitos are not the first indigenous group whose beliefs have been put to the service of their historic enemies by unscrupulous leaders. Brooklyn Rivera was one of the first to acknowledge this when he visited the Miskito refugee camps in Honduras in mid-1981.

FINAL WORDS

In symbolic terms, perhaps the unfinished children's park in Tasbapounie summarizes the current state of affairs between the Sandinista revolution and the ethnic groups of the Atlantic Coast.

As we were told the story by some residents of Tasbapounie, the revolutionary government decided two or three years ago to give materials to the com-munity to build a children's park. The cement quickly arrived with promises that other equipment would come when the community had finished the park. One young man began working immediately and tried to encourage others to help him. But no one did. People would pass by saying that it was a stupid place to build a park; it was swampy and would always be damp. Or probably the government wouldn't give the rest of the park equipment anyway, and why didn't the govern-ment build the park itself? The youth continued work-ing every time he had a few free hours, building a border around the park so that the water couldn't seep in. But without help he couldn't work fast enough, and soon the humidity and rain hardened the sacks of cement. Reluctantly, he abandoned the project.

At first the people felt satisfied; they had been right not to get involved. But little by little, the unfinished park began to tell a different story to some people. Now they pass the abandoned work and say: perhaps the government was trying to do something nice, perhaps if we had helped we would have a park for the children now.

The problem came from both sides. The govern-ment, in all good will, wanted to do something for the people, but without first gaining their interest and receptivity. The people, on the other hand, were locked into an historic fatalism, combined with the alienating effects of centuries of paternalism, and a traditional rejection of anything "Spanish." The result was understandable.

The real problems of the coast are obviously much more profound and complex, but many of the roots of these problems are contained in this anecdote. For example, the socio-economic problem: the region isn't even self-sufficient enough to minimally fill its own basic needs; decades of pillage by the U.S. com-panies have left the area destroyed and dependent on the Pacific. Furthermore, the coastal population demands education, health, transport, food provisions and other kinds of assistance. But these services cannot continue to be provided from Managua. They require the economic development of the region, and this implies, among other things, the reorganization of production and living patterns to make these services feasible.

But the government cannot decide this by fiat. Recent history has shown that the indigenous com-munities resist participation in such changes just as they initially resisted putting their energies into the construction of the park.

For example, the first steps have been taken to address the question of land tenure and usufruct, but in the fullest sense this issue cannot be separated from the one above. The government and the coastal peoples together have to resolve the contradictions that exist between traditional modes of living and the desire for improved socio-economic wellbeing.

In short, solutions have to come through the parti-cipation of the people themselves in the political decision-making process, and on this, the principles of the revolution are clear. The revolution is based fundamentally on developing the possibilities for true popular democracy.

Given the failure of Misurasata to provide the vehicle for progressive participation, it has been necessary to seek other means. In the last two years, this has meant opening dialogue at the level of community leaders, church functionaries and others who represent the progressive aspirations of the national minorities on the coast. It has also meant promoting the formation of authentic organizations that can carry these aspira-tions forward at a regional level. This need for organ-ized participation was publicly addressed during the celebration of the amnesty for Miskito prisoners in December 1983 by Minerva Wilson, a director of

Tasba Pri. Speaking Miskito and Spanish, she urged the creation of a grassroots indigenous organization, and added that she had asked the government that such an organization be represented in the Council of State.

In a certain sense, the communities of Tasba Pri have offered an alternative. Despite the unfortunate reason for their creation, they have demonstrated the real concern of the government to improve the living conditions of the indigenous peoples. In these communities schools, health programs, decent housing and services such as electricity, drinking water and transport are becoming a tangible reality. In Tasba Pri as well, community members are increasing their participation in administration and decision-making. Their religous leaders are playing a positive role that raises the position of the communities in their relation with the government and FSLN cadres there.

The process is slow and not free of difficulties. It cannot be denied, for example, that some, particularly the elders, dream of a future when the war has ended and they can return to their home on their river "Wanki". But Tasba Pri has also produced a change of attitude toward the revolution on the part of many there.

Given the "urbanization" of these previously dispersed river communities, Miskito cultural expressions have flowered in Tasba Pri. Music and folklore have undergone a vibrant rebirth, and the people are now openly proud of their language.

In other areas of the coast as well, efforts to understand and preserve what is vital within the Miskito culture continues. One pillar of Miskito identity is language. A Spanish-Miskito grammar is about to be published and oral narratives and histories are being collected for use in the bilingual–bicultural education project and other publications. The latter include translations for the Pacific to help break the wall of ignorance about the coast. The daily radio program in Miskito and Sumu, "La Costa Atlantica Presente" ("Kus Uplika Nani Narasna") receives hundreds of letters weekly to be read directly on the program for relatives and friends. The program has thus become an active medium of popular communication.

The peoples of the Atlantic Coast have, throughout their history, experienced long periods of relative autonomy, followed by a situation of abandonment under oligarchic or dictatorial forms of centralized government. In the latter period their lands and labor were exploited by economic interests whose goals did not take them into account at all. Each one of these experiences has left the coastal people deeper in misery.

The challenge still remains for the Sandinista revolution to give an integrated answer to the real economic, cultural, political and social demands of the coast. Nevertheless, four years of struggle show that substantial human and economic resources have been and continue to be dedicated to overcoming the complexities and contradictions involved in this effort. It is evident that the revolution is committed to assure the survival and prosperity of Nicaragua's ethnic groups.

It is also evident that as long as the war on the coast and in the rest of the country is kept alive through the assistance of the U.S. government, the search for new solutions will be more difficult. Resources, energies and creativity will continue to be divided between dialogue and defense.

In the final analysis, one last thing is equally clear: whatever the cost in suffering and sacrifice, the Nicaraguan revolution is unswervingly dedicated to building a new society, one that is more just and human, multi-ethnic and multilingual.

SELECTED BIBLIOGRAPHY

ON POPULAR CULTURE AND COMMUNICATION IN NICARAGUA

1. Books

ALDARACA, B., ed. *Nicaragua in Revolution: The Poets Speak*. Minneapolis: University of Minnesota, 1980.

ALEMAN OCAMPO, C., ed *Y tambien enseñenles a leer: Alfabetización en Nicaragua*. Managua: Editorial Nueva Nicaragua, 1984.

ARRIEN, J. B. *Nicaragua: Revolución y proyecto educativo*. Managua: Publicaciones del Ministerio de Educación, 1980.

—; et al. *Educación y dependencia: El caso de Nicaragua*. Managua: Ediciones el Pez y la Serpiente, 1977.

ASOCIACION NICARAGUENSE DE CIENTIFICOS SOCIALES (ANICS). *Estado y clases sociales en Nicaragua*. Managua, 1982.

ASSMANN, Hugo. *Nicaragua: Triunfo en la alfabetización*. San José (Costa Rica): Departamento Ecumenico de Investigaciones, 1981.

BARRICADA, ed. *Corresponsales de guerra*. Managua: Editorial Nuevo Amanecer, 1983.

BIRRI, F., et al. *Nicaragua: No interrumpaís que coman su naranja*. Rome: Laboratorio de poéticas cinematográficas, 1985.

BLACK, G. *Triumph of the People: The Sandinista Revolution in Nicaragua*. London: Zed Press, 1981.

—; J. BEVAN. *The Loss of Fear: Education in Nicaragua Before and After the Revolution*. London: NSC/WUS, 1980.

BORGE MARTINEZ, T. *El axioma de la esperanza*. Bilbao: Desclée De Brouwer, 1984.

BRANDAO, C., ed. *Lições de Nicaragua: A experiencia de esperança*. Campinas (Brazil): Papirus Livraria Editora, 1982.

CABESTRERO, T. *Blood of the Innocent: Victims of the Contras' War In Nicaragua*. New York: Orbis, 1985.

—. *Revolucionarios por el Evangelio*. Bilbao: Desclée de Brouwer, 1983.

CABEZAS, O. *La montaña es algo mas que una immensa estepa verde*. Havana: Casa de las Américas, 1982.

CARDENAL, E. *Apocalypse and Other Poems*. New York: New Directions, 1977.

—. *La democratización de la cultura*. Managua: Ministerio de la Cultura, 1982.

—. *The Gospel in Solentimane*. New York: Orbis Books, 1982.

—. *Love*. New York: Crossroads, 1981.

—. *Nostalgia del futuro*. Managua: Editorial Nueva Nicaragua/Editorial Monimbó, 1984 (2nd Edition).

—. *Zero Hour and Other Documentary Poems*. New York: New Directions, 1980.

CAROIT, J.-M.; V. SOULE. *Nicaragua, le modèle sandiniste*. Paris: Le Sycomore, 1981.

CASALIS, G. et al. *Libération et religion. Défis des thèologies de la libération*. Paris: INODEP, [1983?].

CENTRO DE INVESTIGACIONES Y DOCUMENTACION DE LA COSTA ATLANTICA (CIDCA), ed. *Trabil Nani: Historical Background and Current Situation on Nicaragua's Atlantic Coast*. New York; Managua: CIDCA; Riverside Church Disarmament Project, 1984. Mimeographed.

CENTRO DE INVESTIGACIONES Y ESTUDIOS DE LA REFORMA AGRARIA (CIERA). *Lunes socio-económico de Barricada*. Managua, 1984.

—. *La democracia participativa en Nicaragua*. Managua, 1984.

—. *La mujer en las cooperativas agropecuarias en Nicaragua*. Managua, 1984.

CHACON, M. A.; M. A. TALAVERA. *Refugio noticieros radiales en las iglesias (Periodismo de Catacumba)* Managua: Universidad Nacional Autonoma de Nicaragua, Facultad de Humanidades, 1978.

Mimeographed.

COLLINS, J.; et al. *Nicaragua: What Difference Could a Revolution Make?* San Francisco: Institute for Food and Development Policy, 1985.

CORAGGIO, J. L. *Nicaragua: Revolución y democracia.* Mexico City: Editorial Linea/CRIES, 1985.

CORTAZAR, J. *Nicaragua tan violentamente dulce.* Managua: Editorial Nueva Nicaragua, 1983.

CRAVEN, D.; J. RYDER. *Art of the New Nicaragua.* New York: [Funded by the New York Council for the Humanities], March 1983.

CRIQUILLION, A.; et al. *Revolución y mujeres del campo.* Managua: Asociación de Trabajadores del Campo, 1985.

DE CASTILLA, M. *Educación y lucha de clases en Nicaragua.* Managua: UCA, 1980.

DIXON, M.; S. JONAS, eds. *Nicaragua Under Siege.* San Francisco: Synthesis Publications, 1984.

DONAHUE, J. M. *The Nicaragua Revolution in Health.* South Hadley (MA): Bergin & Garvey, forthcoming 1986.

DUFLO, M.; F. RUELLAN, eds. *Le volcan nicaraguayen.* Paris: La Découverte, 1985.

EPIC TASK FORCE. *Nicaragua: A People's Revolution.* Washington, D.C., 1980.

ESCUELA DE PERIODISMO; UNIVERSIDAD CENTRO-AMERICANA. *Para una lectura crítica del diario "La Prensa".* Managua, 1985.

ESPEJO, P. *Femmes du Nicaragua.* Paris: Editions des Femmes, 1980.

EZCURRA, A. M. *Agresión ideológica contra la revolución sandinista.* Mexico City: Nuevomar, 1983.

FAGEN, R. R. *The Nicaraguan Revolution: A Personal Report.* Washington, D.C.: Institute of Policy Studies, 1981.

Fe cristiana y revolución sandinista. Managua: Instituto histórico centroamericano, 1979.

FEDERATION INTERNATIONALE DES DROITS DE L'HOMME. *La realidad actual de Nicaragua.* Paris: CIAL-Université de Paris VIII, 1985.

FESTA, R.; VIGIL LOPEZ, M. *El Tayacán. La innovación del periodismo popular en Nicaragua.* Lima: IPAL, October 1985.

FONSECA, C. *Bajo la bandera del sandinismo. Textos políticos.* Managua: Editorial Nueva Nicaragua, 1981.

—. *Obras.* Managua: Editorial Nueva Nicaragua, 1982.

GIRARDI, G. *Fe en la revolución: Revolución en la cultura.* Managua: Editorial Nueva Nicaragua/Ediciones Monimbó, 1983.

GOROSTIAGA, X. *Los dilemas de la revolución popular sandinista.* Managua: Cuadernos de Pensamiento Propio, 1982.

—. *Geopolitica de la crisis regional.* Managua: INIES, 1984.

GUEVARA, O.; C. PEREZ BERMÚDEZ. *El movimiento obrero nicaragüense.* Managua: Ediciones Davila Bolaños, 1981.

HARRIS, R.; C. M. VILAS. *Nicaragua: A Revolution*

Under Siege. London: Zed Press, 1985.

HIRSHON, S.; J. BUTLER. *And Also Teach Them to Read.* Westport (CT): Lawrence Hill, 1983.

Historia de la iglesia de los pobres en Nicaragua. Managua: El Tayacán, [ca 1980].

INSTITUTO NICARAGUENSE DE CINE (INCINE). *El Cine en la revolución.* Managua: Segundo Seminario de capacitación para proyeccionistas del EPS, February 1981.

—. *El Instituto Nicaragüense de cine presenta.* Managua, 1985. Mimeographed.

INSTITUTO NICARAGUENSE DE INVESTIGACIONES ECONOMICAS Y SOCIALES (INIES). *Nicaragua revolucionaria: Bibliografía 1978–84.* Managua, July 1984.

JARA, O. *Educación popular: La dimensión educativa de la acción politica.* Panama: CEASPA–ALFORJA, 1981.

JENKINS MOLIERI, J., ed. *Testimonios sobre la realidad miskita.* Stockholm: Cono Sur Press, 1984.

KAHN, D.; D. NEUMAIER, eds. *Cultures in Contention.* Seattle: The Real Comet Press, 1985.

LAPPLE-WAGENHALS, D. *A New Communication Model — A New Communication Policy?: On Communications in Nicaragua before and after July 19, 1979.* Frankfurt/Main: Verlag Peter Lang, 1984.

LEVIE, A. *Nicaragua: The People Speak.* South Hadley (MA): Bergin & Garvey, 1985.

MARMENTINI, V.; A. GUERRERO. *La manipulación de la información: Tratamiento del caso nicaragüense en la prensa.* Bogota: CINEP, 1982.

MATTELART, A., ed. *Communicating In Popular Nicaragua.* New York; Bagnolet: International General, 1986.

—; G. ROTHSCHUH VILLANUEVA. *Guerra, ideología y comunicación.* Managua: Ediciones Nicaragua al Dia, 1985.

MEISELAS, S. *Nicaragua.* New York: Pantheon, 1980.

MELROSE, D. *The Threat of a Good Example?* Oxford (UK): Oxfam, 1985.

MINISTERIO DE LA CULTURA. *Hacia una politica cultural de la revolución popular sandinista.* Managua: Ministerio de la Cultura, 1982.

MINISTERIO DE LA EDUCACION (MED). *Documentos primer congreso nacional de la alfabetización "Georgino Andrade Rivera".* Managua, 9–10 June 1980.

—. *Documentos segundo congreso nacional de la alfabetización "Héroes y martires por la alfabetización".* Managua, 5–6 September 1980.

—. *Documentos primer congreso nacional de educación popular de adultos "Augusto César Pinell".* Managua, 6–7 June 1981.

—. *Documentos de lineamientos 1982, programa de educación popular básica de adultos.* Managua, 1982.

—. *Evaluacion 1981–plan 1982, programa de edu-*

cación de adultos. Managua, 1982.

—. *Quiénes son y a qué aspiran los estudiantes de los CEP, programa de educacion de adultos*. Managua, 1982.

—. *Los cortes de café y sus implicaciones en el programa de educación de adultos, programa de educación de adultos*. Managua, 1982.

—. *La educación en el primer año de la revolución popular sandinista*. Managua, 1980.

—. *La educación en dos años de revolución*. Managua, 1981.

—. *La educación en tres años de revolución*. Managua, 1982.

—. *La educación en cuatro años de revolución*. Managua, 1983.

—. *Cinco años de educación en la revolución*. Managua, 1984.

MINISTERIO DEL INTERIOR. *Hacia un nueva educación en Nicaragua*. Managua: Publicaciones del Ministerio del Interior, 1980.

NOLAN, D. *The Ideology of the Sandinistas and the Nicaraguan Revolution*. Miami (Florida): Institute of Inter-American Studies, 1984.

ORTEGA HEGG, M. *El conflicto etnia-nación en Nicaragua*. Managua: Ministerio de la Cultura, 1981.

ORTEGA SAAVEDRA, H. *Sobre la insurrección*. Mexico City: Editorial Nuestro Tiempo, 1980.

PASQUINI, J. M. *Nicaragua: Formación de especialistas de comunicación y desarrollo de las instituciones y programas de formación*. Paris: UNESCO, 1983. Mimeographed.

RAMIREZ, S. *El alba de oro: La historia viva de Nicaragua*. Mexico City: Siglo XXI, 1983.

—, ed. *El pensamiento vivo de Sandino*. Managua: Editorial Nueva Nicaragua, 1981.

—; O. CABEZAS; D. M. TELLEZ. *La insurrección de las paredes*. Managua: Editorial Nueva Nicaragua, 1984.

RANDALL, M. *Todas estamos despiertas*. Mexico City: Siglo XXI, 1980.

—. *Cristianos en la revolución*. Managua: Ediciones Monimbó, 1983.

ROTHSCHUH TABLADA, G.; C. TAMEZ. *La cruzada nacional de alfabetización de Nicaragua: Su organizacion y estrategias de participación y movilización*. [Managua], August 1983.

ROTHSCHUH VILLANUEVA, G. *Anotaciones sobre periodísmo y revolución en Nicaragua*. Mexico City: Ediciones Mex-Sur, 1983.

—; et al. *La mentira: Arma del imperialismo contra Nicaragua*. Managua: Ediciones Nicaragua al Dia, 1980.

—. *El problema de la comunicación en un estado de transición*. Managua: Ediciones Nicaragua al Dia, 1980.

SANDINO, A. *Pensamientos*. Managua: Ministerio de Educación, 1979.

STRAUBHAAR, J.; E. MAHAN, eds. *Broadcasting in Latin America*. Philadelphia: Temple University Press, forthcoming 1986.

TORRES, R. M. *De alfabetizando a maestro popular: La post-alfabetización en Nicaragua*. Managua: Cuadernos de Pensamiento Propio, 1983.

—. *Los CEP: Educación popular y democracia participativa en Nicaragua*. Managua: CRIES/INIES, 1985.

—. *Nicaragua: Revolución popular, educación popular*. Mexico City; Managua: INIES; Editorial Linea, 1985.

TÜNNERMAN, C. *La contribución del periodísmo a la liberación nacional*. Managua: Publicaciones del Ministerio de la Educación, 1980.

UNION NACIONAL DE AGRICULTORES Y GANADEROS (UNAG). *Nuestra comunicación*. Managua: Programa de capacitación de los consejos zonales, 1984.

—. *Nuestra historia nacional*. Managua, 1984.

VAYSSIERE, P., ed. *Nicaragua: Les contradictions du sandinisme*. Paris: Editions CNRS, 1985.

VILAS, C. M. *Perfiles de la revolución Sandinista*. Havana: Casa de las Américas, 1984.

WALKER, T. W., ed. *Nicaragua: The First Five Years*. New York: Praeger, 1985.

—, ed. *Nicaragua in Revolution*. New York: Praeger, 1982.

WEBER, H. *Nicaragua: The Sandinist Revolution*. London: Verso Editions, 1981.

WHEELOCK ROMAN, J. *Nicaragua: El gran desafío*. Managua: Editorial Nueva Nicaragua, 1983. Interview by Marta Harnecker.

—. *Raíces indígenas de la lucha anticolonialista en Nicaragua*. Managua: Editorial Nueva Nicaragua, 1981.

ZWERLING, P.; C. MARTIN, eds. *Nicaragua: A New Kind of Revolution. Forty-Five Key Spokespeople Interviewed*. Westport (CT): Lawrence Hill, [1985?]

2. Reviews

Amanecer, Apartado Postal 3205, Managua, Nicaragua.

Barricada Internacional, Apartado Postal 576, Managua.

Cuadernos de Periodísmo, Journal of the School of Journalism, Recinto Universitario "Ricardo Morales Aviles", Managua.

Envío, Apartado Postal A-194, Managua. Also in English.

Nicaráuac, Ministerio de la Cultura, Managua.

Pensamiento Propio, Apartado Postal C-16, Managua.

El Tayacán, Apartado Postal 447, Managua.

ON POPULAR CULTURE AND COMMUNICATION IN LATIN AMERICA

1. Books

ARDILES, O., et al. *Cultura popular y filosofia de la liberación*. Buenos Aires: F. Carcia Cambeiro, 1975.

ARTUR DE LIMA, V. *Comunicação e cultura:As ideias de Paulo Freire*. Rio de Janeiro: Paz e Terra, 1981.

BARREIRO, J. *Educación popular y proceso de concientización*. Mexico City: Siglo XXI, 1977.

BOAL, A. *Teatro del oprimido*. 2 vols. Mexico City: Nueva Imagen, 1980.

—. *Técnicas latinoamericanas del teatro popular*. Mexico City: Nueva Imagen, 1982.

—. *The Theater of the Oppressed*. New York: Urizen Books, 1979.

CAMACHO, D.; R. MENJIVAR, eds. *Movimientos populares en Centroamérica*. San José (Costa Rica): Educa, 1985.

CARVALHO-NETO, P. *El folklore de las luchas sociales*. Mexico City: Siglo XXI, 1973.

COLOMBRES, A. et al. *La cultura popular*. Mexico City: Premiá Editora, 1982.

Comunicación y cultura (Mexico City), Number 10. On popular cultures.

DE KADT, E. *Catholic Radicals in Brazil*. London: Oxford University Press, 1970.

ESTEINOU, J. *Los medios de comunicación y la construcción de la hegemonía*. Mexico City: Nueva Imagen, 1983.

FERNANDEZ, F. et al. *Video, cultura nacional y subdesarrollo*. Mexico City: Filmoteca UNAM, 1985.

FREIRE, P. *Pedagogy of the Oppressed*. New York: Herder & Herder, 1971.

—. *Cultural Action for Freedom*. Harmondsworth (UK): Penguin, 1970.

GARCIA CANCLINI, N. *Arte popular y sociedad en América Latina*. Mexico City: Grijalbo, 1977.

—. *Las cultures populares en el capitalismo*. Havana: Casa de las Américas, 1982.

GARGUREVICH, J. *Historia de los medios masivos de comunicación en el Peru*. Lima: APEIC, 1984.

GONGORA, A. *La televisión del mundo popular*. Santiago de Chile: ILET, 1983.

GONZALEZ SANCHEZ, J. *Sociología de las culturas subalternas*, an issue of *TICOM* (Mexico City), 11 October 1981.

GRIMBERG SIMPSON, S. ed. *Comunicación alternativa y cambio social*. Mexico City: Universidad Autonoma de Mexico, 1982.

LINS DA SILVA, C. E., ed. *Comunicação, hegemonía e contra-informação*. Sao Paolo: Cortez Editora-Intercom, 1982.

MATA, M. C. *Radio Enriquillo en dialogo con el pueblo*. Quito: Asociación latinoamericana de educación radiofónica, 1985.

MATTELART, A. *Mass Media, Ideologies and the Revolutionary Movement*. Brighton (UK): Harvester Press; Atlantic Highlands (NJ): Humanities Press, 1980.

—; S. SIEGELAUB, eds. *Communication and Class Struggle: 1. Capitalism, Imperialism*. New York, Bagnolet (France): International General, 1979.

—; —, eds. *Communication and Class Struggle: 2. Liberation, Socialism*. New York, Bagnolet (France): International General, 1983.

NETHOL, A. M. *La comunicación participativa*, an issue of *TICOM* (Mexico City), 7, [ca 1980].

ORTIZ, R. *A consciencia fragmentada: Ensaios de cultura popular e religião*. Rio de Janeiro: Paz e Terra, 1980.

OSSANDON, F. *Lugar de la comunicación popular en la democratización de las comunicaciones en Chile*. Santiago de Chile: ECO, 1983.

PUIGGROS, A. *La educación popular en América latina: Origenes, polémicas y perspectivas*. Mexico City: Nueva Imagen, 1984.

REYES MATTA, F., ed. *Comunicación alternativa y busquedas democraticas*. Mexico City: ILET–Friedrich Ebert Stiftung, 1984.

SOL, R. *El Salvador: Medios masivos y comunicación popular*. San José (Costa Rica): Editorial Porvenir, 1984.

THIOLLENT, M. *Crítica metodológica, investigação social e enquete operária*. Sao Paulo: Polis, 1985.

2. Reviews

Amérique Latine, CETRAL, 35 rue Jeûneurs, 75002 Paris, FRANCE.

Areito, PO Box 1124, New York, N.Y. 10009.

Casa de las Americas, Havana.

Cahiers des Amériques Latines, IHEAL, 27 rue Saint Guillaume, 75007 Paris.

Cine Cubano, Havana.

Cine sí, 1719 Butler Avenue, Los Angeles, CA 90025.

Cineaste, 200 Park Avenue South, New York, N.Y. 10003.

Comunicación, Apartado Postal 20133, 1020 Caracas, Venezuela.

Comunicación y cultura, Calzada del Hueso 1100, 04960 Mexico City, Mexico.

Comunicação & politica, rua do Catete 311/813, CEP 22220 Rio de Janeiro (RJ), Brazil.

Comunicação & sociedade, rua Bartira 387, SP 05009 Sao Paulo, Brazil.

Chasqui, Apartado Postal 584, Quito, Ecuador.

Cuádernos del TICOM, Universidad Autonoma Metropolitana-Xochimilco, Calzada del Hueso 1100, 04960 Mexico City, Mexico.

Cultura popular, CELADEC, General Garzón 2267, Lima 11, Peru.

ININCO, Instituto de investigaciones de la comunicacion, Universidad Central de Venezuela, Apartado Postal 47339, 1041 Caracas, Venezuela.

Journal of Latin American Studies, Cambridge University Press, The Edinburgh Building, Shaftesbury Road, Cambridge CB2 2RU, UK.

Jump Cut, PO Box 865, Berkeley, CA 94701; and, 2620 North Richmond, Chicago, IL 60647.

Latin American Perspectives, Sage Publications, PO Box 11017, Beverly Hills, CA 90213.

Materiales para la comunicación popular, IPAL, Centro de estudios sobre cultura transnacional, Apartado Postal 270031, Lima 27, Peru.

Le Monde Diplomatique, 7 rue des Italiens, 75009 Paris.

NACLA Report on the Americas, 151 West 19 Street (9th floor), New York, N.Y. 10011.

Problémes d'Amérique Latine, La Documentation Française, 29–31 quai Voltaire, 75007 Paris.

Signo y pensamiento, Facultad de comunicación social, Pontificia Universidad Javeriana, Carrera 7a, 40–62 Bogota, Colombia.

Studies in Latin American Popular Culture, c/o Harold E. Hinds Jr., Division of the Social Sciences, University of Minnesota, Morris, MN 56267.

Notes On Contributors

Tomás BORGE MARTINEZ was born in Matagalpa, Nicaragua in 1930, and is the last surviving founder (in 1961) of the Sandinista National Liberation Front (FSLN). In addition to his poetry, he is a "Commander of the Revolution", and is presently the Minister of the Interior.

Julianne BURTON is Assistant Professor of Latin American Literature, Culture and Film at the University of California, Santa Cruz. She has written extensively on Latin American film including *The New Latin American Cinema: An Annotated Bibliography (1960–1980)* (1983), and is an associate editor of the review *Cineaste*. Currently she is completing a book on documentary film in Latin America.

David BUXTON, the translator of the Armand Mattelart text, was born in Oamaru, New Zealand in 1955. He is the author of *Le Rock: Star-système et société de consommation* (1985), and presently teaches communication at the Université de Rennes 2 (France).

Omar CABEZAS was born in Nicaragua, and just after finishing high school joined the FSLN and participated actively throughout the war of liberation. He has written a book about his experiences in guerrilla struggle entitled *La montaña es algo más que una immensa estepa verde*, which won the Casa de las Américas (Havana) Prize in 1982.

Fernando CARDENAL was Vice-Rector and Professor of Philosophy and Education at the Catholic University, Managua, and National Co-ordinator of the Nicaraguan Literacy Crusade. He is presently the Minister of Education. His brother, the poet Ernesto Cardenal, is Minister of Culture. Valerie MILLER was a Planning Advisor to the Nicaraguan Literacy Crusade, and is a Fellow at the Center for International Education, University of Massachusetts.

CENTRO DE INVESTIGACIONES Y DOCUMENTACION DE LA COSTA ATLANTICA (CIDCA; the "Center for Atlantic Coast Research and Documentation") is an independent research center originally founded in 1982 under the auspices of the Ministry of Agrarian Reform. It is linked to the ethnic movement MISATAN, and has offices in Managua, Bluefields and Puerto Cabezas.

Don CLARK, the translator of two of the Spanish texts, was born in Coshocton (Ohio) in 1948, and at five his family joined the great post-war migration west to California, where he had his first contact with the Spanish language and culture. He took his B.A. in Spanish at the San José State University, and in 1983 his M.A. in Spanish Literature at the University of California Santa Barbara where he has taught Spanish. In addition to his interpreting and translation work, he has published a book of poetry, *Islands* (1981). Despite great odds he remains a hispanophile and visits Mexico and Spain as often as possible.

José Luis CORAGGIO was born in Argentina and is an economist. He has taught in Argentina, Mexico and the U.S., and has been living in Nicaragua since 1981. He is presently head of the research project "The Popular Project and Social Transition in the Small Peripheral Countries" organized by the Coordinadora Regional de Investigaciones Económicas y Sociales (CRIES). His most recent publication is *Nicaragua: Revolución y democracia* (1985).

Howard H. FREDERICK is a political scientist with a Ph.D. from the School of International Relations at the American University. His area of research concerns communication systems in Central America and the Caribbean. He presently teaches international telecommunications at the School of Telecommunications at Ohio University, and is the author of the forthcoming *Cuban–American Radio Wars: Ideology in International Communication* (Ablex).

Dee Dee HALLECK produces Paper Tiger Television, a weekly series on Manhattan Public Access Cable TV. For many years she has been involved in directing and producing films, including *Peliculas, Haiti: Bitter Cane*, and *Waiting for the Invasion: US Citizens in Nicaragua*. She works at Xchange TV, POB 586, New York, N.Y. 10009.

Janette JAMIESON, the translator of three of the Spanish texts, has a B.A. in Language and Literature at the Universidad de las Americas, Puebla (Mexico), and has studied at the Universidad Nacional Autonoma de Mexico. In addition to graduate work at the University of California, Santa Barabara, she has worked as a translator, interpreter and bilingual instructor at schools and colleges in both the U.S. and Mexico.

David KUNZLE teaches Art History at the University of California, Los Angeles and is author of *U.S. Posters of Protest 1966–1970, The Early Comic Strip* (1973), *The Nineteenth Century Comic Strip* (forthcoming) and *Fashion and Fetishism* (1981). He has written extensively on popular and revolutionary art, especially that of Cuba, Chile and Nicaragua. Presently he is working on a social history of 17th-century Dutch art.

Armand MATTELART, born 1936 in Belgium, has a Ph.D. in Law and Political Economy from the Université de Louvian and a post-graduate degree in Sociology from the Université de Paris. During 1962–73 he was Professor at the Universidad de Chile and during the Popular Unity government he was involved in numerous popular communication projects. He is a founder and co-editor of the review *Comunicación y cultura*, published first in Santiago de Chile, and later in Buenos Aires and Mexico City. Presently he is Director of the Faculty of Information and Communication Sciences at the Université de Haute-Bretagne — Rennes 2 in France. He is the author of numerous books including *How to Read Donald Duck* (1975, 1984, with Ariel Dorfman), *Communication and Class Struggle* (2 volumes, 1979 and 1983; with Seth Siegelaub), *Multinationals and the Control of Culture* (1979), *Mass Media, Ideologies and the Revolutionary Movement* (1980), *Transnationals and the Third World* (1983), *International Image Markets* (1984; with Michèle Mattelart and Xavier Delcourt), *Communication and Information Technologies: Freedom of Choice for Latin America?* (1985; with Hector Schmucler), and *Technology, Culture and Communication* (1985).

Guillermo ROTHSCHUH VILLANUEVA was born in Nicaragua and was an editor of *La Prensa* from 1969–1978. After the revolution he was head of the "Media Commission" under the Ministry of Culture, and has been an active member of the Nicaraguan Journalist's Union. In addition to his extensive writings on communication, he presently works with the Agitation and Propaganda Department of the FSLN.

Margaret D. WILDE was born in the USA and has undertaken many study missions to Nicaragua on behalf of the Board of the World Mission Moravian Church in America.

Other CRITICAL BOOKS ON COMMUNICATION, CULTURE AND IDEOLOGY

Armand Mattelart, ed.
COMMUNICATING IN POPULAR NICARAGUA

141pp, 35 BW and line illustrations,
Large-format Paper, 178 × 260mm,
0-88477-024-9, $8.95

This collection of texts, by authors from Nicaragua and the US, is the first critical anthology on the media and culture in Nicaragua, where concern for the "freedom of the press" has become a veritable fetish for the international news media. In analysing numerous aspects of the subject — journalism, the press, the radio, film, video, mural expression, literacy and social movements — in their social-historical dimension, the authors attempt to assess the cultural achievements, problems and future of Nicaragua in its struggle to develop a practice of democratic participation despite the siege conditions of US-imposed warfare: economic and psychological as well as military.

Wolfgang Fritz Haug
COMMODITY AESTHETICS, *Sept* IDEOLOGY AND CULTURE

ca 176pp, Paperback, 140 × 210mm,
0-88477-022-2, ca $8.95.

This collection of texts is the first presentation of the work of the important West German Marxist philosopher Wolfgang Fritz Haug. It brings together an essential selection of his work written since 1970, and sets forth a multi-dimensional analysis of culture integrating three inter-related theories: a theory of commodity aesthetics or the phenomenon and function of the realization of the value of commodities; a theory of the cultural as an omni-present dimension of everyday life, especially "culture from below"; and a theory of the ideological, particularly concerned with ideological powers "from above". It concludes with a complete bibliography of his writings.

Jean-Guy Lacroix
Benoît Lévesque *Dec*
COMMUNICATION IN QUEBEC: THE STATE OF THE ART

ca 96pp, Paperback, 140 × 210mm,
0-88477-026-5, ca $5.95

This original work analyses the social reality of the communication research apparatus in Quebec by studying its two constituent elements: its material basis and its production. To realize its objective this carefully-documented study seeks to identify the specific form of the institutional structure underlying Quebec's communication apparatus, and to show how research is concentrated on certain subjects in function of different areas of expertise and how it is influenced by the major theoretical currents in the field.

Bernard Miège
THE CAPITALIZATION OF CULTURAL PRODUCTION *March 87*

ca 224pp, Paperback, 140 × 210mm,
0-88477-025-7, ca $9.95.

Although the industrial production of culture is not a new phenomenon, in recent years it has undergone a spectacular growth, which, in spite of the crisis, is likely to continue in the coming years. But while the term "cultural industries" since the Frankfurt School has become well-accepted on the left — and elsewhere — there are still very few critical left studies analysing how the sphere of cultural activities function within capitalism, both on a national as well as an international scale.

RECENT AND BACKLIST TITLES

Sakari Hänninen
Leena Paldàn, eds.
RETHINKING MARX

202pp, Paperback, 120 × 190mm,
0-88477-021-4, $8.50

In the more than 100 years since Marx's death in 1883, the theory and practice of the ruling and subaltern classes have evolved radically, introducing new unforseen forms and problems in the struggle for a truly liberated society. The Marxist heritage, however, has rarely been the object of a systematic critical analysis by those working within the Marxist tradition, and it is the purpose of *Rethinking Marx* to propose a new critical reading of Marx in light of — or in dark of — current problems. This book contains the principal papers presented at the "Internationale Konferenz Aktualisierung Marx" held in West Berlin. The contributions range from questions on historical materialism, the State, economic and class analyses, culture and ideology, new social movements, politics and socialist perspectives, and the renewal of Marxism.

Sakari Hänninen
Leena Paldàn, eds.
RETHINKING IDEOLOGY: A MARXIST DEBATE

158pp, Paperback, 120 × 190mm,
0-88477-015-X, $7.50

With Gramsci's ground-breaking work over 50 years ago, Louis Althusser "Ideology and Ideological State Apparatuses" (1970), and the present world economic and political crisis, the need to formulate a theory of ideology is increasingly posed as a central element in the analysis of existing society as well as in a political project for its transformation. Developing on the analyses of the research group PIT ("Projekt Ideologie Theorie"), *Rethinking Ideology* contains the principal papers presented at the "International Seminar on Problems of Research On Ideology" held in West Berlin. The contributions range from highly conceptual texts to those on politics, education, aesthetics, fascism and feminism; all together they offer a rare confrontation between a wide spectrum of theoretical positions on questions of ideology.

Yves de la Haye, ed.
MARX AND ENGELS ON THE MEANS OF COMMUNICATION: A SELECTION OF TEXT

173pp, Paperback, 100 × 185mm,
0-88477-013-3, $6.95

This collection of Marx's and Engels' basic texts on the means of communication, information and transportation is the first volume of its kind ever published. Edited with an essential introduction by Yves la Haye, its purpose is to contribute to the development of a materialist analysis of the media, and to combat the concepts underlying dominant communication theory. In presenting the work of Marx and Engels, its intention is not to provide a Marxist communication "catechism", but rather to explain how the analytic method of historical materialism served to understand the complex relations between the media and society which arose during the nineteenth century, and how this critical method can form the basis for an understanding of the new communication forms developing in our time.

iel Dorfman
rmand Mattelart
OW TO READ
ONALD DUCK:
MPERIALIST
DEOLOGY IN THE
ISNEY COMIC

1 Enlarged Edition,
pp, 66 Cartoon illustrations,
ge-format Paper, 178 × 260mm,
8477-023-0, $6.95.

is book was first published in Chile
'1 as part of a Popular Unity govern-
nt study to develop a new education
licy, and since the fascist coup in 1973,
as been banned and burned there with
er literature. In 1975, in the U.S., the
glish edition was seized and banned
more than a year by the U.S. govern-
nt. A product of the political struggle,
w to Read Donald Duck is a profound
1 imaginative critique of how the
sney fantasy world reproduces the
merican Dream" fantasy world, and
disastrous effect of Disney comics and
er "mass" cultural merchandise on the
velopment of the Third World. Pub-
hed in hundreds of thousands of copies
more than 13 languages, this book has
eady become the popular classic study
cultural imperialism, and children's
rature. In comic book format, with car-
n examples, translation and introduc-
n by David Kunzle, a new preface by
authors, and an annotated biblio-
phy of Marxist writings on cultural
perialism, and the comics. This new
arged edition also contains an appen-
x by John Shelton Lawrence on the
ok's U.S. censorship and the legal-
litical aspects of the right to criticize
sney.

FOLLOW THEM.
MAYBE WE CAN
SAVE THE KING.

has become a handbook of de-colonization.
xamines the meaning of Walt Disney
nics: in doing this one thing precisely and
ofoundly, it illuminates a global situation.
e clinical writings of Frantz Fanon worked in
imilar way."
John Berger, *New Society* (London)

his expose should be in libraries as another
ample of America's role in world politics."
avonne Jacobsen, *Booklegger* (San Francisco)

"Closes a long standing gap in the subject of
imperialism and ideology in Latin America."
Arturo Torrecilla,
Insurgent Sociologist (Eugene, OR.)

"The report on Donald Duck that Walt Disney
doesn't want you to read."
Jim Hoberman, *Village Voice* (New York)

"Ideology even in the most innocent antics of
Donald Duck? . . . Alas, the day will come
when ignorance is no longer permissible."
France-Soir (Paris)

tional image."
E. J. Hobsbawm, *Studio International* (London)

". . . the best epitome of Marxist aesthetics in
English, and so far as I know, in any language."
Melvin Rader,
The Journal of Aesthetics and Art Criticism
(New York)

"In the crucial but problematical field of
Marxist aesthetics, Morawski is surely the
greatest living authority."
Frederic Jameson

Lee Baxandall
Stefan Morawski, eds.
MARX AND ENGELS
ON LITERATURE
AND ART:
A SELECTION OF
WRITINGS

[8], 179 pp, 115 × 195mm,
Cloth: 0-88477-000-1, $17.50
Paperback: 0-88477-001-X, $6.95

This collection of Marx and Engels *On
Literature and Art* is the first English
edition to be published in almost thirty
years. Edited by Lee Baxandall and Stefan
Morawski, it is a concise selection containing all Marx's and Engels' basic
aesthetic writings, organised to reflect the
principal themes underlying their
thought on literature and art: "capitalist
alienation", "communism", "class
values", "realism", and "form and style",
among others. It contains many new
translations, and includes a major introductory essay by Polish aesthetician
Stefan Morawski. In addition, it includes
a full bibliography of Marxist books in the
English language on aesthetics.

"He [Stefan Morawski] is keenly aware that in
developing a Marxist aesthetic, we are building not so much on Marx's texts, which may or
may not imply but certainly do not contain a
'rounded, balanced aesthetic theory', but on
our knowledge of Marx's general thought and,
hopefully, on a command of his method. His
own extremely intelligent version has the
advantage of seeking to emancipate Marxist
criticism from some of the more primitive versions which long monopolized its conven-

International Mass
Media Research
Center, ed.
MARXISM AND THE
MASS MEDIA:
TOWARDS A BASIC
BIBLIOGRAPHY

Now Available:
No. 1–2–3, Revised Ed. (Catalogue
Nos. 1–453)
105pp, Paperback, 140 × 210mm,
0-88477-009-5, $8.00
No. 4–5 (Catalogue Nos. 454–658)
95pp, Paperback, 140 × 210mm,
0-88477-007-9, $8.00
No. 6–7 (Catalogue Nos. 659–825)
128pp, Paperback, 140 × 210mm,
0-88477-008-7, $8.00

This is an ongoing bibliographic research
series published irregularly. Its purpose is
to provide a global, multi-lingual annotated documentation of past and current
Marxist and critical studies on all aspects
of communications: the press, radio, television, publishing, public opinion,
advertising, journalism, cultural imperialism, and film and mass culture, among
other subjects. Each issue contains
approximately 500 entries indexed by
subject, author, and country. *Marxism and
the Mass Media* is the only bibliographic
series of its kind in the world, and is available on a per-copy or standing-order as-
published basis.

". . . an indispensable reference source for
those doing critical research . . ."
Communication Perspectives (Urbana, Illinois)

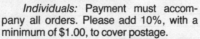

ORDERING

Individuals: Payment must accompany all orders. Please add 10%, with a
minimum of $1.00, to cover postage.
Forthcoming Publications: Prepaid
orders received before scheduled publication date will be sent postage-free when
available.
Trade Discounts: 1–4 copies (mixed),

25% (Proforma only); 5–9, 33⅓%; 10 plus,
40%; post additional. Payment net 30 days.
*College/University Bookstore (Course
Use) Discount:* 25%.
Payment should be made to the order
of "International General" in US$ payable
against a bank in the USA unless otherwise
agreed.

international general

PO Box 350, New York, N.Y. 10013, USA.
173 av de la Dhuys, 93170 Bagnolet, FRANCE.

Armand Mattelart
Seth Siegelaub, eds.
COMMUNICATION AND CLASS STRUGGLE:
1. CAPITALISM, IMPERIALISM

445pp, Large-format Paper, 178 × 260mm,
0-88477-011-7, $21.95

COMMUNICATION AND CLASS STRUGGLE, a two-volume work, is the first general Marxist anthology of writings on communication, information and culture. Its purpose is to analyse the relationship between the practice and theory of communication and their development within the context of social struggle on a world scale. Armand Mattelart and Seth Siegelaub, the editors, have selected 128 essential Marxist and progressive texts originating in over 50 countries and written since the mid-nineteenth century to explain three interrelated phenomena: (1) how basic social, economic and cultural processes condition communication; (2) how bourgeois communication practice and theory have developed as part of the capitalist mode of production; and (3) how in the struggle against exploitation and oppression, the popular and working classes have developed their own communication practice and theory, and a new, liberated mode of communication, culture and daily life.

This first volume, 1. CAPITALISM, IMPERIALISM, provides the basic Marxist theory essential to an analysis of the communication process and studies the formation of the capitalist communication apparatus, ideology, and "mass" culture. Volume 1 contains 64 texts. More than one-third are published for the first time in English, and some texts appear for the first time in any language. In addition, it includes a 500-entry bibliography.

Contents: A. Basic Analytic Concepts; B. The Bourgeois Ideology of Communication; C. The Formation of the Capitalist Mode of Communication (Bourgeois Hegemony, Colonialism, Industrialization, Fascism); D. Monopoly Capitalism/ Imperialism and Global Ideological Control (Concentration and Standardization, New Technology, Imperialist System, Militarization of Culture); Selected Bibliography; Notes on Contributors.

The authors: S. Siegelaub, A. Mattelart, K. Marx, F. Engels, A. Gramsci, V. I. Lenin, Mao Tse-tung, P. Bourdieu, Revolutionary Left Movement (Chile), H. Lefebvre, L. Acosta, M. Mattelart, D. W. Smythe, S. Finkelstein, T. Wengraf & R. Murray, F. Mehring, R. Escarpit, J. Habermas, Y. de la Haye, A. Cabral, R. Constantino, C. Ortega & C. Romero, R. Frederix, J. D. Bernal, S. Ewen. N. R. Danielian, The Film Council (UK), R. Lindner, R. Williams, R. A. Brady, D. Sington & A. Weidenfeld, Free Communications Group, R. Peron, French Communist Party-Chaix Printers, R. Bonchio, J. Strasser, M. Janco & D. Furjot, J.-M. Caroit, M. O. Caollai, Science for the People, L. A. Perez Jr, H. I. Schiller, R. Drinot Silva, T. H. Guback, S. Perez Barreto, J. Aronson, Phong Hien, Le Van Hao, C. Brightman & M. Klare.

Armand Mattelart
Seth Siegelaub, eds.
COMMUNICATION AND CLASS STRUGGLE:
2. LIBERATION, SOCIALISM

438pp, 63 BW and line illustrations, Large-format Paper, 178 × 260 mm, 0-88477-018-4, $21.95

The second volume, 2. LIBERATION, SOCIALISM, provides an analysis of the development of popular and working class communication and culture, in theory and practice under different political-social and historical conditions, and its contemporary expression. Volume 2 contains 64 texts, 38 are published for the first time in English, and some texts appear for the first time in any language. In addition, it includes a 650-entry bibliography.

Contents: E. Popular Culture and Communication: Elements Towards a Definition; F. Popular Communication and Cultural Practices (The Formation of Proletarian Organization and Communication, Clandestine Communication, National Liberation Movements); G. Socialist Communication Processes; H. Towards A Globalization of Struggle (The Interior of the Capitalist Communication Apparatus, Intensification of Struggle, New Struggles — New Communication Practices); Selected Bibliography; Notes on Contributors.

The authors: S. Siegelaub, A. Mattelart, A. Gramsci, M. Mattelart, L. Trotsky, O. Negt & A. Kluge, W. F. Haug, E. Cabet & L.-A. Pagnerre, K. Marx, A. Fornet, R. Lavroff, V. I. Lenin, Communist International, D. Tartakowsky, B. Fogarasi, *Worker's Life,* B. Hogenkamp, G. Barone & A. Petrucci, B. Brecht, H. Eisler, F. Hollering, E. Hoernle, W. Munzenberg, P. Gaudibert, L. Basset, Che Guevara, A. Sibeko, A. Dorfman, F. Fanon, O. Getino & F. Solanas, H. Ab Ghanima, A. B. Khalatov, S. Tretiakov, L. Lissitsky, T. Kurtovic, F. Castro, J. Garcia Espinosa, S. Coelho, MPLA, J. Rebelo, FRELIMO, M. Chanan, Unified Federation of Printing & Paper Workers, Democratic Federation of PTT Workers-CFDT, P. M. Manacorda, S. Allende, D. Kunzle, Armed Forces Movement, Portuguese Communist Party, Strike Committee of the Ecole Nationale Superieure des Beaux Arts, Directors of Popular Theatres and Cultural Centres, Council for the Development of Community Media, G. Richeri, J. Lindsay, J.-M. Piemme.

"With its 128 texts and bibliographies, almost 900 pages and 800,000 words, this 2-volume anthology is by far the most impressive attempt to date to lay the groundwork for a critical theory of communication and culture... Destined to be a classic!"

ORDER FORM

Please send the following books:

_____ Communicating in Popular Nicaragua _____
_____ Commodity Aesthetics, Ideology and Culture _____
_____ Communication in Quebec _____
_____ The Capitalization of Culture _____
_____ Communication and Class Struggle 1 _____
_____ Communication and Class Struggle 2 _____
_____ Rethinking Marx _____
_____ Rethinking Ideology _____
_____ Marx and Engels On Communication _____
_____ Marx and Engels on Literature and Art _____
_____ How To Read Donald Duck _____
_____ Marxism and Mass Media 1–2–3 _____
_____ Marxism and Mass Media 4–5 _____
_____ Marxism and Mass Media 6–7 _____

Date: _____ PO No: _____

+ 10% Postage